Montaigne and Shakespeare

Montaigne and Shakespeare

The emergence of modern self-consciousness

Robert Ellrodt

Manchester University Press

Copyright © Robert Ellrodt 2015

The right of Robert Ellrodt to be identified as the author of this work has been asserted by him in accordance with the Copyright, Designs and Patents Act 1988.

Published by Manchester University Press
Altrincham Street, Manchester M1 7JA, UK
www.manchesteruniversitypress.co.uk

British Library Cataloguing-in-Publication Data is available

ISBN 978 0 7190 9108 7 *hardback*
ISBN 978 1 5261 1685 7 *paperback*

First published by Manchester University Press in hardback 2015

This edition first published 2018

The publisher has no responsibility for the persistence or accuracy of URLs for any external or third-party internet websites referred to in this book, and does not guarantee that any content on such websites is, or will remain, accurate or appropriate.

Printed by Lightning Source

Contents

Preface	vii
Acknowledgements	xi

1 New forms of self-consciousness in Montaigne   1
   1. Calling the self into question   1
   2. Persistence and coherence of the self   8

2 The progress of subjectivity from Antiquity to Montaigne   25
   1. The Hellenic world   25
   2. The Roman world   32
   3. Christian spirituality: St Augustine   38
   4. The Middle Ages   40
   5. From the troubadours to Petrarch   43
   6. The Italian and French Renaissance   46

3 Shakespeare and the new aspects of subjectivity   59
   1. The medieval heritage in England   59
   2. The Shakespearean moment: the English Renaissance at the turn of the century   61
   3. The self in Shakespeare's *Sonnets*   65
   4. The dramatic self: from the medieval monologue to the Shakespearean soliloquy   73
   5. A reassessment of the influence of Montaigne on Shakespeare   92

4 Complexity and coherence of the Shakespearean characters   102
   1. Hamlet   102
   2. Macbeth and Lady Macbeth   108
   3. The characters in *King Lear*   110

5	Subjective time in Montaigne and Shakespeare	126
	1. From Antiquity to Montaigne	126
	2. Shakespearean time in the *Sonnets*	132
6	Scepticism and stable humanistic values	144

Epilogue. The wisdom of Montaigne and Shakespeare — 173

Select bibliography — 175
   Critical studies on Montaigne — 176
   Critical studies on Shakespeare (including studies on
      Shakespeare and Montaigne) — 180
   General studies (literary, historical, philosophical) — 185

Index — 191

Preface

This book is at once a rewriting, a revisiting and a revision of my *Montaigne et Shakespeare* (2011). It has been adapted to Anglophone readers by changes in the quotations and references. Where some notes have been suppressed, others have been extended, and the bibliography includes more recent publications.

The original subtitle has had to be modified. 'L'émergence de la conscience moderne' played on the ambiguity of the French word 'conscience', which can be deployed for both consciousness and moral conscience. The modernity of Montaigne and Shakespeare can be viewed from both perspectives, but chapter 6 alone illustrates the modernity of some of their depictions and readings of moral values. This aside, my main concern throughout is with the historical evolution and illustration of self-consciousness.

The original's 'annexe', 'Et Shakespeare créa la jeune fille', has been left out, for two reasons. Firstly, it concerned only Shakespeare. While Montaigne often speaks of women and sex in a modern way, he displays no particular interest in 'la jeune fille' and thus there is no obvious parallel. Secondly, while diverting, it was rather loosely related to the main theme – the emergence of modern self-consciousness. While I included it in the French book as another illustration of Shakespeare's modernity, and believe it provided a further opportunity of tracing, though much more briefly, an evolution from Antiquity to the Renaissance, I have excluded it here for those reasons.

A brief account of a long journey

To see in Montaigne and Shakespeare the fountainhead of an evolution beginning in early modern times and culminating in our own age is not surprising given the canon of extant literary and philosophical studies that have viewed their works from a post-modern or post-structuralist perspective. However, the situation was different in 1952, when I published an essay on the genesis and dilemma of 'la conscience moderne'. Perhaps prematurely given the prevailing theoretical preoccupations of the time, it juxtaposed the two possible meanings of the word 'conscience' in French: 'consciousness' and 'moral conscience'. While researching the English Metaphysical poets for a French doctorate, I had noticed in John Donne's writings the presence of a phenomenon earlier illustrated in Montaigne's *Essays* that might be characterized as a calling into question of the self. I thought one could discern in such self-scrutiny a foreshadowing of the doubts concerning the existence or accessibility of the self later expressed by Henri Frédéric Amiel and modern authors, notably Paul Valéry and Jean-Paul Sartre. My essay thus attempted to suggest an outline of the evolution of subjectivity from Antiquity to the present age. As I was writing in a moment of existentialist excitement, it was maybe inevitable that I sought an explanation for this apparent paradox in Sartre's *Being and Nothingness: An Essay on Phenomenological Ontology* (1943), describing a trajectory towards an intense self-consciousness that resulted in a dissolution of the self.

In my *L'inspiration personnelle et l'esprit du temps chez les poètes Métaphysiques anglais* (1960), I focused attention on the individual structures of thought, imagination and sensibility present in each author. Implying a stable self despite obvious evolutions or 'conversions', I detected various forms of self-consciousness, apparently unprecedented in the history of literature, and alluded to similarities between Montaigne and Shakespeare's *Hamlet*. A later essay, 'Self-consciousness in Montaigne and Shakespeare', published in *Shakespeare Survey* (1975), further explored convergences between the Elizabethan dramatist and the author of the *Essays*. I returned to these themes in *Seven Metaphysical Poets: A Structural Study of the Unchanging Self* (2000), and in several lectures and articles, some of which have been included in volumes often inaccessible nowadays. This work builds on these foundations. Yet it also presents a profound expansion of the presentations and conclusions of my earlier research. Based on a historical approach, it includes fresh material, opens new perspectives on the thematic concerns highlighted above and seeks a mediation between theses that I recognized as related but perhaps antagonistic in my earlier interventions in the field.

Chapter 1 calls attention to a special kind of self-consciousness displayed by Montaigne: its instantaneity in the very moment of experience. It suggests that it may account for his doubts concerning the stability or the very existence of the self, thus anticipating Hume's analysis and the later interrogations of modern and post-modern writers. However, it also proposes that a fuller examination of the *Essays* reveals that their author was aware of the coherence and continuity of his own self from youth to old age: his conception of his 'essential form' is clarified. This view of the self can be read from the psychological perspectives of Cornelius Castoriadis or the philosophy of Paul Ricoeur rather than post-modern theory.

Chapter 2 traces the evolution of subjectivity from Greek and Roman Antiquity to the Renaissance in literary, philosophical and religious works. Against a prevailing objectivity, growing attention to the self and its conflicts can be seen in the Roman elegists and satirists as well as in the Stoics, something which culminates in the *Confessions* of Augustine. By contrast, the allegorization of the inner life in literature and its purely objective description in scholastic treatises blurs any sense of progress in this regard in the Middle Ages. While Petrarch's introspection can be viewed as reviving Augustinian interrogations, later Renaissance poets on the Continent display a marked tendency to indulge in expressions of sentiment rather than intense self-analysis. Viewed from this cultural-historical perspective, Montaigne's mode of self-scrutiny is thus unprecedented.

Chapter 3 is divided into five distinct yet interrelated sections. Reacting and responding to the trajectory and contexts established in the preceding chapters, sections 1 and 2 turn attention to the English predecessors and contemporaries of Shakespeare, scrutinizing their evolution from a moral insistence on self-knowledge to an emphasis on self-assertion, but discovering only in Donne the kind of self-consciousness displayed by Montaigne. Section 3 explores the various forms of subjectivity and self-consciousness manifested in the *Sonnets* of Shakespeare, traceable even though their autobiographical significance is doubtful. Section 4 traces the slow growth of subjectivity from the medieval dramatic monologue to the Shakespearean soliloquy, positioning the character of Hamlet as a turning point in this evolution. Finally, section 5 assesses the extent of the influence of Montaigne on Shakespeare.

Chapter 4 offers a study of three tragedies, *Hamlet*, *Macbeth* and *Lear*. The analysis demonstrates that the complexity of Shakespeare's characters and their occasional evolution does not impair the essential coherence of their individual selves, often denied nowadays.

Disclosing the kind of evolution from objectivity to subjectivity discerned in the modes of self-consciousness traced earlier, chapter 5 explores changes in the perception and conception of time from Antiquity to the Renaissance, notably emphasizing the personal and distinctive apprehension of time revealed by the analysis of Montaigne's *Essays* and Shakespeare's *Sonnets*.

Chapter 6 qualifies the scepticism and moral relativism nowadays generally ascribed to Montaigne and Shakespeare. Their adherence to universal humanistic values is demonstrated; its emotional and religious bases are investigated and its modernity acknowledged. Their quest for truth can thus be viewed as inseparable from a belief in essence, and the originality of their aesthetic intuitions of transcendence is highlighted.

Finally, as each chapter has its own conclusion, the Epilogue serves only to restate their findings, reminding us that, unlike many of our contemporaries, both Montaigne and Shakespeare 'saw life steadily and saw it whole' (Matthew Arnold, 'To a friend', 1849).

Acknowledgements

Éditions Corti have authorized this translation of my book *Montaigne et Shakespeare: l'émergence de la conscience moderne* (Paris, 2011).

Several publishers had given their agreement to the reproduction of passages borrowed from my earlier publications, more or less modified and inserted into a new whole:

- Oxford University Press for a few pages in chapters 16 and 17 of my *Seven Metaphysical Poets: A Structural Study of the Unchanging Self* (2000);
- University of Delaware Press for part of my International Shakespeare Association lecture 'Self-consistency in Montaigne and Shakespeare', in *Shakespeare and the Mediterranean* (2004);
- Éditions Gallimard (Pléiade) for part of my 'Notice' on 'Le Roi Lear' in *Shakespeare: Tragédies II* (Pléiade, 2002) and Cambridge Scholars Publishing for the use of a translation of this 'Notice' in *'And That's True Too': New Essays on King Lear* (eds François Laroque, Pierre Iselin and Sophie Alatorre, 2007);
- Éditions Actes Sud for the use of parts of my 'Présentation' in my edition of *William Shakespeare: Sonnets* (2007);
- Publications de l'Université de Saint Etienne for part of my article 'La perception du temps dans les Sonnets de Shakespeare', in *Le char ailé du temps* (ed. Louis Roux, 2003);
- Société française Shakespeare for the use of my article (much augmented) in *Shakespeare et Montaigne: vers un nouvel humanisme* (2003).

I also wish to thank Professor François Laroque and Professor Gilles Monsarrat for their help on various occasions.

Chapter 1

New forms of self-consciousness in Montaigne

An acute and original attention to the self is noticeable in the writings of several authors by the end of the sixteenth century and at the beginning of the seventeenth. Most intensely manifested by Michel de Montaigne in France, it was mirrored by William Shakespeare's and John Donne's engagements with the same concepts in England. This development may be aligned to our own views of the modern and modernity, not just because it occurred in a period called the 'early modern' by historians, philosophers, linguists and literary critical commentators alike, but also because it announces an engagement with the question of personal identity, whose character the same observers have largely ascribed to our modern and post-modern age. When I suggest such contiguities, of course, it is with the awareness that there are nonetheless fundamental differences. In proposing these confluences, I do not have in mind the emergence of the individualism which Jacob Burckhardt, in his epoch-making *Die Kultur der Renaissance in Italien* (1860), considered to be a distinctive feature of the Renaissance. This is not to wholly reject Burckhardt's position, but to suggest that assumptions surrounding the nature of individualism and its relationship to the individual self must be tempered. As such, I intend to call attention to a phenomenon of self-consciousness manifested in particular moments of self-observation: that which is characterized by doubts concerning the nature and at times the very existence of a self, which cannot be defined, or even discerned.

1. Calling the self into question

Our discussion can take as its starting point Montaigne's description of his own character in the essay 'Of the inconstancy of our actions':

> Every sort of contradiction can be found in me, depending upon some twist or attribute: timid, insolent; chaste, lecherous; talkative, taciturn; tough, sickly;

clever, dull; brooding, affable; lying, truthful; learned, ignorant; generous, miserly and then prodigal – I can see something of all that in myself, depending on how I gyrate, and anyone who studies himself attentively finds in himself and in his very judgement this whirring about and this dissonance. There is nothing I can say about myself as a whole simply and completely, without intermingling and admixture.[1]

In essaying a dialogue of self-description, Montaigne was not the first to discern this changeableness, of course. It had been observed by the Roman moralists, satirists and elegists, but they pointed out this instability only in the succession of our actions and emotions. In Montaigne's *Essays*, the contradictory aspects also appear at times in succession, as in the claim that 'I now and I then are certainly twain' (III, ix: 1091 C; VS 964). But in the passage quoted above the different aspects of the self are embraced in a single glance, as if the motions of the soul were so many possibilities rising to consciousness at the same moment, 'depending on how I gyrate'. Indeed, in the same paragraph Montaigne begins by noting that he is not moved by the wind of chance: 'I also shake and disturb myself by the instability of my stance'.

In 1952 I proposed that Montaigne's *Essays* contained an intuition of an absolute freedom which would confer on our individual consciousness a Sartrian 'for-self', a possibility of choosing itself at all moments, albeit in a nascent, imperfect form.[2] While this early engagement with the author, the text and these ideas perhaps went too far in its assertion of this, I still think it certain that although he achieved self-formation through the very process of writing, Montaigne went through an initial phase approximating a dissolution of the self under the observant gaze of his protracted attention to himself. I have not only in mind the kind of difficulty we meet when 'swept on downstream' we 'struggle back towards our self against the current […]; thus does the sea, when driven against itself, swirl back in confusion' (III, ix: 1132 B; VS 1000). As he noted earlier, 'it is a thorny undertaking – more than it looks – to follow so roaming a course as that of our mind's, to penetrate its dark depths and its inner recesses' (II, vi: 424 C; VS 378). This descent into 'dark depths' had not been unknown to St Augustine, in whose *Confessions* a forethought of the unconscious may be discerned.[3] Yet when Montaigne at other times writes 'every moment it seems to me that I am running away from myself' (I, xx: 97 A; VS 88) he might be only stating his impression of drifting towards the ultimate dissolution of his conscious being. However, the tone is intensely personal and the Heraclitean vision it presents is invested with a new meaning when the inner landscape is described in this way:

This is a register of varied and changing occurrences, of ideas which are unresolved and, when needs be, contradictory, either because I myself have become different or because I grasp hold of different attributes or aspects of my subject. [...] If my soul could only find a footing I would not be assaying myself but resolving myself. But my soul is ever in its apprenticeship and being tested. (III, ii: 908 B; VS 805)

This description gives us more than the various meanings ascribed by critics to the term 'essay' chosen by Montaigne: it reveals that the author himself is 'essaying', trying out his own virtualities in order to achieve a self-revelation in this 'account of the essays of [his] life' (III, xiii: 1224 B; VS 1079).[4] Yet, at least in a first stage, he apparently could not achieve fixity, nor give himself a foundation: 'the more I haunt myself and know myself, the more my misshapenness amazes me and the less I understand myself' (III, xi: 1164 B; VS 1029). He found he kept escaping from himself: 'I drip and drain away from myself' (III, xiii: 1251 B; VS 1101).[5] To define himself was the constantly repeated effort of the essayist, ever resumed since it was always frustrated. His perplexity deepened in the attempt at analysis and his very clear-sightedness blurred his vision.

Montaigne intended to persist in his quest for an uncertain or elusive self to the very last moments of his life, as if he hoped to discover his identity in the experience of death. According to Hugo Friedrich, it is impossible to have a clear and distinct idea of his conception of death, since he himself failed to realize it.[6] Yet whether we choose to consider him as a fundamental sceptic or a convinced Christian, one trait is obvious: Montaigne wished to experience his death as an ultimate assertion of his identity. He wanted to remain conscious in his very last moments, for 'it is to go far beyond having no fear of death actually to want to taste it, to savour it' (II, xiii: 689A; VS 609). Death, in his eyes, was a part of life. He spoke of wanting to 'cajole it' and 'concentrate' on it, for 'death forms a big chunk of [life]' (III, ix: 1112 B; VS 983). He also viewed it as a moment of self-revelation, as the individual confronts it alone: 'This event is not one of our social engagements: it is a scene with one character' (III, ix: 1107 B; VS 979). And Montaigne could face this final event without anxiety because his attention was not focused on the dissolution of his being but on the expectation of 'a death which will withdraw into itself, a calm and lonely one, entirely my own' (*ibid.*). Friedrich noted that 'my own' is a possessive pronoun: 'death is absorbed in myself; confused with myself'.[7] One may go further: to a self so often perceived as fragmented and mutable, death for Montaigne can be seen as imparting a final consistency and wholeness at the very moment when it will be dissolved. Thus perfect self-possession will be achieved only on that 'Master-day' (I, xix: 87 A; VS 80), in the miraculous instant the essayist elsewhere defines as a leap 'from a wretched existence to non-existence' (I, xx: 101B; VS 91). For him, indeed, the rest is silence.

An ability to detach himself from himself at the very moment of experience, which I shall call instantaneous self-reflexivity, characterizes Montaigne's self-consciousness, and I suggest that it inaugurates a notion of subjectivity more readily associated with the modern and modernity. It is not limited to the critical detachment required for self-examination practised by the Stoics or recommended by Christian moralists, even when it turns into a dissection or anatomization of oneself, as John Donne characterized it, an image itself anticipated by Montaigne in his description of his self-portrait: 'a SKELETOS on which at a glance you can see the veins, the muscles, [and] the tendons' (II, vi: 426 C; VS 379). I have in mind more the deliberate effort of self-examination practised by the essayist when he writes 'I turn my gaze inwards' (II, xvii: 747 A; VS 657).

In my previous writings I have made it clear that I commonly use the term 'self-consciousness' to characterize an ability to think and feel while setting oneself simultaneously at a distance from oneself.[8] The following passage bears testimony to this reading. Montaigne denies that our experience when 'lying with women' so 'transports us' that 'we are entirely transfixed and enraptured by the pleasure', arguing:

> I know it can go otherwise and that, if we have the will, we can sometimes manage, *at that very instant*, to bring our soul back to other thoughts. But we must vigilantly ensure that our soul is taut and erect. (II, xi: 481 A; VS 429–30; my italics)

This control of one's emotions makes a concomitance of feeling and irony possible: hence the appearance of humour, to which I shall return when speaking of Shakespeare.[9] This distancing also leads to the kind of irresolution confessed by Montaigne as well as by Hamlet.[10] Its constant presence in the *Essays* accounts for his ability to 'bridle' even his 'pressing desires' (II, xi: 478 A; VS 427) and 'violent emotions' (I, ii: 10 B; VS 14), and for his effort 'to extend by reason and reflection this privileged lack of emotion which is by nature well advanced in me' (III, x: 1134 B; VS 1003).

In explaining this distancing, Montaigne states 'I cannot get so deeply and totally involved' (III, x: 1144 B; VS 1012). 'Involved' is Michael Screech's translation of 'engagé'. To take both the statement and the possibilities suggested by this translation of the word as anticipating the rejection of 'engagement' by Jean-Paul Sartre's Hugo in *Les mains sales* (1948) would be to anticipate too far. Yet, as I have consistently suggested from my early engagements with Montaigne, the *Essays* offered a foretaste of a modern phenomenon: both a sense of pure gratuitousness and entire 'disponibilité' in the Gidian sense, as well as the Sartrian claim that our convictions and affections are never rooted in us deeply enough at any moment to prevent us from discarding them and embracing different or even opposite convictions and affections.[11] Montaigne had already noted that 'within ourselves we are, I know not how, double, with the result that what we believe we do not believe' (II, xvi: 704 A; VS 619).[12] For the author of *Being and Nothingness* we never believe enough in what we believe in, since at the very moment when I become aware of it, my belief is no longer my belief: I am detached from it by the very act which allows me to become conscious of it.[13] In this context, I admit that Montaigne usually presents as successive sincerities what later thinkers will experience as a perpetual, ontological insincerity. But I do not intend to ascribe to a Renaissance author a philosophy and a conception of man inconceivable in his own age. I claim only that similar modes of consciousness may be discovered in different individuals living in distant ages and affect in the same way their expression of different ideas and beliefs.[14]

When Montaigne notes that his mind gives birth to 'so many chimeras and fantastic monstrosities, one after another, without order and fitness' (I, viii: 31 A; VS 33), he seems to anticipate the description of mental activity presented by Hume. The author of *A Treatise of Human Nature* (1739–40) writes:

> The mind is a kind of theatre, where several perceptions successively make their appearance; pass, repass, glide away, and mingle in an infinite variety of postures and situations. There is properly no simplicity in it at one time, nor identity in different times, whatever natural propensity we may have to imagine that simplicity and identity.

The consequence is that the self is an illusion:

> Self or person is not any one impression, but that to which our several impressions or ideas are supposed to have a reference. If any impression gives rise to the idea of self, that impression must continue invariably the same, through the whole course of our lives; since self is supposed to exist after that manner. But there is no impression constant and invariable. Pain and pleasure, grief and joy, passions and sensations succeed each other, and never all exist at the same time. It cannot therefore be from any of these impressions, or from any other, that the idea of self is derived; and consequently there is no such idea.[15]

From a philosophical point of view, this negation of identity had become inevitable after Locke's reduction of it to the continuity of individual consciousness.[16] Once this is assumed, 'personal identity can only be defined in terms of appearance – of consciousness – not in terms of essence'.[17] Locke thought he had found in memory a guarantee of continuity which Hume's analysis showed to be an illusion. Though free from any deep anxiety, he confessed that his meditation on the problem of identity bred in him melancholy, until he discovered a solution: the imagination can fill the blanks of memory and impart to the self some sort of identity and permanence.[18]

Was the imagination responsible for the pre-eminence the Romantics granted to self-consciousness, raising it to a degree of acuity best represented by the young Browning's assertion 'I am made up of an intensest life / Of a most clear idea of consciousness / Of self' (1833)? In its manifold aspects, however, Romantic egocentrism must be seen as paving the way for 'the destructuration of the subject which Nietzsche and psychoanalysis effected and which is now a component of modernity', as Bernard Brugière insists when discerning 'a quasi impossibility of coinciding with himself' in the melancholy hero of Sénancourt.[19] This possibility, as I have pointed out, was already latent in Montaigne, as in John Donne.[20] I am inclined to ascribe Jacques Lacan's and Jacques Derrida's negation of the self to a similar exacerbation of their own self-consciousness. An anticipation of this negation may be traced not only in Nietzsche but in many nineteenth-century writers, albeit for different reasons and in different ways.[21]

Henri-Frédéric Amiel's diary was supposed to consecrate 'the triumph of the self'.[22] Yet this self always evades the grasp of the diarist:

> My former states, my outlines and metamorphoses, evade me as transitory accidents. They have become foreign to me, objects of curiosity, contemplation or study; they do not affect my inner substance; I do not experience them as belonging to me, as being in me; they are not me. Consequently I am not a will in continuous operation, an ever enlarging activity, a consciousness in process of enrichment; I am a flexibility which becomes more flexible, an accelerating mutation, a negation of a negation, and a reflection which is reflected like two mirrors placed in front of each other.[23]

To this flexibility, already noticed by Montaigne and Hume, Amiel adds the metaphor of the reflection of the same image in two mirrors facing each other, a metaphor Paul Valéry and Sartre also used in their conception of self-reflexivity. The diarist therefore perceives himself 'as an angle of vision and perception, as an impersonal person, as a subject without a determined individuality'.[24] This absorption of all phenomena in the substance of the self and the vanishing of the self into a void leads to a conclusion that we would not be surprised to see adopted by Valéry: 'A nothingness which perceives itself, this is pure thought'.²⁵ This goes far beyond Montaigne.

As the nineteenth century unfolded, however, introspection gave way to scientific observation in the study of the self, reducing it to the sum of the changing sensations produced in an organism. This self, therefore, always incomplete, could be subjected to a total metamorphosis in pathological cases of multiple personality disorder.²⁶ The undetermined or disseminated 'subject' of empirical psychology may have later inspired and perhaps can be seen in Proust's creation of an anonymous narrator as well as Musil's portrait of the 'Man without qualities'.²⁷

Nevertheless, the attention paid by novelists to the 'stream of consciousness' by the end of that century probably had a greater impact on a perceived vanishing of the subject. As in Montaigne's essays, through the simple means of inner observation, doubt was thrown on the unity and permanence of the self when the novel as a form began to focus attention on the myriad of impressions assailing the mind as an incessant shower of innumerable atoms. As Woolf imaginatively demonstrated between *Jacob's Room* (1922) and *To the Lighthouse* (1927), the world can be reflected in an 'I' which is its sum but whose essence becomes elusive.²⁸ Through fluid characters the author obviously calls in question their own personalities: 'Who am I?' asks Bernard in *The Waves* (1931), uncertain whether he has a unique and distinct identity. In *The Years* (1937) Maggie wonders whether we are one or several, yet admits there may be an I, a knot, a centre in the midst of this confusion.²⁹ This centre, however, seems to be inaccessible. It is because of such engagements with the nature of the individual and the self that Maxime Chastaing placed Virginia Woolf in the lineage of Hume, because her 'sensationnalisme' reduced all realities to a 'halo of impressions'.³⁰

Different was the point of view of Nietzsche, whose admiration for the essays of Montaigne is well known and who laid stress on the plurality of the self:

> We concentrate in ourselves the *possibility* of many persons. Only out of circumstances does a *single* form emerge. [...] The 'character' we believe to be ours, inalienable, constant, [...] is only one of the personages equally possible for us, equally alien to us; one of the masques we might have worn.³¹

From another perspective Valéry characterized 'the pure *Self* [moi]' as least personal (*Variété*, vol. V), since he described it as 'absolute, impersonal consciousness, [...] purified of the *I*' (*Variété*, vol. I). To assert the freedom of the mind, Valéry had to overcome the kind of difficulty Nietzsche had initially met: when reflected, the act of the mind gives birth to a soul within a soul and, as in parallel mirrors, an object is perceived between them: 'But which object? In fact, there is no object.'[32]

The originality of the structuralists and the post-modernists mainly lies in the justification of similar views by the ascription of language's pre-eminent role. This primacy of language, however, is now disputed even by philosophers who are not traditionalists. Francis Jacques, for instance, rejects the assumption that 'language alone founds in its own reality, which is the reality of being, the concept of the ego'. He argues that 'subjectivity, however we choose to conceive of it, remains an extra-linguistic presupposition of language'.[33] Besides, post-modernist theories do not seem to be reconcilable with the fact that thought may exist without language.[34] The existentialism of Martin Heidegger and Sartre – which, though in a different way, also tends to negate the reality of the self – is generally silent about animal consciousness.[35] That the latter can exist in the absence of language is admitted by modern scientists as well as by Montaigne, who demonstrated that animals possess intellectual faculties comparable to those of humans in 'Apology for Raymond Sebond' (II, xii).[36] I do not develop this parallel, for the author of the *Essays* resorts to arguments which were already commonplace in his time.

One may conclude, then, that the calling into question of the self by the author of the *Essays* opened the way to its modern dissolution – even if only the germ of this development is necessarily present in his writings. As the following pages will show, the acknowledgement of the instability of the self is counterbalanced by the recognition of its permanence. My purpose in this book is to bring to light an equipoise which preserved the 'modernity' of Montaigne from the excesses of our post-modernity.

2. Persistence and coherence of the self

Though the author of the *Essays* was at times uncertain about the stability and even the unity of the self, he generally acknowledged its presence and did not proclaim its dissolution. Why?

The first reason – as André Gide and other readers noted – was that he never immersed himself in introspection after the manner of Amiel. He was always conscious of the existence of the world and other people. He reminds us that 'he who does not live a little for others hardly lives at all for himself' (III, x: 1138 C; VS 1007). He acknowledges that 'There seems to be nothing for which Nature has better prepared us than fellowship' (I, xxviii: 207 A; VS 184). Speaking from his own experience he declares: 'My essential form is prone to communication' (III, iii: 928 B; VS 823; my translation).³⁷ He knows that our soul 'loses itself in itself when shaken and disturbed unless it is given something to grasp on to, and so we must always provide it with an object to butt up against and to act upon' (I, iv: 19 A; VS 22). With Amiel, and even with Valéry at times, an individual consciousness takes itself for its only object; that is why the subject, separated from objective reality, loses itself in a play of reflections. This radical subjectivity of consciousness is not found in the *Essays*. With Montaigne the self is elusive, but never isolated. He even claims: 'No powerful mind stops within itself' (III, xiii: 1211 C; VS 1068).

Furthermore, the knowledge of the world is indispensable to one who wants to know himself: 'This great world of ours [...] is the looking-glass in which we must gaze to come to know ourselves from the right slant' (I, xx: 177 A; VS 157). The mayor of Bordeaux laid stress on the fact that his belonging to a community and a church constituted a part of his identity, though not the most intimate. Géralde Nakam has rightly emphasized 'the centrality of the town hall of Bordeaux in the experience of the *Essays*', asserting that his own self was revealed to Montaigne in his political action before a deeper revelation through writing.³⁸

An attention to the world perceived by the senses is also denoted by Montaigne's keen interest in the body and its functions.³⁹ The attention he paid to outward appearance led him to make physiognomy an essential element in self-portraiture, for 'there is nothing more probable than the conformity of the body and the mind' (III, xii: 1198 B; VS 1057). The presence of the body is required to constitute the identity of the person: 'limbs wrought together into so interlocked and kindly a compact' cannot be torn 'asunder in divorce' (III, xiii: 1266 B; VS 1114).⁴⁰ He claims that 'anything we do reveals us' (I, l: 338 C; VS 302). He narrates an accident (II, vi), and evokes vividly his 'wrestling with the worst of all diseases' (II, xxxvii: 860 A; VS 760; cf. III, xiii: 1237 B; VS 1090). The sufferings of the body may have stimulated his attention to the self. His health was impaired; his kidneys 'changed their condition' shortly after he started composing his *Essays*, which were at first rather impersonal (III, xiii: 1241 B; VS 1093). An increased attention to the body unified the subjective and the objective, precluded a total absorption of his attention in the labyrinth of an exploration cultivated after the manner of Amiel. Jean Starobinski rightly spoke of Montaigne as 'a body wholly bent on hearing itself live, distinct from itself but wholly orientated towards itself'.⁴¹ Now, with the exception of pathological cases, the body-self cannot suffer a dissolution. The attention Montaigne dedicated to it reinforced his sense of identity.

There is another reason for tempering the occasional description of the self in the *Essays* as unstable, undetermined, a crowd of contradictions.

These are general assertions emphasized by the critics. Yet numerous and precise examples of these contradictions are seldom supplied.[42] In chapter 6, I shall show that Montaigne's preferences for certain 'values' are definite and constant. Nor does he contradict himself in his judgements on the characters and actions of the many historical personages he speaks of, or in his remarks on his own behaviour and his reactions to the events in his life. It is only when he tries to apprehend his 'self' directly that he discovers multiplicity and changeableness. He considers himself from every possible point of view: 'I describe myself standing up and lying down, from front and back, from right and left, and with all my inborn complexities' (III, viii: 1068 C; VS 943). He is thus at once singular and plural, after the manner of the persons represented by Leonardo da Vinci in successive drawings.

However, Montaigne's reflections more often concern his fundamental inclinations and his ordinary behaviour than the aspects of his inner life. He comes thus to discover constant traits in himself, as in the essay 'On presumption', in which he offers a self-portrait which leaves little room for inconstancy and variety, even with the passage of time.[43] He can thus assert 'My Soul is herself alone and used to acting after her fashion' and speak of his 'heavy, lazy, dilatory nature' (II, xvii: 730 A; VS 643). He notes that 'few emotions have disturbed [his] sleep' (II, xvii: 732 B; VS 644). He makes a long enumeration of all the modes of behaviour he cannot naturally practise: 'I cannot, without turning it into an assay of myself, sleep by day, eat snacks between meals, nor eat breakfast, nor go to bed after supper without having a considerable gap, say three hours or more, nor have sexual intercourse except before going to sleep, nor do it standing up' (III, xiii: 1230 B–C; VS 1083).

Even contrasts between some of his attitudes have a permanent character: 'In events I act like a man; in the conduct of events, like a child' (II, xvii: 733B; VS 644). Furthermore, these essential traits of character can be traced to his childhood:

> You cannot extirpate the qualities we are originally born with. There is hardly an emotion in me which sneaks away and hides from my reason, or which is not governed by the consent of almost all of my parts, without schism or inner strife [...], because virtually since birth it has always been one: the same bent, the same route, the same strength. And as for all my general opinions, I have from childhood lodged me where I was to remain. (III, ii: 914–16 B; VS 810–12)

Inconstancy, no doubt, appears in certain motions of the soul, but Montaigne ascribes this instability to conflicting humours, which are conceived according to the physiological model of his times: 'sometimes a melancholic humour gets hold of me; at others, a choleric one; sometimes grief or joy dominate me' (II, xii: 637 A; VS 566).[44] He justifies this changeableness: 'Of my own physical endowments the best is that I am flexible and not stubborn; some of my inclinations are more proper to me than others, more usual and more agreeable, but with very little effort I can turn away from them and glide easily into an opposite style' (III, xiii: 1229 B; VS 1083). He considers it unfitting that you 'should be so beholden to your predispositions that you cannot stray from them nor bend them' (III, iii: 922–3 B; VS 819). This, however, requires an involvement of the will: 'Not being able to control events I control myself' (II, xvii: 732 B; VS 644). This intervention calls for a distinction between the self, the 'moi' and the ego, the 'I'. It is the 'I' that declares 'I study nothing but me': 'Je n'ai que moi pour visée à mes pensées' (II, vi: 424 C; VS 378).

Such a statement implies that the I and the self exist. From a post-structuralist perspective, the self of Montaigne has been denied any reality outside of the *Essays*.[45] I have stated my convictions concerning theoretical issues in my introduction to *Seven Metaphysical Poets*, but I think it unnecessary to reopen this debate, for what matters here is to test the coherence shown by Montaigne in his presentation of his perceptions of his own self.[46] I feel it is obvious that his 'I' here is not simply the 'I' of enunciation, the 'I' of Benveniste, which reduces the 'subject' to its function in language. Nor is it the Lacanian 'I' reduced to a 'shifter' or 'index term' to show 'the problematic and undecidable nature of the I'.[47] It is at once a consciousness and a faculty, a power of directing one's attention, selecting a point of view, inflecting a tendency, modifying an emotion.[48] Here is a testimony:

> Some painful idea gets hold of me; I find it quicker to change it than to subdue it. If I cannot substitute an opposite one for it, I can at least find a different one. Change always solaces it, dissolves it and dispels it. If I cannot fight it, I flee it; and by my flight I make a diversion and use craft. (III, iv: 941 B; VS 835–6)

Montaigne, indeed, is once more cautious in avoiding any commitment and he does not lose himself, but discovers himself in a moment of intense pleasure:

> Is there some pleasure that thrills me? I do not allow it to be purloined by my senses. I associate my soul with it, not so that she will bind herself to it [*s'y engager*], but take joy in it: not losing herself but finding herself in it. (II, xiii: 1263 B–C; VS 1112)

This is a mode of self-control different from the mastery over one's passions illustrated by the Stoics, for he did not hope he could achieve it. It proceeds from a distinction between his soul, or mind, and his consciousness of their common operations. Donald Frame has minutely studied 'the dialogue of Montaigne with his faculties', pointing out that each of them, as well as the soul as a whole, is clearly distinct from the *Je* and subjected to it.[49] I do not, however, agree with his conclusion when he claims that the self for Montaigne is 'primarily soul (the active part), not body (the passive), but it is not soul itself. [...] It seems to be an admixture of all the parts of the soul.'[50] This would lead to an acceptance of a total absence of unity. By contrast, to my mind a sense of continuity and identity is obvious when the author of the *Essays* asserts: 'My doings are ruled by what I am and are in harmony with how I was made ["ma condition"]' (III, ii: 916 C; VS 813).[51]

Though not necessarily related to psychoanalysis, my conception of the ego is in harmony with the Freudian conception as set forth by Castoriadis when he claims that the *Ich*, the conscious *I*, is characterized by a power of self-reflexivity which can turn the activity of the subject into an object, but only by position, not by nature. Though its action is exercised at different levels – biological, sociological and social – each individual psyche is thus endowed with a certain unity, at least as the common origin and combination of united forces, for the conscious subject alone can say: 'I am the cause of my action as a performing activity'.[52] Montaigne would have agreed that one should seek this unity which proceeds at once from the reflected representation of the self and from a power of initiative of the I.[53] According to Geoffrey Miles, Montaigne certainly was capable of associating an ideal of coherence for the self with an acceptance of diversity and change.[54]

The author thus discovers in himself an unexpected constancy. Though claiming he achieved it through an effort of his will, he is also convinced he does not depart from his 'natural' temper: 'This very awareness of my mutability has had the secondary effect of engendering a constancy in my opinions. I have hardly changed any of my first and natural ones' (II, xii: 641 B; VS 569). He acknowledges that 'natural tendencies are helped and reinforced by education, but they can hardly be said to be altered or overmastered. [...] You cannot extirpate the qualities we are originally born with' (III, ii: 913–14 B; VS 810). He does not hesitate to assert: 'the firmest imaginations that I have, and the most general were, so to say, born with me' (II, xvii: 747 A; VS 658; my translation). Comparing his behaviour in youth and in old age he acknowledges that 'in like circumstances, I would still be thus [*tel*]' (III, ii: 917 B; VS 813); he finds that his reason 'is just the same as in my more licentious years' (919 B; VS 815) and concludes: 'I said so when I was young [...]. And I still say so now that my grey hair lends me credit' (921 B–C; VS 816–17).[55]

Montaigne admits, however, that he did not hesitate to wear masks and take delight in playing parts, recalling that in childhood he had 'an assured countenance and a suppleness of voice and gesture when [he] undertook to act various parts in plays' (I, xxvi: 198B; VS 176; my translation). He could 'conceive and believe that there are thousands of different ways of living' and, though he did not later attempt to stage them as Shakespeare did, he always could 'insinuate himself in their place through his imagination' (I, xxxvii: 257 C; VS 229). His enjoyment of theatrical performances is obvious: as a magistrate he would never have banned them and would even have found it 'reasonable' to 'offer such amusements to the people for nothing' (I, xxvii: 199 B; VS B). Yet Montaigne discriminates between the 'role' and the 'person', for he knows that one betrays one's 'identity' when acting a part: 'We should play our role properly, but as the role of a character, which we have adopted. We must not turn masks and semblances into essential realities, nor adopted qualities into attributes of our self' (III, x: 1143–4 B; VS 1011).[56] That he was adept at assuming various roles does not therefore imply the inexistence of a stable individuality; it denotes only a particular faculty in a man whose own features are at once distinctive and constant in other respects.

The origin of his search for self-knowledge, and the composition of his *Essays*, was, according to Montaigne, a 'melancholy humour', which he declares, however, 'most inimical to [his] natural complexion': it was 'brought on by the chagrin caused by the solitary retreat I plunged myself into'. Therefore, he states, 'finding myself quite empty with nothing to write about, I offered myself to myself as theme and object matter' (II, viii: 433 A; VS 385). He left his mind 'in total idleness, caring for itself, concerned only with itself, calmly thinking of itself', conversing with itself (I, viii: 31 A; VS 33). Renaissance treatises underlined the fact that melancholy could be engendered by inactivity as well as by absorption in intellectual work. Yet whatever the origin and nature of Montaigne's black bile may have been, fits of melancholy, while fostering introversion, would not have inevitably led to interrogations of his own identity, since the same phenomenon is not noticeable in other Renaissance writers affected by the same humour.

The part played by Montaigne's close links with Étienne de La Boétie and his mourning for the death of his friend in causing or contributing to this melancholy has been variously interpreted. It is possible that he allowed himself to be absorbed by his friendship to such a point that the death of his friend would have led him to fill a void which had opened in him: 'He alone had the privilege of my true image, which he took away with him. That is why I decipher myself so inquisitively' (III, ix: 1112, note;

VS 983, note 4; my translation). From a different perspective, one might find in this evolution a particular case of a modern philosopher's general claim that 'the relationship with the other precedes the self's experience of itself'.[57]

In this context, Starobinski's note that Montaigne keeping the lost friend in memory constitutes an element of constancy and continuity – 'the only one perhaps in a life which knows itself subjected to inconstancy and discontinuity' – is instructive.[58] But it also raises the question that while this may be true, why should a realization of discontinuity arise only after the death of La Boétie? Montaigne had 'plunged' and 'lost' himself in his friend (I, xxviii: 212 A–C; VS 189), whose death, according to Regosin, would have provoked a sort of vertigo in his realization of his own nothingness.[59] Without denying the intensity and the durableness of Montaigne's affection for his friend, I wonder whether the link established by the author of the *Essays* between this bereavement and the composition of his book might not have been a reconstruction of his experience inspired by and impregnated with the time-honoured commonplaces of Antiquity and the Renaissance about friendship, notably the conviction that the lover lives in the beloved. The perfect union he celebrated might be a posthumous appropriation of the beloved, as if he had absorbed the lost friend. Another point of view is offered by Gisèle Mathieu-Castellani. Relying on circumstantial evidence, she suggests that Montaigne, considering himself his friend's heir, practised a double operation of appropriation: at once of his writings and of his personality.[60]

Lending credence to this interpretation, Géralde Nakam has established that Montaigne persisted in patterning his life and philosophy on external models after his friend's death. Nakam has linked Montaigne's projections to different personages: 'Pyrrho, the just (II,12), Alcibiades, the many-faceted (I,26), Julian, a realist in politics with a horror of cruelty (II,19), Epaminondas for his sense of honour and his reluctance to shed blood (III,1), and of course Socrates [...] (III, xii and xiii)'.[61] This is not an act of slavish imitation. As Starobinski has suggested, channelling these exemplary figures can be seen as allowing Montaigne to gain access to the truth that it is 'the act of self-assertion which constitutes our personal identity'.[62] The choice of model is always dictated by individual tendencies: one does not select indifferently a Stoic sage or a movie star. The text of the *Essays* is therefore doubly mimetic: in a first phase it reveals the bent of Montaigne's mind; in a second phase it becomes consubstantial with an author thus constrained to imitate his model.[63]

Nor is it only 'the publication of [his] manners' that leads Montaigne to think at times that he 'should not prove disloyal to this account of [his] life' (III, ix: 1108 B–C; VS 980). He identifies himself with the image of himself projected on this book which he presents to Madame de Duras as 'some solid body which is able to outlive me by a few years – or a few days' (II, xxxvii: 885 A; VS 783). It is unnecessary to dwell on this point since Starobinski and the best critics have expatiated on his progressive transfer of the responsibility of fixing his identity to writing, to his book, to an image of himself, so that Montaigne does not hesitate to write: 'I am not at all sure whether I would not much rather have given birth to one perfectly formed son by commerce with the Muses than by commerce with my wife' (II, viii: 451 B; VS 401).[64] In his unceasing revisions of the text one can also discern the 'auto-textual motivation, or auto-referentiality' stressed by Rigolot.[65] One may also interpret it as an aspect of self-reflexive consciousness, the natural bent of his mind.

It is therefore through writing that stability is achieved: 'I realize that there is an unexpected benefit from the publication of my manners: in some ways it serves me as a rule' (III, ix: 1108 B; VS 980). This 'account of the assays of my life' (III, xiii: 1224 B; VS 1079) becomes 'a book of one substance with its author' (III, xviii: 755 C; VS 665). In the same paragraph, however, Montaigne acknowledges some colouring: 'By portraying myself for others I have portrayed my own self within me in clearer colours than I possessed at first'. The reason may be that the attempt to stabilize his identity, dictated by a moral ambition at first, became an artistic endeavour, as Starobinski has suggested.[66] Philippe de Lajarte also proposes that when identifying himself with his book Montaigne must have been conscious of bringing about 'a properly Copernican revolution in the history of fiction'.[67]

Montaigne, like Erasmus, believed that 'each mind has a particular face [*faciem*] which his way of speaking must reflect as a mirror'.[68] He further claimed: 'Everyone recognizes me in my book, and my book in me' (III, v: 989 B; VS 875). He had elsewhere noted: 'my book and I go harmoniously forward at the same pace' (III, ii: 909 B; VS 806). Begun after the death of La Boétie, this book became a 'surrogate self', in Terence Cave's phrasing.[69]

This, however, became possible only because the book remained a faithful reflection of what its author named 'my native form' ('To the Reader': lxiii; VS 1), or 'a form entirely his own, a master-form' (III, ii: 914 B; VS 823), or again 'the proper essence of my own form' ('ma forme essentielle') (III, iii: 928 B; VS 823).[70] I find it noteworthy that although the essayist discovered a Heraclitean flux in himself, he thought it best to remind us of the existence of definite forms. By contrast, Renaissance writers such as Ronsard and Spenser insistently evoked the transience of phenomenal forms: 'La matière demeure et la forme se perd' ('Matter endures and the form is lost').[71] This, I think, reveals Montaigne's desire to recover in the very experience of life the stability and permanence a Platonist poet like Spenser needed less on earth since he found it in the transcendence of immutable ideas.

The word 'form' is used in the *Essays* with a particular frequency partly because it is often taken in a loose or general sense to define a condition: 'I am merely a man with a base Form' (III, ix: 1117 B–C; VS 988); an austere way of life (I, xiv: 65 B; VS 61); a mode of speaking ('ma forme de parler') (I, xl: 67 B; VS 63); a mode of writing or even of philosophizing ('cette forme de philosopher') (II, xii: 568 B; VS 509).[72] Screech claims that 'form', when used as a precise philosophical term, is always taken in an Aristotelian sense, implying a close and constant conjunction with matter or a body.[73] However, one may discern particular features which seem to me distinctive. In the address 'To the Reader', this 'forme naïsve' (native form) must emerge from the portrait in which the author describes himself in his 'simple, natural, everyday fashion'. Yet, when Montaigne asserts 'I myself am the subject [*matière*] of my book', this claim reminds us of a warning of Erasmus: a painter can convey only the living outward features of a man, *vivam hominis speciem*, whereas the essential task is to recover the at once native and natural true form of a man: *vera ac nativa hominis forma*.[74] This is the 'form' which can survive all assaults, according to Montaigne:

> Provided that he listen to himself there is no one who does not discover in himself a form entirely his own, a master-form which struggles against his education as well as against the storm of emotions which would gainsay it. In my case I find I am rarely shaken by shocks or agitations, I am virtually ever settled in place. (III, ii: 914 B; VS 811)

Resisting all of the pressures of the institutions of education and society, this individual form seems to me closer to the *haecceitas* of Duns Scotus than the Aristotelian *entelécheia*, since Montaigne insists on the unique character of each individual: 'In the whole world there has never been two identical opinions any more than two identical hairs or seeds. Their more universal characteristic is diversity' (II, xxxvii: 887 A–C; VS 786). To acknowledge the presence of 'diversity' in each individual does not gainsay their essential individuality: 'Souls are most beautiful when they show most variety and flexibility' (III, iii: 922 B; VS 818). Thus, to acknowledge that 'man, totally and throughout, is but patches and many-coloured elements' (II, xx: 766 B; VS 675) is an admission of complexity, not a negation of the existence of a self. That this unique self should happen to be 'various and wavering' ('divers et ondoyant') (I, i: 5 A; VS 9) does not necessitate the attribution of 'several' selves to each individual.

In the celebrated assertion that 'Each man bears the whole form of the human condition' (III, ii: 908 B; VS 805; my translation) Montaigne did not write 'la forme de l'homme', but 'la forme entière de l'humaine condition'. He did not merely mean that we can find in any man the 'form' that distinguishes human nature from animal or angelic nature. Read in its context, this assertion means that the private life of an individual can bear testimony to all the possibilities offered to each individual by their human condition.[75] The particular and the universal are closely associated, but the essence, the reality of existence, is always situated in the individual. As Tzvetan Todorov argues, the nature of man lies precisely in the capacity of all men for developing a culture, a history, an individual identity; their nature consists in not being wholly determined.[76] One might go further, drawing on Ian Maclean's assimilation of this absence of determination and framing it as 'an absence of essence and substance', which 'becomes thereby its own contrary, that is the substance and essence of humanity'.[77] Nevertheless, I think that Montaigne paints himself with such precision that it is impossible to reduce his essence to a mere absence. Though influenced by the Sceptics, he belongs to another line of descent in his self-scrutiny. In his translation of Raymond Sebond he had written: 'there is nothing more familiar, more inward and more closely adapted to each individual than oneself to oneself'.[78] This is already pure Montaigne, but it is also a continuation of the Augustinian tradition, as my next chapter will show.

Some will say that Montaigne entertains an illusion about the reality of the subject. I do myself. Were it true, the way in which this deluded consciousness functions in the *Essays* would remain interesting. My analyses do not require an acceptance of the Cartesian conception of the ego, provided you grant that a synthetic ascription of experience to a unique subject is possible, as Kant argued when he modified the Cartesian intuition and yet rejected the reduction of the subject to a mere succession of impressions, as Hume had done.[79] According to Thomas Powell:

> as Kant said, it must be possible for the 'I think' to accompany all my representations, for experience would be impossible if a single consciousness did not bracket all one's experiences into a unified whole. Whether there is a single unitary *self* underlying this representation of a single unitary consciousness is something that cannot be known but I think it is at least probable.[80]

Echoing the philosopher E. J. Lowe, I do not think the self can be only a bundle of different perceptions. I believe that 'mental states have to be individuated as states of a person'.[81] Ricoeur saw in the ego at least the intentional pole of a field of experience.[82] He went further in *Time and Narrative*:

> To answer the question 'who?', as Hannah Arendt has so forcefully put it, is to tell the story of a life. The story told tells about the 'who' of the action. And the identity of this 'who' therefore itself must be a narrative identity. Without the recourse to narration, the problem of personal identity would in fact be condemned to an antinomy with no solution. Either we must posit a subject identical with itself through the diversity of its different states, or, following Hume and Nietzsche, we must hold that this identical subject is nothing more than a substantialist illusion, whose elimination merely brings to light a pure manifold of cognitions, emotions, and volitions. The dilemma disappears if we substitute for identity understood in the sense of being the same (*idem*), identity understood in the sense of oneself as self-same ['soi-même'] (*ipse*). The difference between *idem* and *ipse* is nothing more than the difference between a substantial or formal identity and a narrative identity.[83]

This is true of the subject as Montaigne presents it. The painting and gradual retouching of the self through writing has been, indeed, a narrative operation. Yet it may have been the reflection of a substantial reality, since *ipse* seems to imply the constant presence of the overarching *I* assumed in my analysis of various texts in the *Essays*. I am willing to grant that any discourse may be criss-crossed by other discourses, as many linguists insistently warn us.[84] One may see a Bakhtinian polyphony in the *Essays*, studded with quotations and allusions. Yet when borrowing other voices, at times their author nevertheless makes a personal choice which does not stifle his own voice and makes such borrowings consubstantial. I could even admit that I do not really care whether the *ego* present in the *Essays* is or is not an illusion, inasmuch as my essential purpose in this book is to trace the evolution of subjectivity from Antiquity to the Renaissance. As such, devotees of Mikhail Bakhtin and Lacan could retain their convictions and yet take some interest in the following chapter. What I hope to make evident is that the forms of self-consciousness observed in the *Essays* are absent or only dimly discernible in the literature of the Western world before Montaigne.

Notes

1   *Essays*, II, i: 377 B–C; VS 335. All references to the *Essays* cite, respectively, the book, the number of the essay and the page number in the translation by M. A. Screech (*Michel de Montaigne. The Complete Essays*, Harmondsworth:

Penguin Books, 1991; reprinted with corrections, 2003), followed by the page number in the Villey–Saulnier (VS) edition of *Les Essais* (*Michel de Montaigne. Les Essais*, Édition Villey–Saulnier, augmentée en 2004 d'une préface et d'un supplément de Marcel Conche, Paris: Quadrige/Presses Universitaires de France, 2004). The letters A, B, C indicate the successive texts: 1580–2, 1588, 1592–5.

2 'Genèse et dilemme de la conscience moderne', *Revue de la Méditerranée*, XII, 1952–3, p. 398. James J. Supple and Noël Peacock later called attention to the presence in this text of an 'I' which dominates the changing dispositions but without linking his action to a particular form of self-consciousness. James J. Supple and Noël Peacock, eds, *Lire* Les Essais *de Montaigne: perspectives critiques* (Paris: Champion, 2001), p. 118.

3 See *infra*, chapter 2, p. 38.

4 Géralde Nakam has listed these meanings in *Le dernier Montaigne* (Paris: Champion, 2002), p. 236.

5 Cf. 'Every moment it seems to me that I am running away from myself' (I, xx: 97A; VS 88). Yves Delègue ascribes this impression to the 'discovery of a void at the heart of the subject', but Montaigne never speaks of a void. Yves Delègue, *Montaigne et la mauvaise foi. L'ecriture de la vérité* (Paris: Champion, 1998).

6 Hugo Friedrich, *Montaigne*, trans. R. Rovini (Paris: Gallimard, 1968), p. 274.

7 *Ibid.*, p. 298.

8 See R. Ellrodt, *L'inspiration personnelle et l'esprit du temps chez les poètes Métaphysiques anglais* (Paris: Corti, 1960, new edition, 1973); vol. I, ch. iv; R. Ellrodt, *Seven Metaphysical Poets: A Structural Study of the Unchanging Self* (Oxford University Press, 2000), p. 22.

9 See *infra*, chapter 3, p. 81. Self-deprecation is another aspect of this distancing noted by Nakam in *Le dernier Montaigne*, pp. 246–9.

10 Montaigne confesses and even praises this irresolution (II, xvii: 743 A–B; VS 654). For a comparison with Hamlet, see *infra*, chapter 4, section 1.

11 See R. Ellrodt, 'La conscience moderne de saint Augustin à Jean-Paul Sartre', in *Actes du groupe de recherche sur la conscience de soi* (Publications de la Faculté des Lettres et Sciences Humaines de Nice, first series, vol. XVIII, 1980); and R. Ellrodt, ed., *Genèse de la conscience moderne* (Presses Universitaires de France, 1983), épilogue. In 'Lecture de Montaigne', first published in *Les Temps Modernes*, 27 (1947), Maurice Merleau-Ponty had chosen Montaigne's statement 'Je m'engage difficilement' for his epigraph, but curiously abstained from any comment on it. See Maurice Merleau-Ponty, 'Lecture de Montaigne', in *Signes* (Paris: Gallimard, 1960).

12 My translation; 'double creatures' in Screech.

13 J.-P. Sartre, *L'être et le néant* (Paris: Gallimard, 1943), p. 110.

14 In *Route par ailleurs*, André Tournon recently noted that one could find approximations of some statements of Montaigne in 'existentialist' philosophy, which explains why Merleau-Ponty and Francis Jeanson took an interest in the *Essays*. He adds, however, that the parallel may be misleading, which is

true but does not make it irrelevant. André Tournon, *Route par ailleurs: le 'nouveau langage' des Essais* (Paris: Champion, 2006), p. 217, note 1.
15   David Hume, *Treatise of Human Nature* (1739–40), I, 4, vi.
16   John Locke, *An Essay Concerning Human Understanding* (1689), II, xxvii: 'since consciousness always accompanies thinking, and it is that which makes every one to be what he calls self, [...] in this alone consists personal identity, i.e. the sameness of a rational being'. Quote taken from the edition collated and annotated by A. C. Fraser (Mineola, NY: Dover, 2003), vol. I, p. 449.
17   Emilienne Naert, in Ellrodt, ed., *Genèse*, p. 176.
18   Alain Bony, *ibid.*, p. 184.
19   Bernard Brugière, *ibid.*, p. 239.
20   On Donne see my *Seven Metaphysical Poets*, ch. 1.
21   In *Beyond Good and Evil*, vol. I, p. 17, Nietzsche wrote: 'a thought comes to my mind when "it" wants and not when "I" want. [...] Something is thinking, but that this something precisely is the ancient and famous "I" is a mere hypothesis'. Quoted by Alain de Libéra, *Archéologie du sujet: vol. I, Naissance du sujet* (Paris: Vrin, 2007), p. 41 (my translation).
22   H.-F. Berchet, in *Encyclopaedia universalis*, 'Amiel'.
23   Entry for 19 April 1876 in Amiel's *Journal intime*, eds Bernard Gagnebin and Philippe Monnier (Paris: L'Age d'homme, 1990), vol. X, p. 681 (my translation).
24   Entry for 8 March 1868, *ibid.*, vol. VII, p. 12.
25   Entry for 9 September 1876, *ibid.*, vol. X, p. 902.
26   See Jean Starobinski, 'Sur quelques formes de critique de la notion d'identité (remarques historiques)', in Odo Marquard and Karlheinz Stierle, eds, *Identität* (Munich: Wilhelm Fink, 1979), pp. 644–53.
27   According to Judith Ryan, 'Proust's nameless narrator, Musil's "man without qualities", Woolf's world "seen without a self" are all direct descendants of empiricist psychology with its indeterminate or disseminated subject'. Judith Ryan, *The Vanishing Subject* (University of Chicago Press, 1991), p. 228.
28   Virginia Woolf, *The Common Reader* (London: Hogarth Press, 1925), vol. I, p. 189.
29   Virginia Woolf, *The Waves* (London: Hogarth Press, 1931), p. 205; *The Years* (London: Hogarth Press, 1937), pp. 150, 395.
30   Maxime Chastaing, *La philosophie de Virginia Woolf* (Presses Universitaires de France, 1951), p. 12.
31   Nietzsche quoted by Edouard Gaède, *Nietzsche et Valéry* (Paris: Gallimard, 1962), p. 192 (my translation); Gaède cites the Musarion edition of Nietzsche, vol. xvi, pp. 304–5. See also Brendan Donellan, 'Nietzsche and Montaigne', *Colloquia Germanica*, 19 (1986), pp. 1–20. According to Nietzsche, Montaigne initiated a movement for the liberation of thought which inspired Shakespeare only from an artistic point of view: *Kritische Studien Ausgabe*, vol. xi, p. 159, quoted by Donellan, 'Nietzsche and Montaigne', p. 6. See also Nicola Panichi, *Montaigne e Nietzsche* (Paris: Champion, 2008). Alain

Renaut discerns a continuity between the 'I' of Leibnitz, based on the monad, and the Nietzschean interpretation of the Cartesian *cogito*, thus rejecting the empirical *cogito* of Locke and Hume. A twofold influence is possible. Alain Renaut, *L'ère de l'individu: contribution à une histoire de la subjectivité* (Paris: Gallimard, 1989).

32 Paul Valéry, *Mauvaises pensées et autres* (Paris: Gallimard, 1942), p. 166.
33 Francis Jacques, *Difference and Subjectivity: Dialogue and Personal Identity* (Yale University Press, 1991), p. 30.
34 See Dominique Laplane, *La pensée d'outre-mots: la pensée sans langage et la relation pensée-langage* (Paris: Institut Synthélabo pour le progrès de la connaissance, 2000).
35 This silence is justified by Heidegger's distinction between people and animals deprived of world consciousness: see Luc Ferry and Alain Renaut, *Heidegger et les Modernes* (Paris: Grasset, 1988.), pp. 201–2. But animals may be conscious without having a world consciousness.
36 See Henri Ey, *La conscience* (Presses Universitaires de France, 2nd edn, 1968), pp. 7–11; C. Allen and M. Bekoff, *Species of Mind* (Cambridge, MA: MIT Press, 1997), ch. 8; P. Carruthers, *The Animals Issue* (Cambridge University Press, 1997).
37 Cf. 'I am sociable to the point of excess' (III, ix: 110 C; VS 982).
38 Gérald Nakam, 'Montaigne maire de Bordeaux: à la mairie et dans les Essais', *Bulletin de la Société des Amis de Montaigne*, 8e série, 13–14 (1983), pp. 7–28.
39 See Jean Céard, 'Montaigne et l'intériorité', in M. T. Jones-Davies, ed., *L'intériorité au temps de la Renaissance* (Paris: Champion, 2005), pp. 144–8.
40 Cf. II, xvii: 727 A; VS 639: 'Those who wish to take our two principal pieces apart ... are wrong'.
41 Jean Starobinski, *Montaigne en mouvement* (Paris: Gallimard, 1982), p. 266.
42 Jean-Yves Pouilloux, *Lire les 'Essais' de Montaigne* (Paris: Maspéro, 1969), p. 180, had noted that Montaigne, unable to give a positive definition of himself, resorts to a series of negations: 'no memory, no concentration' (III, x: 1137 B; VS 1005).
43 II, xvii, throughout; cf. III, ii: 915B; VS 812 ('My custom is to be entirely given to what I do'); III, iii: 924–5 B; VS 820–1; III, xiii, *passim*.
44 'On physiognomy' offers another instance of his adhesion to the psycho-physiological theories of his time.
45 See Richard L. Regosin, 'Recent trends in Montaigne scholarship: a post-structuralist perspective', *Renaissance Quarterly*, 38 (1984), pp. 34–54.
46 See also Robert Ellrodt, 'Literary theory and the search for certainty', *New Literary History*, 17 (1996), pp. 529–43; Robert Ellrodt, 'Unchanging forms of identity in literary expression', *European Review: Interdisciplinary Journal of the Academia Europaea*, 7:1 (1999), pp. 113–26.
47 See 'Shifter' in Dylan Evans, *An Introductory Dictionary of Lacanian Psychoanalysis* (London: Routledge, 1996).
48 For Rigolot, 'the "I" speaking in the *Essays* stands for the man speaking

in the present moment, a moment which is paradoxically eternized when painted on the page'. François Rigolot, *Les métamorphoses de Montaigne* (Presses Universitaires de France, 1988), p. 100. But this 'I' of the moment knows he is, outside the page, an 'I' identical with the 'I' speaking in all the moments past or to come, since dwelling in the same body, reassembling the same remembrances. That is why Montaigne can say: 'For many years now the target of my thoughts has been myself alone' (II, vi: 424 C; VS 378).

49 Donald M. Frame, 'Montaigne's dialogue with his faculties', *French Forum*, 1 (1976), p. 198.
50 *Ibid.*, p. 207.
51 His attention to the body also contributes to his perception of his 'essential uniqueness', as Glyn Norton noted in *Montaigne and the Introspective Mind* (La Haye: Mouton, 1975), p. 169.
52 Cornelius Castoriadis, 'L'état du sujet aujourd'hui', *Topique. Revue Freudienne*, 38 (1986), pp. 13, 26, 37. Cf. Yves Lebeau, 'Je, sujet et identification', *Topique: Revue Freudienne*, 37 (1986), pp. 77–92.
53 Castoriadis, 'L'état du sujet aujourd'hui', p. 37; cf. Ellrodt, *Seven Metaphysical Poets*, p. 8.
54 Geoffrey Miles, *Shakespeare and the Constant Romans* (Oxford: Clarendon Press, 1996), pp. 97, 109.
55 This continuity of the inner self is the more remarkable since Montaigne underlines the changes in outward physical appearance: 'in how many ways it [my portrait] is no longer me!' (III, xiii: 1251 B; VS 1102).
56 Omitting the second sentence in this quotation, Rigolot comes to write: 'The theatrical illusion allows to become another thus in a way to become oneself'. About another statement, 'I only quote others the better to quote myself [*me dire*]' (I, xxvi: 166 C; VS 148), he concludes: 'to tell oneself means trying to act successively the parts of David and Goliath, of Alexander and Socrates, while hoping to discover oneself one day'. Rigolot, *Les metamorphoses*, p. 213 (my translation).
57 Jacques, *Difference and Subjectivity*, p. 12.
58 Starobinski, 'Sur quelques formes', p. 29.
59 Richard L. Regosin, *The Matter of My Book: Montaigne's 'Essais' as the Book of the Self* (University of California Press, 1977), pp. 22ff.
60 Gisèle Mathieu-Castellani, *Montaigne ou la vérité du mensonge* (Geneva: Droz, 2000), p. 105.
61 Nakam, *Le dernier Montaigne*, pp. 241–2.
62 Starobinski, *Montaigne en mouvement*, pp. 29–30.
63 Cf. Steve Rendall, *Distinguo: Reading Montaigne Differently* (Oxford: Clarendon Press, 1992), p. 6.
64 Starobinski, *Montaigne en mouvement*, p. 43.
65 Rigolot, *Les metamorphoses*, p. 147.
66 Jean Starobinski, 'Montaigne et la dénonciation du mensonge', in Odo Marquard and Karlheinz Stierle, eds, *Identität* (Munich: Wilhelm Fink, 1979), p. 478. Cf. Nakam, *Le dernier Montaigne*, p. 73.

67 Philippe de Lajarte, 'Les Essais de Montaigne et la naissance de l'auteur moderne', in J. R. Fanlo, ed., 'D'une fantastique bigarrure'. Le texte composite à la Renaissance. Études offertes à André Tournon (Paris: Champion, 2000), p. 174.
68 Desiderius Erasmus, Ciceronianus, in Opera Omnia (Leyden, 1703–6), vol. I, fol. 1022 B.
69 Terence Cave, The Cornucopian Text: Problems of Writing in the French Renaissance (Oxford University Press, 1979), pp. 273–4.
70 Marcel Conche points out that this master form 'is not consciousness, but the singular nature of each man, the *idios poion* of the Stoics'. Marcel Conche, Montaigne et la philosophie (Presses Universitaires de France, 1996), p. 114.
71 Ronsard, Élégie xxiv ('Aux bûcherons de la forêt de Gastine'); Spenser, Faerie Queene, III, vi, 38: 'The substance is not chaungd nor altered / But th'only forme and outward fashion'.
72 I give priority to VS when Screech substitutes another term for 'forme', which is justified in the absence of a philosophic meaning.
73 M. A. Screech, Montaigne and Melancholy (London: Duckworth, 1983), pp. 78–9, 107–8, 143.
74 Desiderius Erasmus, Ciceronianus (1528), LB, I, 988 C–E; quoted by Gérard Defaux, Marot, Rabelais, Montaigne: l'écriture comme présence (Paris: Champion; Geneva: Slatkine, 1987), pp. 190–1.
75 Hamlin suggests that Montaigne himself felt capable of experiencing imaginatively whatever people experience, 'totalizing in his own individual form all the forms of mankind'. William M. Hamlin, The Image of America in Montaigne, Spenser, and Shakespeare (New York: St Martin's Press, 1995), p. 63. In his Montaigne, une vérité singulière (Paris: Gallimard, 2012), published shortly after my Montaigne et Shakespeare and shortly before this translation, Jean-Yves Pouilloux devotes a chapter to an elaborate and brilliant interpretation of this 'phrase emblématique'. I would not do justice to it if I tried to sum it up. His views and mine, though different, do not seem to me irreconcilable.
76 Tzvetan Todorov, Le jardin imparfait: la pensée humaniste en France (Paris: Grasset, 1998), p. 82.
77 Ian Maclean, Montaigne philosophe (Presses Universitaires de France, 1996), p. 83.
78 Montaigne, La théologie naturelle de Raymond Sebond (Paris, 1581), ch. 1, fol. 5r.
79 Thomas Powell, Kant's Theory of Self-consciousness (Oxford: Clarendon Press, 1990), pp. 28, 46.
80 Ibid., pp. 55–6.
81 E. J. Lowe, Subjects of Experience (Cambridge University Press, 1996), p. 31.
82 See L. E. Hahn, The Philosophy of Paul Ricoeur (Chicago: Open Court, 1994), p. 587.
83 Paul Ricoeur, Time and Narrative, vol. III, trans. Kathleen Blamey and David Pellauer (Chicago University Press, 1988), p. 246. In this translation of a

passage from *Temps et récit, vol. III: Le temps raconté* (Paris: Éditions du Seuil, 1985), p. 355, I have corrected the second sentence.

84 For instance, Mirna Velcic-Canivez, 'La polyphonie: Bakhtine et Ducrot', *Poétique*, 131 (September 2002), pp. 359–82. With Francis Jacques, *Difference and Subjectivity*, p. 285, I accept Bakhtin's claim that 'no individual voice could make itself understood without integrating itself into the complex chorus of the other voices that are already present, in relation to which it must situate itself'. In other respects we both part company with Bakhtin.

Chapter 2

The progress of subjectivity from Antiquity to Montaigne

During my exploration of the wide field of this subject I have, naturally, relied many times on previous research, while reserving the right to check, adopt, temper and occasionally reject its conclusions. Within these parameters, I claim that my constant confrontation of literary, philosophical and religious sources in various countries and languages and my contribution to the debates highlighted in this book are original.[1]

1. The Hellenic world

In European literature, the calling into question of the self we can observe in the *Essays* of Montaigne anticipates later interrogations in modern and post-modern literature. The question of how far this was an innovation can be answered only after briefly surveying the evolution and trajectory of subjectivity in the Western world.

Montaigne himself stressed the influence of Greek thought:

> It must be important to put into effect the counsel that each man should know himself, since that god of light and learning [Apollo] had it placed on the tympanum of his temple as comprising the totality of the advice which he had to give us. (III, xiii: 1219 B; VS 1075)

The Delphic injunction 'Know thyself' has been so often repeated by philosophers and priests, moralists and poets, and pagans and Christians, that one may be forgiven for thinking that humanity has always been concerned with its identity. Yet the quest for self-knowledge has been differently understood and practised from Plato to St Bernard, or from St Bernard to Erasmus, or indeed to Montaigne. The successors of Socrates invited man to realize he was not a god but a mortal who had to shun *hubris*: he had to know what he was capable of doing and achieve self-mastery rather than mere self-consciousness.² The Socratic injunction was linked to the Greek precept *Mêden agan*, echoed in the Latin *ne quid nimi*s, 'nothing in excess', in Plato's *Protagoras*. Ultimately, what can be viewed as a search for self-knowledge can be more accurately positioned not as a questioning of his identity, but man's quest to estimate his own capacities – a reading supported by Xenophon's and Epictetus's insistence on this.

Michel Foucault has called attention to another precept, originally associated with the *gnôthi seauton*, but less widespread, *epimeleia heautou* or 'care of the self'. Involving 'all the transformations of the self required for having access to truth', Foucault's position is that the Stoic will be led to 'attend to himself as the object of his care'. Nevertheless, this 'would not make the self the essential object of knowledge; it is a knowledge concerned with things, concerned with the world', yet 'its effect and function is to modify the being of the subject'.³ I would suggest that, read this way, this 'care of the self' has little connection with the quest for self-knowledge illustrated by Montaigne.

Richard Broxton Onians insists that in archaic Greek literature the representation of states of consciousness was materialistic.⁴ This led to a fragmentation of the soul into a 'plurality of organs, each of them endowed with an autonomy which allowed them to be treated almost as individuals'.⁵ Within this, therefore, the self appears to be absent – an interpretation supported by Bruno Snell's assertion that 'the archaic Greeks do not perceive the human body as unitary'.⁶ Nor, I suggest, are they able to conceive a fundamental opposition between the body and the mind. Only by the end of the fifth century BC would the psyche become a unitary soul.⁷

Augmenting these interrelated yet distinct interpretations, mystical sects had earlier posited a conception of the soul as a *daemon*, 'a being coming from outside, kin with the divine'.⁸ The psyche was then at once 'an experience lived intimately by the subject' and 'the first frame allowing the inner world to become objective and progressively elaborate the structure of the self'. Jean-Pierre Vernant, however, adds a precise modifier to this concept, stating that 'since the soul is divine, it exceeds, it outpasses the individual'.⁹ It is this impersonal character, I feel, which is retained in the thoughts of the Greek philosophical canon on the subject.

Does this separation mean that the heroes and gods are individualized? In Hesiod's *Works and Days*, men of the 'third race' went to 'Hades' house of decay leaving no names'.¹⁰ The hero, a demi-god, retains his proper name in the world beyond death but he is defined only by his achievements, which 'are not the displaying of a personal virtue, but the sign of a divine grace'.¹¹ Even among the gods, the self is ill defined, if not absent. The Hellenic gods 'are Powers, not persons' according to Jean-Pierre Vernant, who quotes Walter Friedrich Otto: 'among the Greek gods no feature calls attention to a *self*, none speaks of an *ego*' (Otto's italics). Thus the representation of the god 'does not set forth a subject in its singularity, but an impersonal type'.¹²

Passions, then, are ascribed to the intrusion of a god in the human mind, rather than an emotional or intellectual act of self-agency. When a hero says a god has 'inspired' an action, he means that the god has literally 'breathed' it into him. This does not free the individual from all self-responsibility, of course, but it changes the nature of that responsibility. For example, in the *Iliad* (XIX, 86–9) Agamemnon, guilty of stealing Briseis from Achilles, claims he was not the sole cause of this act: 'Zeus and my fate and the Erinyes that walk in darkness, they it was who put wild Ate in my mind on that day when of myself [*autos*] I took Achilles' captive from him.' Following E. R. Dodds, A. D. Nuttall concludes there is no contradiction for Agamemnon between 'Zeus [and not I] did this in me' and 'I myself have done it'.¹³ Though it was caused by a divine intervention, the individual is the author of his action: he cannot exculpate himself. As such, and certainly logically, Agamemnon therefore accepts responsibility for his actions and agrees to pay restitution. However, as Nuttall also pointed out, this arrangement means that the Homeric hero is conscious of alternatives: he does not know 'whether he went to Pylos incited by some God or by his own *thumos*' (*Odyssey*, IV, 712–13).¹⁴ The *thumos*, however, is not the mind, but 'the vital principle that thinks and feels and prompts to action', and its physical link with the lungs has been stressed.¹⁵

When Onians insists on the physiological origins of the Greek or Latin terms used for the mind and the emotions, I am inclined to think he did not take into account the historical evolution which gradually effaced their etymological meaning, although the original sense is very much present in Greek tragedy up to Euripides. I am not sure Martial still thought of wisdom as being associated with 'moisture in the chest', or that Lucilius, Horace and Lucretius 'connected the mind with *venae* in the chest' when they spoke of the *venae*, or sources of their genius.¹⁶ I also think it likely that the ascription of passions or actions to the intervention of a god progressively became a metaphor for the Ancients as well as for Racine when he described the love of Phaedra: 'C'est Vénus toute entière à sa proie attachée' (*Phèdre*, I, iii, 306).

In studying the 'genesis of European thought' from these antiquarian roots, Bruno Snell argues that a suggestion of the individual as we might know him becomes perceptible in Greek lyrical poetry in its emergence from anonymity. This materialization of personality is said to be perceptible in the poems of Archilochus, yet when he declares himself 'slain by desire', he claims that his sufferings are due to 'the gods that pierce him to the bone'.[17] Snell noted his self-absorption, but it does not lead to self-analysis. This is also true, much later, of Callimachus, although importantly he no longer ascribed passion as a form of divine intervention.[18]

Likewise, it has been claimed that Sappho endows her personages with a true identity, which may be granted when you add: 'yet this consciousness of their self is experienced in passivity and powerlessness'.[19] Love for Sappho continues to be considered as the intervention of a divine power and her most famous poem is, indeed, the expression of a consciousness of the body rather than a manifestation of self-consciousness.[20] The paraphrase of Catullus quoted by Montaigne preserved its characteristics and its special intensity due to the very absence of any pronoun or grammatical sign that would associate the primary sensation with a 'person':

> lingua sed torpet, tenuis sub artus
> flamma dimanat, sonitu suopte
> tintinnant aures, gemina teguntur
> lumina nocte.[21]

Anacreon, mentioned by Montaigne (III, v: 892 B), will later grow more conscious of the psychological complexities of love, anticipating the paradoxes of Catullus and Ovid (constantly repeated in later ages), when he writes: 'Once more I love and I love not / I am infuriated, yet I am not'.[22] Perhaps equally pertinently, through his satirical inspiration Archilochus had earlier revealed his personality. To experience frustrations leads one to the expression of demands and the assertion of personal values; this will be confirmed by Elizabethan satire in chapter 3.[23] Nevertheless, his apostrophes to his heart are soliloquies but still devoid of introspection.

Greek tragedy seems to have had its origin in satire, relying on the soliloquy. Within this an evolution is traceable from Aeschylus to Euripides. While Vickers assumes that, in a general way, 'in Greek tragedy [...] man is free and responsible', and although Creon and other characters acknowledge they are the authors of their actions and admit their guilt, they are still convinced that they acted under the influence of a god or a passion unrelated to their conscious will.[24] Suzanne Saïd, like Vernant, maintains that the decisions of the heroes of Aeschylus cannot be interpreted as the result of an inner process.[25] But unlike them, the Sophoclean hero asserts his self-determination when facing the gods, rejecting advice and ignoring threats when acting in accordance with his own nature.[26] Nevertheless, she concludes, 'Antigone's reliance on her self-consciousness should not be interpreted as the realization of an irreducible singularity'.[27]

According to Saïd, 'it is only with Euripides that the self takes on an individual character', but she does not offer an illustration of this in her essay.[28] Nevertheless, I think it is fair to agree with and yet temper this assertion. It is indisputable that the characters of Euripides are individualized. An instance of this is when Medea sees herself as she is, not as she appears to others.[29] Like Medea, they may be agitated by contrary passions and 'devoid of steadfastness'; like Agamemnon, they may 'shift yet again'.[30] They are conscious of their versatility. Medea proclaims her character is made up of contrasts, going so far as to debate the matter with herself.[31] The heroes of Euripides also have a moral conscience and they acknowledge their individual responsibility. Orestes, for example, says he 'both wanted and did not want to go' into exile.[32] Nevertheless, the characters still often claim that the gods inspired their passions and their actions, as Electra does for the murder of her mother: 'What Apollo, what oracle ordained that I should be the murderer of my mother?'[33] Similarly, Orestes worries he 'might be overcome by the goddesses' madness' and when Heracles asks who killed his children Amphitryon answers: 'You, your arrows, and whichever of the gods is responsible'.[34] Also Theseus says: 'Here we see how Hera fights'.[35] Thus it can be seen that passions and pains are externalized, grasped in their corporeal effects. Awakening after a fit of madness, Heracles declares: 'a wave overran me, disrupting my soul', adding 'my breathing is hot and shallow, not a steady stream from my lungs'.[36] A devastating remorse also afflicts the body of Orestes: 'when the madness subsides, my body is limp and drained'.[37]

The self-consciousness that emerges in the tragedies of Euripides seems to me to be still in a period of transition, perhaps on account of the influence of the myths preserved for dramatic requirements when sceptical tendencies are already apparent in anxious questionings:

> What is god, or not god, or what is in between?
> Which of mortals can say after searching?
> He who can see the divine
> leaping this way and that and back again
> in contradictory unexpected shifts of fortune.[38]

For similar reasons Roman Seneca, when taking up the Greek myths, left little room for the expression of inwardness, although it can be found in his letters. A few moments of introspection barely emerge from a flood of descriptions, ravings or lamentations. The sufferings and the frenzy of Clytemnestra and Deianira, Oedipus, Thyestes and Atreus are exteriorized. There are frequent monologues, but inner debates are rare, even when a character feels the strain of 'opposite currents' (*Agamemnon*, l. 138). Charles and Michelle Martindale speak of 'obsessive introspection'; yet, in the only passage they quote from Seneca's *Hercules Furens* (ll. 1258–61), the hero describes his new states of mind objectively and I fail to discover in his speech an interiority that could lead to a thoughtful self-questioning.[39]

In this analysis, I pass over the historians Herodotus and Thucydides, as their primary concern was with objective facts, and so I come to the philosophers.[40] Plato, who founded the Academy in 387 BC, spread the Socratic invitation to self-knowledge. He seems to have approached an intuition of individuality but his philosophy of love led to a process of 'disindividualization'.[41] When calling man to ignore emotions and follow reason, Socrates refused to seek a foundation for moral conduct in subjective states and sought to discover universal standards for behaviour. Plato originated a philosophical and mystical tradition of an obvious continuity, which may therefore be examined now, since it will have no bearing on Montaigne's conception of individuality. When Socrates undertakes to prove that neither the body, nor the union of body and soul, is man, and asserts that 'the soul is man' (1 *Alcibiades* 130e), his position is, of course, antipodal to the conception of Montaigne, with his constant attention to the body and his conviction that the union of body and soul characterizes man and constitutes the personality of each individual. Socrates assumes that, if the soul is to know herself, one must look at the soul (he does not say 'at oneself') and especially at 'that part of the soul which resembles the divine', that is, the part of the soul 'which has to do with wisdom and knowledge'. He who looks at this part of the soul is 'most likely to know himself' (1 *Alcibiades* 133). In the Platonic tradition, followed by Plotinus (*Enneads* VI, 9, 11), what the soul apprehends is the intellectual soul, united to the body but transcending the personal.

The Platonic introversion, instead of reminding man that he is not God, as Montaigne insistently does, invites him to know himself divine. *Scito te esse deum* is the most insistent expression of this conviction: it will recur in Plutarch, Macrobius, Philo and Plotinus.[42] The Platonic ideal of self-knowledge will turn into self-examination only with Christianity. Its orientation remains impersonal when Plotinus objectively examines the relation between 'the soul, called divine, which is our essential constituent' and 'the other soul, which comes from the universe' (IV, iii, 27).[43] The latter soul remembers the actions done in her life, which is her particular sphere; but the essential soul, who recovers in the moment of death recollections of her previous lives, must free herself of all remembrances of earthly life to enter what Plotinus calls the intelligible world (IV, iii, 27 and 32). Our attention must therefore be always focused on intelligible objects: 'all attention directed to oneself is useless and vain' (IV, iv, 25). When the individual soul is in the intelligible world, 'the self is all things; the self and its object are one' (IV, iv, 2). The philosopher agrees that 'to think and to think that one is thinking are two different things'; but he takes no interest in the individual intuition of a *cogito* (II, ix, 1).

Plotinus condemns the narcissistic love of the soul for herself, for 'individuality and totality are in opposition' in his eyes; one must aim at a union of the self and the all. When this union is achieved, the self is no longer entrenched in his individuality and must be conceived as the interiority of a consciousness which, when apprehending her interiority, gains access to the universal apprehension of the all.[44]

Later, Neo-Platonist thinkers and theologians will perpetuate this conception of self-knowledge. The soul absorbed in herself has her attention constantly directed towards the vision of the all, the vision of God. In the Pseudo-Dionysius of the *Corpus areopagiticum* or *Corpus dionysiacum*, as in Gregory of Nyssa, the absorption in the inner life is always linked to a release from the body.[45] When they follow the Alexandrian Neo-Platonic line of thought, Renaissance thinkers do not show more interest in the operations of individual self-consciousness. After calling man to 'separate his soul from the body', for example, Ficino invites the soul 'to seek herself where her aspiration resides, outside the body' and 'outside the world'.[46]

Returning to our chronological overview, we find in Aristotle the founder of another tradition which hardly proved more favourable to an investigation into the individual processes of self-consciousness. His conception of the *intellectus agens* which produces the intelligible was not centred on thought itself but on the object of this thought.[47] He was, of course, alert to the fact that perception is a sensation of sensation, but ascribed this 'sense of sensing' to a special organ, objectively conceived, which became the Scholastic *sensus communis* (*On the Soul*, III, 1, 425 a–b). The object perceived remains outside the soul; what is intelligible is in the soul and is apprehended by the *intellectus agens*. The personality is in the soul, but the soul, conceived as an entelechy, is always perceived as an object rather than a subject.[48] At no moment does Aristotle introduce the notion of an 'I' (*On the Soul*, III, 3–4). It has been claimed that he anticipated the Cartesian *cogito* in asserting that, if someone perceives himself for a continuous moment, he must necessarily know he exists (*De sensu*, 7, 448 a 25). But this is an argument in a debate concerning the

Pythagorean doctrine of time. I would argue that it is not a living intuition experienced in a moment of reflexive self-consciousness.[49]

In opposition to Plato and Aristotle, Epicure and his disciples elaborated a materialistic conception of the soul which did not invite introspection. Nevertheless, their search for pleasure as the highest good may have called for a keener attention to the desires and emotions of the individual. It was the Sceptics, however, who were primarily responsible for the progress of subjectivity. In calling attention to the relativity of human judgements, they apprehended the unique and original value of each individual experience. As Léon Brunschvicg argues, 'for the Cyrenaics [who had a sceptical theory of knowledge] the only reality is the individual as he appears to himself in the moment of experience'.[50] This is an assertion which does not guarantee the continuity of the self. One must wait for the second century of the Christian era and the *Pyrrhōneioi hypotypōseis* of Sextus Empiricus to discover some remarks on the variety of humours (XIV, 79) and the illusions of lovers (XIV, 100, 109) that may be interpreted as being due to the emergence of a self-consciousness first awakened among the Roman poets, as the following section will show.[51] Yet only with St Augustine will Sceptic doubt become a living experience leading to inward probing. Nevertheless, it is clear that self-consciousness had progressed under the influence of the Stoics.

Like the Cynics before them, those who initiated this current of thought acknowledged that only individuals exist. In the Greek world, however, their attention was focused on physics, with a materialist and deterministic bias, rather than on subjective experience. The early Stoics already invited man to live in accordance with his individuality while obeying the laws of the cosmos, but interrogations on the inner life will mainly appear among the Roman writers they influenced.

2. The Roman world

The *Aeneid* offers a striking illustration of a hesitation between two conceptions of passion and human action, either considered as an impulse due to a god or as the manifestation of a personal desire and an individual will. Feeling suddenly rapt, Nisus wonders 'do the gods, Euryalus, put this fire in our hearts, / or does his own wild longing become to each man a god?' (IX, 184–5).[52] This is almost an echo of *The Odyssey*: 'I cannot say if a god impelled him or if his own heart felt the promptings' (IV, 712).[53] This hesitation recurs throughout the *Aeneid*: now ''tis Venus that upholds the Trojan power, not their own right hands' (X, 608–9); now Juno herself justifies her resentment against Aeneas by asserting he acted on his own initiative – 'Did any man or god constrain Aeneas to seek war?' (X, 65). Yet, on the whole, the intervention of a god seems to be the most frequently favoured hypothesis; nor does it seem to be a mode of expression dictated by a poetic convention, as in Renaissance poetry.

For Virgil the soul still has its seat in the chest and the emotions are denoted by their physical signs.[54] Aeneas 'feigns hope on his face, and deep in his heart strikes the anguish' (*Aeneid*, I, 209). When terrified, Andromache 'stiffened as she gazed and the warmth forsook her limbs' (III, 308). When Dido is 'on fire with love', the madness 'is drawn through her bones' (IV, 101). 'Anger burned deep in the bones' of a young man (V, 172). The characters are often in deliberation, but can we speak of introspection when they seem to contemplate an outward projection of their thought, when Aeneas 'now hither, and now thither swiftly throws his mind, casting it in diverse ways, and turns to every shift'?[55]

Self-consciousness began to appear in its modern form in the Roman elegies and epistles. I feel that Onians perhaps goes too far when he declares the Roman conception and the Greek conception of the conscious self 'virtually identical'; a progression is obvious.[56] One critic has noted a desire to escape from 'a total alienation of the self' evident in Catullus's *Attis* (LXI–LXIII).[57] Ovid has a vivid realization of his singularity, particularly in his *Tristia* (II, 495–6). Most remarkable is the poet's attention to his conflicting passions. This inner duality is no longer due to the coexistence of a supernatural impulse and a human desire, but to the inner rending of the self. When Catullus says 'I hate and love', he adds: 'Perhaps you are asking why I do that? / I don't know, but I feel it happening, and am rack'd.'[58] When Ovid, too, is a prey to 'contrary' passions of love and hate for a woman, and confesses 'he cannot live with her, nor without her', he only realizes a paradoxical fact, but he adds: 'And I myself know not what I desire'.[59] The poet is each time at a distance from his opposite feelings, which he could not apprehend simultaneously if he were wholly loving or wholly hating.

Catullus has been said to display 'an invasive and outspread self through his frequent use of the pronoun *ego* and of the first person singular verb forms'.[60] Linguistic analysis is supposed to furnish evidence of 'the highly self-revealing nature' of the poet's subjectivity: 'he starts by speaking of himself in the third person, then the first person intrudes and the text is invaded by the subjectivity of his passion'.[61] One may agree, remembering how often Montaigne quotes Catullus and borrows images from him, and yet it is noticeable that the Roman poet generally sees himself love, hate and act as if he watched a spectacle by projecting himself out of himself, as we have seen Greek thought apprehend itself by creating an outward object.[62]

Roman elegies offer a behavioural psycho-physiology of love. Passion is expressed through outward signs: sleeplessness, sobs, shivers, angry talk.[63] Propertius even projects on a rival the physical signs of frustrated love one could detect on his own face and body:

> Ah, many's the time you'll run to my door humiliated,
> Your brave boasts sunk to sobs;
> On tearful whining trembling dread will supervene
> And fear leave its ugly mark on your face [...]
>
> You'll cease to express amazement at my pallor,
> Or wonder why I am a mere skeleton.[64]

Introspection is not required to discover that, when the lover shows disdain, the mistress is no longer scornful (II, 14). Objectivity prevails even in poems which claim to be autobiographical. And when Propertius writes *De se*, he tells us only that he was born in Umbria and grieves for a kinsman.[65]

These are all characteristics that I had insisted on in 1960.[66] Paul Veyne went further when he maintained that the Roman love elegies had no 'reference to reality'.[67] He acknowledged the presence of an ego but considered it only a 'humorous fiction' which 'imperfectly hides the objectivity of the third person', claiming that in the eyes of the Ancients one could say more extensively in the third person what was said in the first person.[68] This statement, I think, overlooks the undeniable progress of subjectivity when we pass from Ancient Greece to Rome. Inversely, Veyne neglected the part played by poetic fiction in the Renaissance when he wrote: 'The elegy, produced by aesthetes, is not the expression of an affectivity after the manner of the sonnets of Shakespeare'.[69] Without denying a heightened subjectivity in some Shakespearean sonnets, I still maintain that, by its dramatic intensity, 'the Latin elegy, despite its conventions, artificiality and mythological apparel, creates more vividly than most Elizabethan sonnets the impression of an experience lived through: hence its influence on the *Songs and Sonnets* (1633) of John Donne.'[70] Ovid wrote the first versified autobiography in his *Tristia* (IV, x); may he not rely at times on personal experiences in his *Amores*?

Veyne ascribed to Horace a 'literary' sincerity only when he presented himself as a model of wisdom or an example which should not be followed.[71] Yet one cannot deny that this poet wished to turn an epistle into a self-portrait when he wanted it to reveal that he was 'of small build, prematurely grey and fond of the sun, quick to lose his temper, but not hard to appease' (*Epistles*, I, xx, 24–5).⁷² He reveals his tastes (I, x, 1–11) and his changes of mood: 'In Rome I long for Tibur; at Tibur I long for Rome' (I, viii, 12).⁷³ I admit, however, that moral reflection is dominant herein. His conception of the *vir bonus* calls for self-examination, but the tendency to objectify the inner life persists: 'Your life is in order if you manage to be what you seem' (I, xvi, 17). The *Satires* disclose the same tendency to autobiography, with the same limitations. There is little insistence on the poet's personality. Yet he mentions his origins, 'only a freeman's son', speaks of his childhood and his education (I, vi), describes his life on his farm (II, vi) and reveals that an erotic dream 'spattered [his] nightshade' (I, v). Deriding the illusions of lovers about the charms of their mistresses, he is conscious of his own failings, but ascribes their observation to some friends, as if they could be detected only from outside (I, iii, 38ff.). He can be intensely concerned with himself. He seeks self-knowledge, like the Stoics, by 'turning inward' (I, iv, end). Still, a tendency to see himself from outside persists. He will ask his slave to reveal him to himself as he is: inconstant, subject to passions, incapable of remaining alone with himself for an hour, for tedium oppresses him in solitude (II, vii). Montaigne praised Horace for his art in describing himself, but he was speaking of his style (III, v: 987 B; VS 873). He also found Terence 'wonderful at vividly depicting the emotions of the soul and the modes of our behaviour' (II, x: 461 A; VS 411), but the Roman dramatist was more concerned with the painting of manners than inward probing.

Juvenal seldom obtrudes himself and he depicts his life only in the country (satire IX).⁷⁴ Persius, like Horace, is more inclined to indulge in intimate revelations. He describes his way of life (satire VI), reminisces about his childish wiles (satire III, 44–55) and meditates on his teens, the moment when a lack of experience brings youth to intricate crossways (satire V, ll. 30ff.). Under the influence of Stoicism he urges man to 'search for himself outside himself', deploring that 'No man – no man – tries to delve into his heart: / Every man watches the bag upon the back of the man in front' (satire IV, 24–5).⁷⁵ Yet a tendency to generalize the experience rather than focus attention on the individual is as obvious as the ethical purpose. The satirical epigrammatist Martial practised self-derision, like Montaigne, who mentioned him, but went no further in self-scrutiny: 'Keep your venom for those who admire themselves. I know my work is worthless.'⁷⁶

(One may add in parenthesis that in elegies, as in epistles and satires, this was a *spoken* poetry, which addressed an interlocutor and called for dialogue or pseudo-monologue. It was therefore hardly fit for a revelation of the speaker's inner life. The genuine soliloquy will be a Christian mode of expression.)

Stoic philosophers such as Epictetus and Marcus Aurelius continued to invite men to practise introversion for practical ends.[77] As their interrogations concern our ability to control forces within us, when their scope widens they hardly become a search for a personal identity. It is possible to agree that Epictetus brings into full light the freedom and autonomy of the individual in the moral sphere.[78] But he also invites each man to 'discover in himself what he has in common with other men as a chorister giving attention to the symphony' (*Dissertationes*, III, 22, 53).

Similarly, the *Meditations* of Marcus Aurelius are not intimate revelations but spiritual exercises.[79] He still believed in the presence of a *daemon* or genius within the soul, a notion which does not call for a 'modern' introspection but which does imply a kind of personification of the desires and appetites of the individual.[80] He questioned himself thus:

> How can I use my soul at the present moment? This must be my constant interrogation. I must examine what I find at the present moment in this part of myself which is called the inner guide. Of whom have I the soul at this moment? Would not one say it is the soul of a child, of a youth, of a weak woman, of a tyrant, of a beast of burden, of a wild animal?[81]

Furthermore, through his individual nature the Stoic sage sought an impersonal nature and reason; his own soul was always invited to follow the movements of the universal soul. Concerning the conception of individuality, what was essential, according to Bernard Groethuysen, was 'not the quality of what was proper to him, but the fact that something was proper to him; [...] self-assertion remained the essential principle'.[82]

It is in the *Epistles* of Seneca that an orientation of Stoicism towards the observation of the inner life may be discovered. It influenced the style itself, which became a reflection of the 'pensée pensante', the very activity of thought.[83] Seneca offered a representation of an inner process of the mind, though still imperfectly.[84]

Among the satirists influenced by the Stoics one can also discover some signs of the introversion from which Montaigne's quest for his identity originates. The lapidary injunction of Persius, *tecum habita* (satire IV, l. 52), was Christianized. St Jerome called Augustine's attention to it; Gregory identified it with the *Nosce te ipsum*, and twelfth-century contemplatives interpreted it as an invitation to engage in a conversation with oneself without any disturbance coming from the outside world.[85] Donne will paraphrase it – 'Be then thine own home and in thyself dwell' – in a verse letter to Sir Henry Wotton written in 1597, a period when the influence of Persius and Horace is obvious in his poems. However, the invitation of the Roman satirist, 'nec te quaesiveris extra' (do not seek yourself outside yourself), is only a preliminary for a quest which can take various directions.

In the Greek and Roman perception of personality the aim was not to achieve individuality leading to diversity, but self-mastery by the exertion of one's will. In his *Anthropologie philosophique* (1953), Groethuysen claimed:

> In Antiquity the conception of individuality was close to the conception of man as a product of nature, and this was possible through a classification of men according to types: the particular qualities which distinguish men from one another do not prevent them from sharing a human nature. Attention must not be focused on individual qualities but on a common experience of the world. For a stable personality the central question is: 'what is my relation with the world?'[86]

In this period, then, the search for one's true self will have a different orientation from that of Montaigne.

The difficulty we meet when trying to know ourselves in this way had been acknowledged by Aristotle: we take others to task for what we do ourselves because we are blind to our own actions; the eye cannot see itself.[87] This blindness only led Aristotle to the conclusion that we must use a friend as a mirror to look at ourselves, since the friend is another self.[88] Horace asked his slave to point out to him his deficiencies.[89] Thus a clear tendency is betrayed here, one which objectifies the inner life, and which sustains a belief in distinct and unchanging features corresponding to types.

Even when intimate in tone and demonstrably conveying a revelation of personality, Roman poetry was still *spoken* to an interlocutor. Through the epistle, the dialogue (dominant in satires) and the pseudo-monologue, feelings always found an outward dramatic expression – anything apparently dealing with the internal self is still communicated outwards, directed towards another, rather than remaining an interior dialogue. By contrast, in the soliloquy, Christianity discovered a way of communing with oneself. There is no clearer evidence of the predominant objectivity of consciousness in Antiquity than the surprise of young Augustine when he saw St Ambrose reading without uttering words, sometimes even with closed lips.[90] Silent reading may have appeared earlier, but was certainly not widespread; the instances of it recently collected rest on mere assumptions.[91]

3. Christian spirituality: St Augustine

In the Old Testament, the prophet is conscious of having a personal vocation. Moreover, the lamentations and interrogations of Job and the emotions expressed in the Psalms already seem to be evidence of a more intensely personalized inner life than the first signs of conscious subjectivity in the literature of Ancient Greece. Calvin will later describe the Psalms as a dissection of all the parts of the soul, since there is no affection that is not represented in them as in a mirror.[92] Nevertheless, I am in accordance with Stanley Toliver, who insists that a great distance remains between the 'I' of the Psalms and the autonomous ego.[93]

When St Augustine Christianized Platonic notions, he personalized the soul. As Groethuysen phrased it:

> it is no longer a soul in me, but my soul. Not a spiritual element which may be conceived as cosmic and general [...], but the soul that is wholly mine in a particular way. I no longer say 'I feel a soul within me', but 'I am a soul.'[94]

This was a revolution in the history of self-consciousness. Yet, by itself, it is not enough to cause the interrogations of Montaigne and other writers about their identity, for Augustine went further and sought a centre or summit of the soul 'more inward than my most inward part; and superior then, unto my supremest'.[95] From this point of view one may agree with Pierre Hadot when he claims that 'man in the modern age is mistaken if he thinks he can already discover the Self [*moi*] in the *Confessions*'.[96] This assertion, however, may be qualified, for, unlike other mystics, Augustine dwelt upon the paradoxes of the inner life: 'Lord, I yet labour upon this, yea and I labour in myself, and am become a soil that requires hard labour and very much sweat'.[97] Exploring his psyche, Augustine came to an obscure region:

> the knowledge of mine own abilities so far lies concealed, as that, when my soul makes enquiry into herself concerning her own powers, it conceives it is not safe, too lightly to give credit unto itself; because that what is already in it, lies many times so closely muffled up, as nothing but experience can reveal it.[98]

Discovering the dark core of the self in his *Confessions*, Augustine had a foreboding of the unconscious which is also traceable in the *Essays* when Montaigne, peering into his mind, speaks of 'its dark depths and its inner recesses' (II, vi: 424 C; VS 378). Montaigne, however, is convinced that 'there is hardly an emotion [*mouvement*] in me which sneaks away and hides from my reason' (III, ii: 915 B; VS 812).

Augustine had not discovered the existence of inner conflicts already perceived by Greek and Roman authors, but he rejected the earlier assumption that this conflict could result from the intrusion of exterior powers – whether gods or passions – into one's soul. He also denied that an alien mind could be present in him:

> it was I myself who willed it; it was I myself [...]. Therefore was I at strife with myself, and distracted by mine own self. Which distracting befell me much against my mind, nor yet shewed it forth the nature of another man's mind (*nec tamen ostendebat naturam mentis alienae*), but the punishment of mine own.⁹⁹

Rejecting the Manichaean assumption that two natures, two minds could be present in each man, the theologian maintained that 'in the acts of one man's deliberation there is one soul distracted between two contrary wills' and 'it is but one and the same soul which willeth not this or that with an entire will'.¹⁰⁰ This view of the inner conflict bears testimony to an evolution in the development of self-consciousness. Furthermore, this evolution will lead Augustine to reject the presence in the soul of a 'personal daemon', a Socratic notion popularized by the Stoics. For Epictetus and Marcus Aurelius, self-questioning meant conversing with one's own *daemon*.¹⁰¹ But Augustine addresses himself directly when he insistently asks in the *Confessions*: 'Who am I, and what manner of man'; 'And I turned myself unto myself, and said to myself: Who art thou?'¹⁰² Of course, the question occurs when he is engaged in a dialogue with God, and his purpose is therefore different from Montaigne's, but Augustine's review of the paradoxes in his affections and the mysteries of memory discloses a genuine psychological curiosity. The irruptions of passions in the human soul could no longer be ascribed to the intervention of an exterior agent, though literature, in mimetic fashion, often continued to present it thus. The novelty of Augustine's self-questioning is apparent when it is compared with the interrogations of Marcus Aurelius.

As early as 1952 I had pointed out that the modern form of subjectivity, incipient in the Roman elegies and satires, was for the first time fully attained in Augustine's *Confessions*. From a slightly different point of view Charles Taylor has ascribed to their author the discovery of 'the inwardness of radical reflexivity'.¹⁰³ There seems to be a close relationship between this mode of exploration of the self and Augustine's acute consciousness of his inner conflicts, leading to the conclusion: 'Hence is it that there be two wills'.¹⁰⁴ His deepening perplexity in front of the paradoxes of his inner life led him to this admission: 'I became a great riddle to myself'.¹⁰⁵ The problems evoked were the sweetness of tears, a fear of dying despite a loathing of life, the association of joy and sadness in remembrance, and so on.[106] What is significant is the surprise of Augustine in the face of contradictions which are familiar terrain for us nowadays. Some of them had already been noted in the Roman elegies he had read, but a progress of subjectivity is apparent in the insistence placed by Augustine on the unity of the self, persisting in division. It is in the experience of these contradictions that one can discover the mysterious unity of the self, unsuspected as long as the soul was unaware of them.

Augustine undoubtedly originated a more attentive and penetrating exploration of the spiritual life, and his later influence on Petrarch and on Protestant spirituality later proved decisive. But whether this influence extended to Montaigne is still a matter of debate. Pierre Villey and other scholars have maintained that Montaigne had not read the *Confessions*, since he never mentioned them, and they cite as parenthetical evidence that he refers to *City of God*. Yet silence is not a proof of unacquaintance. One may note that Augustine and Montaigne both expressed their grief for a loved friend lost in their youth, in very similar ways. In Augustine's case:

> I more admired that myself who was to him a second self, should be able to live after him [...] for I still thought my soul and his soul to have been but one soul in two bodies. [...] And even then therefore was I afraid to die, lest he should wholly die, whom so passionately I had loved.[107]

Moreover, as Gisèle Mathieu-Castellani argues, there are many other parallels which to me seem decisive in suggesting that Montaigne possessed an awareness of Augustine – a debt he apparently chose not to reveal.[108]

4. The Middle Ages

It is generally agreed nowadays that Augustine turned the 'confession' into a self-examination, one centred on an interrogation of the ego and aiming at a definition of his personality and his role.[109] Yet from Antiquity to the Renaissance this quest for self-knowledge apparently had one object: the confession of one's sins and the achievement of repentance. A confession, of course, may lead to self-analysis and Alfed de Vigny even claimed that the psychological novel had its origins in the Christian habit of confession.[110] Its appearance, however, was long delayed. Throughout the Middle Ages ethical and poetic works were influenced by the *Psychomachia* of Prudentius (345–c.413), an exact contemporary of

Augustine (345–430). Adopted even in lyrical poetry, it staged a conflict within the human soul. This allegorization of the inner life was further refined in the thirteenth-century French poem *Roman de la rose*.[111] Like Augustine, Prudentius was aware of the presence of contrary inclinations in the human mind and proclaimed 'non simplex natura hominis'.[112] With him, however, this complexity was limited to the coexistence of a soul and a body and to the conflict between virtues and vices.

The interiority of Augustinian devotion was preserved in theological and mystical writings throughout the Middle Ages only by the conviction that man could find the divine in himself since he is *imago Dei* and his soul is an image of the Trinity.[113] Among the Scholastics, however, one does not find the Augustinian insistence on psychological problems. They are more inclined to discuss logical questions or explore the sphere of the physical world and the relations between Christian doctrine and conceptions of the cosmos.[114] Thomas Aquinas often relies on the data of experience, but he always argues from a logical or metaphysical point of view. To perceive how widely his analyses differ *in exposition* from Augustine's vivid intuition of the workings of the human mind, one need only compare Augustine's reflections on memory in the *Confessions* (XI, xxvi–xxviii) with the articles of the *Summa theologica* devoted to the same subject (1a, q. 79, art. 6–7). Another difference must also be noted. The Thomist *quidditas* does not invite an exploration of individuality. This notion of essence or 'whatness' applies to properties shared by an individual with others of the same kind and is apprehended by the intellect alone; the particular can be known only through reflection and imaginary representations. For the Thomist, everything in man is fixed, whether by the *quidditas* or the *habitus*.

Duns Scotus and his disciples, however, ascribed an intuitive knowledge of the particular to the intellect and maintained that the soul can know its own act directly, though this intuition does not give us an immediate knowledge of the essence of the soul. But they did not go much further after stating these principles and they did not tackle psychological problems.[115] Like Aristotle's, their interest in man was centred on 'form'. The *haecceitas* or 'thisness' of Scotus also implied a fixed personality. Gregory Zilborg claimed but did not prove that Scotus and Ockham took an interest in the feelings and individual experiences of men, and the 'modernity' sometimes ascribed to Scotus may be called into doubt.[116] Neither the Scotists nor the Nominalists really founded their principles on psychological evidence. To acknowledge it does not prevent us from admitting the close affinities between Montaigne's thought and Nominalism detected by Antoine Compagnon.[117]

To find something approaching Augustinian subjectivity one must turn to the mystics. Bernard of Clairvaux took the way which leads to God through self-knowledge. He argued that one cannot love what one does not know. Since man is expected to love God and his neighbour as himself, he must find in himself the divine image, just as Augustine had discovered the Trinity in the human soul.[118] Hence Bernard's prayer: 'My God, let me know you and let me know myself'.[119] Self-knowledge without the knowledge of God would only breed despair.[120] This progress invites man to move away from himself. The attainment of the third and fourth degrees in the love of God ultimately requires one to love God not for oneself but for Himself alone.[121]

Yet as the soul must lose itself in God to find itself, the mystic quest throughout the ages has always led to sounding inner depths. Foucault reminds us that the Christian mystical experience is 'if not wholly ordered, consummated, or at least traversed by the theme of self-absorption in God in a loss of identity, individuality and subjectivity, through a privileged and immediate contact with God'.[122] Nevertheless, an acute self-consciousness seems to be present in some of the mystics. Meister Eckhart, one of the most audacious, unhesitatingly declared: 'If I were not, God too would not be' – an assertion taken up by Angelus Silesius. Eckhart, however, was thinking of this 'essential being' which had existed from eternity: 'in this Essence of God [...] I was my self, I wanted my self and knew my self in order to produce the man I am in this lower world'.[123] This intuition of a transcendental 'I' – a 'wholly available and undetermined being'[124] – could not lead to an exploration of an individual self in the diversity of experience, for in this world 'the soul must entirely give up itself and sink in the bottomless ocean of the Deity'.[125]

From another point of view, one must take into account the dictates of medieval society. For centuries, the individual was constrained to adopt a style of life in harmony with his status. Even in an exceptional biography written in the form of a letter, Abelard's *Historia calamitatum*, a personal experience was recorded in conformity with a type. Karl Joachim Weintraub rightly noted that Abelard and Héloïse did not write an original scenario for their lives and personalities; they adapted their lives and personalities to scenarios already written.[126] Michel Zink agrees, arguing that the personalities of Abelard and Héloïse were 'built on ancient literary conventions'.[127]

In the whole field of literature, from the *Psychomachia* of Prudentius to the *Roman de la rose,* the characteristic feature was the constant allegorization of the psychic life. It may be considered a convention, but it seems to reveal the persistence of the mode of consciousness which objectified the thoughts and emotions of man in Antiquity. C. S. Lewis, however, called attention to the rich psychological content of medieval allegory. It is true that these personifications would not appear more arbitrary than the relations between the id, the ego and the super-ego if those personages of the Freudian theatre were considered truly distinct entities. One must admit, however, that the psychic life seemed to be thus frozen – if not reified – for centuries. The literature of the Renaissance would liberate itself only progressively from this vision of the inner life.

5. From the troubadours to Petrarch

It is important to acknowledge that the progress of self-consciousness throughout medieval literature, however slow, was continuous. Zink called attention to a 'literary subjectivity' in the Middle Ages. He admitted, however, that it never was 'the spontaneous revelation or the true expression in a text of the personality, the opinions or emotions of an author', but what in a text revealed the point of view of a consciousness. When this meaning is retained, literary subjectivity defines literature which exists only from the moment when the text neither pretends to give general, objective information on the world nor expresses a metaphysical or sacred truth, but indicates that it is the product of a personal consciousness, depending at once on the arbitrariness of individual subjectivity and on the necessary constraints of language forms.[128] This type of subjectivity, however, would not necessarily lead to self-consciousness and interiority. What various studies have confirmed is the presence of the author as an individual in his poetic works from the thirteenth century, at once in romances and in the '*dit*', as distinguished from the lyrical songs of the first troubadours: '*Vidas* and *razos* then write a romance of the self which is supposed to be hidden behind the *I* of the poem.'[129] Zink cited Rutebeuf as an example; Kimmelman found illustrations in Marcabru, and, extending his analysis to the great poems of Dante and Langland, he ascribed this personalization to the legacy of Augustine, and particularly to the *Confessions*.[130] Yet Gregory Stone maintains, rightly I think, that the language of poetry in these romances of the self generally does not allow us to identify the *I* of the poet with a historical individual.[131] Besides, this 'literary subjectivity', the presence of the poet in his work through the creation of a *persona*, is not necessarily accompanied by an attempt at introspection; I have found no example of it in my investigations, which, I confess, were limited.

There is, however, no reason to deny that, either under the cover of allegory or directly, an intuition of the emotional life which one might call 'pre-modern', together with a deep and genuine sense of the self, was present from the twelfth century in the writings of the first troubadours, from Guillaume d'Aquitaine to Arnaut Daniel and Bernard de Ventadour. Protesting against the assumption that 'the poet only invests his self in a commonplace', Antoine Tavera discovered a remarkable progress in self-knowledge in some of their 'chansons'.[132] Tavera was probably right when rejecting the Lacanian reduction of the self to an 'illusion of the subject' and in acknowledging each poet's desire to distinguish himself from other authors. Yet he had to admit that the 'painful introspection of the troubadours was only revealed through their search for difficult and varied forms'.[133] It was by this process that they opened the way for the *dolce stil novo* in Italy.

This search does not appear to me to have led to a discovery which would herald the new forms of self-consciousness detected in Montaigne's essays. Their analysis of feelings is underdeveloped and does not extend beyond changing moments of delight or pain, even when a narcissistic tendency is disclosed as in a poem of Bernard, 'Can vei la lauzeta mover'.[134] Paul Zumthor's thesis on the impersonality of courtly love poetry has been challenged by critics who claim to discover in it the author's personality and a tendency to autobiography.[135] One may, however, side with Olivia Holmes in concluding that there is 'a great distance' from the simple narrative of the *vidas* and the *razos* of the troubadours to the elaborate self-portrait presented by Petrarch on the pattern of the *Confessions* in the *Canzoniere*.[136]

Before Petrarch, a more elaborate dialectical presentation of the inner life had been sought in thirteenth-century Italy by the poets of the *dolce stil novo*, sometimes considered forerunners of the English Metaphysical poets on account of their reliance on Scholastic notions.[137] However, I have shown elsewhere how superficial the resemblances are.[138] Dante himself has affinities with Donne only in his physiology of love, not in the acuity of his introspection; he even felt obliged to apologize for talking about himself (*Convivio*, I, ii).

One might, of course, maintain that from the *dolce stil novo* to Petrarch and from Petrarch to John Donne or the Shakespeare of the *Sonnets*, there was an evolution but no discontinuity. An intense interest in psychological analysis has been ascribed to Cavalcanti.[139] But general resemblances should not obscure the fact that these poets do not analyse the inner life in the same way. All of them resort to a philosophy of love which weaves Scholastic notions with literary conventions, but the poets of the *dolce stil novo* wearisomely use the same notions with slight variations. Their psycho-physiology of the amorous passion rests on stereotypes which do not highlight the complexity of the experience lived and their passion is hardly individualized. This constant allegorization of the inner life, with the monotony of the personifications, is tedious: these poets offer no new observations on human nature. In Guinizelli and Cavalcanti, self-consciousness is present but exercised objectively, a projection of the self which only allows them to see themselves from outside. Guinizelli stiffens 'like a brass statue' and 'wears death inscribed on his face'.[140] Cavalcanti, in *Tu m'ai si plena*, is similar to 'one who seems to the onlooker made of brass, or stone, or wood'.[141] Cino da Pistoia never wearies of expressing his grief through exterior signs in *Omo lo cui nome, I'no spero, Non credo che'n Madonna*.[142] Similarly, the poet may also describe himself as onlookers see him, as Cino does in *Si mi distinge*.[143]

The inner life is most often described through the personification of the faculties and the virtues of the heart, the mind or the spirits. The personality is then dissolved in a series of distinct entities animated by their own impulsions.[144] These tendencies are also present in the love poetry of Dante, for whom 'the face shows the colour of the heart' and the various 'spirits' are often in conflict.[145] It is true that the movements of the soul were still at times allegorized in seventeenth-century poetry, but it was a means of expressing the inner conflicts of a soul more attentive to such contradictions since it had a sharper feeling of the spiritual unity of the individual.

Was Petrarch the first of the moderns when he asked himself in the *Secretum*: 'Who am I really?' It was not by chance that the problem was raised in a dialogue with St Augustine, strewn with quotations from Seneca and Juvenal. The self here presented is a *multivolum pectus*, a self subject to many contradictory impulses, and the poet is invited by Augustine to unify his personality and no longer be *nusquam integer, nusquam totus*.[146] And when we are reminded that the soul is a riddle, it is not the mystery of a Neo-Platonic universal soul, but the mystery of an individual soul and the experiences lived through. We are already close to Montaigne and Donne, and it should be noticed that Petrarch was trying, like them, to escape from melancholy in this dialogue. The difference lies in the religious orientation of this exploration of his personality and in his attempt to make his self conformable to a universal and unique ideal of Christian perfection.

The lover of Laura was undoubtedly an egotist who composed the epistle *Ad seipsum* and was affected by his awareness of his own emotions. The ebb and flow of the inner life are dramatized in the *Canzoniere*, as they are in the *Songs and Sonnets* of Donne. The reader has the impression of watching the spontaneous welling forth of nascent thoughts and emotions:

> My song I feel my pen already weary
> Of the long, sweet intercourse I have had with her;
> But my thought never wearies of talking with me.[147]

Petrarch is perplexed by the nature of his love and his contradictions, uncertain about his own desires, but the range of his emotions remains limited when compared with Donne's. He has not freed himself from the conventions of courtly love; hence there is a stylistic artificiality and a lesser density of human experience. The complexity of the feelings is only apparent: passion is broken up into mechanical antitheses, which may be traced back to the 'bitter-sweet' of the Latin elegiac poets.[148] The salt of irony is missing, particularly the ironic self-consciousness which the next chapter will highlight in some poems of Donne and Shakespeare.

6. The Italian and French Renaissance

For this period my enquiry was limited to the Italian and French literatures, both influential in England.[149] In both of them the emergence of autobiography might reveal a keener interest in the 'I' and a deeper self-consciousness.

Forms of autobiography had appeared by late classical Antiquity. After the triumph of Christianity and the *Confessions* of Augustine, these tended towards the production of narratives of conversion and self-examination through to the Middle Ages. As he extended the definition of autobiography to include 'any kind of information an author gives about himself', the many examples offered by Georg Misch in his encyclopaedic volumes do not discriminate with enough nuance for our purposes.[150] The more precise study by Zink bears on the 'monodic discourse' which may develop from a 'narrative of one's own life, illuminated by contemporary events into a committed comment on these events'.[151] From this perspective, in the rare examples of it discovered in the Middle Ages, no attempt at introspection is apparent.[152] The flourishing of profane autobiography in the Renaissance betrays the desire for self-assertion emphasized by Burckhardt, yet without a concomitant disclosure of a deeper insight into the inner life.

The study of personality took on a scientific aspect with Cardan's *De vita propria*. It has sometimes been compared with Montaigne's *Essays*, but the differences are obvious.¹⁵³ This physician methodically draws up a list of the characteristics of his temperament which he ascribes to the influence of the stars. We may grant he is conscious of his 'singularities', yet he patterns himself on the *Characters* of Theophrastus. He focuses his attention on 'facts' but is profuse in details.¹⁵⁴ He lays stress on exterior compulsions and even reintroduces the notion of the 'familiar genius', or *daemon*, who endows him with exceptional aptitudes (*De vita propria*, XLVII). The chapter 'De me ipse' is oddly brief. Cardan does not devote it to an engagement with his identity or personality but instead asks himself whether he should feel regret for having lived.

In his *Memoirs*, Cellini, too, is not inclined to self-scrutiny.¹⁵⁵ His personality comes to the fore in them, but it is by the way of a self-assertion which characterized the earliest manifestations of Renaissance individualism in the *condottiere* dear to Burckhardt, or in the self-portrait sketched by Agrippa d'Aubigné in his autobiography, aptly described by a recent editor as a 'parade of the self'.¹⁵⁶ Though Burckhardt's views have been severely criticized by modern historians, one may yet think he was right in calling attention to the emergence of individualism in this period, provided it is sharply distinguished from introspective forms of subjectivity. The individualism which developed in society with the merchant or the *condottiere* was bent on action, acquisition and enjoyment. It was not fundamentally concerned with or engaged in an exploration of the self, nor inclined to call its permanence into question.

In the literary works of many Renaissance authors, individualism and humanism were associated.¹⁵⁷ Rabelais tempered his famous 'Do what thou wilt' by his overoptimistic trust in an instinct given by nature to men 'who are free, well-bred, well-taught'.¹⁵⁸ Among those writing books affording 'plain delight', Rabelais was the only French author Montaigne considered 'worth spending time on' and Rabelais's taste for the Pyrrhonian sceptics was shared by the author of the *Essays*.¹⁵⁹ There is, however, no indication that his reading of Rabelais prompted his self-examination.

In the religious domain, Protestant individualism undoubtedly deepened the interiority of the spiritual life. It also favoured the keeping of private diaries. I have not explored this field on the Continent but I am inclined to think that I would not have discovered more evidence of acute introspection than in the English diaries.¹⁶⁰ The same remark may apply to the expression of Catholic spirituality. When Jean-Claude Margolin analyses 'the inner life according to Charles de Bovelles', he describes an activity which reveals the inner presence of the whole universe in the individual soul but which does not invite an analysis of the self.¹⁶¹

From a philosophical point of view, the problem of personality was always related to a cosmology by the Neo-Platonists, to a theology by the Reformers. After claiming that 'to know oneself in the cosmological anthropology of the Renaissance meant to define oneself in one's relations with the world', Groethuysen added:

> with Luther self-knowledge can only mean achieving self-consciousness through one's relation with God. *Homo cosmologicus* and *homo theologicus*: in both cases man's effort to know himself leads him beyond himself.[162]

With Erasmus, however, man seeks to know himself and accept himself as he is. Like Montaigne, Erasmus acknowledged he could not change his nature, 'ego alius quam sum esse non possum'.[163] He paid heed to the individual and private physiognomy of the soul, 'interna species animi'.[164] Nature having endowed each man with an individual 'genius', he found it difficult to find men with similar skills and similar tastes.[165]

In France, the lyrical poetry of the Renaissance offered large possibilities for self-expression and meditation. By the end of the fifteenth and the beginning of the sixteenth century, the so-called *grands rhétoriqueurs* still practised the mediaeval technique tending to an objectification of the subject. In his *Séjour d'honneur*, Octavien de Saint-Gelais aimed at 'an understanding of the general data of the human condition by the way of history' rather than through individual experience. With Jean Lemaire de Belges, however, the play of irony, directed at the poet himself rather than the lover, had already caused the emergence of a split subject (*sujet dédoublé*).[166] In the fifteenth century the melancholy lyricism of Charles d'Orléans was more personal, but often still allegorical.[167] Villon, in the opening of a poem, named after himself, defined his condition: 'Je, François Villon, escolier' (*Petit testament*), 'En l'an de mon trentiesme aage' (*Grand testament*). He twice wrote his epitaph.[168] Yet his *Débat du cueer et du corps de François Villon* is an objective self-examination which does not reveal his inner life. The author of 'La ballade des pendus' is a great poet but he moves us by appealing to our emotions and he does not separate his own fate from the fate of his 'Frères humains'.

Among the poets of the French Pléiade, according to Nathalie Dauvois, the 'lyrical subject' is constantly present, but the 'I' remains a 'pure instrument of enunciation' and in theoretical descriptions lyrical poetry only began to be 'characterized by its subjective expression by the end of the 16th century'.[169] Marot, however, had already begun to weave together 'the voice of the poet, the "I" speaking in the text, and the "I" of the author, who has an existence outside the text'. The pronouns 'je' and 'moi' are swarming in the poems of Ronsard and Du Bellay, but we are told that they most often denote 'an activity of the *je* rather than an expression of the *moi*'.¹⁷⁰ This 'dialogic lyricism' reveals 'an *I* oriented towards a *thou*' and Ronsard, like Marot, alternately stages an 'I' with a definite authorial referent (for instance in the elegies to Genèvre) and an abstract universal 'I'.¹⁷¹ It is, however, obvious that this was a period of transition in which the poet's subjectivity had a tendency to assert itself continuously, notably by staging 'a subject in an itinerary within a story', as in the *Regrets* expressed by Joachim Du Bellay.¹⁷² One may also note that the landscape came now 'to represent a subjective choice' and express the individuality of a poet who seems to say: 'The world is such as I have seen it: here it is.'¹⁷³ The natural elements are evoked in order to contribute to the emergence of the subject. Self-scrutiny and introspection, however, are seldom noticeable. It has been pointed out that 'the constitution of the poetic self in Ronsard is not so much characterized by a permanent staging of the subject than by the adoption of a deliberately subjective point of view'.¹⁷⁴ In the 'Voyage de Tours' (*Second livre des amours*) 'rather than engaging in an introspective narration Ronsard musters observations of the outer world to support his cause'.¹⁷⁵ This, I think, can apply to all Renaissance poets. They sang their loves, vented their feelings, but did not call their self in question, nor doubted its stability. Montaigne, who had read and admired them, owed nothing to them in this respect.¹⁷⁶

This vast historical enquiry has shown, I hope, that the undeniable progress of subjectivity from Greek Antiquity to the Renaissance had not brought to maturity the particular modes of self-consciousness that the preceding chapter traced in the *Essays*.

Notes

1   In his epoch-making *Sources of the Self* (Cambridge University Press, 1994), Charles Taylor has traced the historical evolution of subjectivity from Antiquity to the early modern age but confined his attention to the major philosophers. In *Aspects of Subjectivity – Society and Individuality: From the Middle Ages to Shakespeare and Milton* (Duquesne University Press, 2003), Anthony Low includes all manifestations of individuality and inwardness in his quest. I am concerned with the peculiar forms of self-consciousness I have traced in the *Essays* of Montaigne and think them much more dimly anticipated in Greek, Roman and medieval literature than Low assumes.

   In *L'invention du moi* (Presses Universitaires de France, 2010), Vincent Carraud narrows his point of view excessively in his grammatical and metaphysical approach. He reduces the history of the concept of the ego to a history of the substantivizing of the pronoun which allowed Pascal first and

Descartes next to say 'le moi', turning it into a noun. He therefore has to demonstrate that this was not anticipated by Socrates, Epictetus, Augustine, Aquinas, Bernard of Clairvaux or Eckhart. Confining his attention to philosophical and religious works, he never takes literary works into consideration. In a footnote (p. 238) he argues that Montaigne never wrote 'le moi' because he was concerned only with 'le moi empirique' and its 'singularité événementielle'. I need not dispute his thesis since my own concern is with this 'empirical I' and its 'singularity'.

In *Shakespeare's Individualism* (Cambridge University Press, 2010), Peter Holbrook offers a stimulating survey of the dominant values in his plays: freedom, individuality and authenticity. He is concerned with the modernity of his point of view, his affinities with Blake, Emerson, Kierkegaard, Nietzsche, Oscar Wilde and Gide. He touches on his affinities with Montaigne, but he is not concerned with the development of subjectivity before the Renaissance.

Ugo Thiel starts from Descartes in his study of *The Early Modern Subject: Self-consciousness and Personal Identity from Descartes to Hume* (Oxford University Press, 2011).

2   See J. Defradas, *Les thèmes de la propagande delphique* (Paris: Klinksieck, 1954), ch. 3; quoted by Michel Foucault, *L'herméneutique du sujet* (Paris: Gallimard, Seuil, 2008), pp. 5–6.
3   Foucault, *L'herméneutique*, pp. 10–20 and 233 (my translation).
4   Richard Broxton Onians, *The Origins of European Thought* (Cambridge University Press, 1991), see part I, ch. 1, and ch. 3, pp. 53–8, and part II, ch. 1.
5   See Suzanne Saïd, 'La conscience de soi dans la tragédie grecque', in R. Ellrodt, ed., *Genèse de la conscience moderne* (Presses Universitaires de France, 1983), p. 26.
6   Bruno Snell, *La découverte de l'esprit: la genèse de la pensée européenne chez les Grecs* (Paris: Éditions de l'Éclat, 1994), pp. 24 and 118 (my translation); cf. Jan Bremmer, *The Early Greek Concept of the Soul* (Princeton University Press, 1983), p. 54.
7   Bremmer, *The Early Greek Concept of the Soul*, pp. 24, 68.
8   Among the Pythagoricians, *daemon* remained an outside as well as inside reality according to Marcel Detienne, 'Ébauche de la personne dans la Grèce archaïque', in I. Meyerson, ed., *Problèmes de la personne* (La Haye: Mouton, 1973), p. 50.
9   Jean-Pierre Vernant, *Mythe et pensée chez les Grecs* (Paris: Maspéro, 1969), pp. 280–2.
10 In Hesiod, *Theogony and Works and Days*, trans. M. L. West (Oxford University Press, 1988), pp. 41, 154.
11 Vernant, *Mythe et pensée*, pp. 277–8.
12 Ibid., p. 274; Walter Friedrich Otto, *Die Götter Griechenland* (Bonn: Hädecke, 1929), translated by Moses Hadas as *The Homeric Gods: The Spiritual Significance of Greek Religion* (London: Pantheon, 1954).
13 A. D. Nuttall, *Openings* (Oxford: Clarendon Press, 1992), p. 5.
14 Ibid., p. 7.

15 Onians, *The Origins*, part I, ch. 3, 'The stuff of consciousness'. It is the *thumos* which is most often mentioned when the poet is describing emotion. The consciousness is naturally identified with the breath (p. 49).
16 *Ibid.*, part I, ch. 3, pp. 64–5.
17 Snell, *La découverte de l'esprit*, p. 93.
18 *Ibid.*, p. 360.
19 Saïd, 'La conscience de soi', p. 27.
20 Snell, *La découverte de l'esprit*, p. 95.
21 The translations given here are from *Essays* (I, ii: 9 A) because in *Essais* (VS 13) personal pronouns are *introduced*: '*my* tongue sticks in *my* mouth; a fiery flame courses through *my* limbs; *my* ears are ringing and darkness covers both *my* eyes'.
22 Anacreon 79; cf. Snell, *La découverte de l'esprit*, p. 100.
23 Cf. Zevedei Barbu, 'The emergence of personality in the Greek world', in *Problems of Historical Psychology* (New York: Grove Press, 1960), pp. 79–80.
24 Brian Vickers, *Towards Greek Tragedy: Drama, Myth, Society* (London: Longman, 1973), p. 136.
25 The language of Aeschylus 'constantly privileges co-responsibility with terms such as *mel-aitios, sun-aitios, par-aitios* and *ep-aitios*': Saïd, 'La conscience de soi', p. 31.
26 *Ibid.*, p. 33. Francis Jacques, *Difference and Subjectivity*, also notes a progression in the exploration of individual differences from Aeschylus's *Oresteia* to Sophocles: 'in the *Oresteia* the pairs of brothers and sisters were still more or less interchangeable individuals, with Sophocles Antigone and her sister are differentiated' (p. 304).
27 Saïd, 'La conscience de soi', p. 35.
28 *Ibid.*, p. 39.
29 'I am clever, and so to some I am a butt for their odium, to others I seem wrapped up in myself, to others quite the opposite'. Euripides, *Medea and Other Plays*, trans. James Morwood (Oxford University Press, 1997), p. 9, ll. 302–5.
30 See *Medea, ibid.*, pp. 28–9, 1048 ff.: 'I must face the deed [...]. My hand will not weaken. – Ah, Ah, do not my heart, do not do this.' Cf. Euripides, *Iphigenia Among the Taurians, Bacchae, Iphigenia at Aulis, Rhesus*, trans. James Morwood (Oxford University Press, 1999), pp. 93–4, ll. 333, 366.
31 Euripides, *Medea*, p. 22, ll. 808–10, p. 24, l. 872.
32 Euripides, *Iphigenia Among the Taurians* (l. 515), p. 15.
33 Euripides, *Electra*, ll. 1306–7, in *Medea and Other Plays*, p. 117.
34 *Orestes*, l. 792, in Euripides, *Orestes and Other Plays*, trans. Robin Waterfield (Oxford University Press, 2001), p. 70.
35 *Heracles*, ll. 1135, 1188, in Euripides, *Heracles and Other Plays*, trans. Robin Waterfield (Oxford University Press, 2003), pp. 64, 66.
36 In the first instance, I follow here the translation of Henri Berguin and Georges Duclos in *Théâtre d'Euripide* (Paris: Garnier, 1955), vol. III, p. 164; in the second instance, *Heracles*, 1091–4, in Euripides, *Heracles and Other Plays*, p. 62.

37 *Orestes*, l. 229, in Euripides, *Orestes and Other Plays*, p. 54.
38 *Helen*, ll. 1138-42, in Euripides, *Medea and Other Plays*, p. 152.
39 Charles Martindale and Michelle Martindale, *Shakespeare and the Uses of Antiquity* (London: Routledge, 1990), p. 37. Gordon Braden's claim that the rhetoric of Seneca became 'the language of the self's autarceia, its selfhood and self-sufficiency' seems to me also an overstatement. Gordon Braden, *Renaissance Tragedy and the Senecan Tradition: Anger's Privilege* (Yale University Press, 1985), pp. 40, 57, 184.
40 See Barbu, 'The emergence of personality', p. 127.
41 See Yvon Brès, *La psychologie de Platon* (Presses Universitaires de France, 1968) and Yvon Brès, 'La connaissance de soi chez Platon', in R. Angelergues, ed., *Psychologie de la connaissance de soi: 15e symposium de l'Association de psychologie scientifique de langue française, Paris, 1973* (Presses Universitaires de France, 1975). Charles Taylor, in *The Sources of the Self*, p. 174, says bluntly: 'Introspection had no significance for Plato'.
42 Pierre Courcelle, *Connais-toi toi-même: de Socrate à saint Bernard* (Paris: Études augustiniennes, 1974), pp. 41-4, 87, 114.
43 I follow here the translation of Émile Bréhier, *Plotin: Ennéades* (Paris: Les Belles Lettres, 1924-31, 6 vols).
44 Pierre Hadot, *Plotin, porphyre: études néoplatoniciennes* (Paris: Belles Lettres, 1999), p. 253.
45 See J. Meyendorff, 'Le thème du 'retour en soi' dans la doctrine palamite du XIVe siècle', *Revue de l'histoire des religions*, 145 (1954), pp. 188-206.
46 Marsilio Ficino, in his *Correspondence*, quoted by A. Chastel, 'Lettres sur la connaissance de soi etsur l'astrologie', *La Table Ronde*, 2 (1945), pp. 198-9.
47 Léon Robin, *Aristotle* (Presses Universitaires de France, 1944), p. 201.
48 See Marie-Louise Gill, 'Individuals and individuation in Aristotle', and Michael Woods, 'The essence of a human being', both chapters in T. Scaltsas, ed., *Unity and Explanation in Aristotle's Metaphysics* (Oxford: Clarendon Press, 1994).
49 See Jacques Chevalier, *Histoire de la pensée antique, vol. II: D'Aristote à Plotin* (Paris: Éditions Universitaires, 1991), p. 257.
50 Léon Brunschvicg, *Le progrès de la conscience dans la philosophie occidentale* (Paris: Presses Universitaires de France, 1953 [1927]), p. 16.
51 See Sextus Empiricus, *Oeuvres choisies de Sextus Empiricus*, trans J. Grenier and G. Goron (Paris: Aubier, 1948).
52 Quotations are taken from Virgil, *Aeneid*, trans. H. R. Fairclough (Harvard University Press, 1966).
53 Quotations are taken from Homer, *The Odyssey*, trans. Walter Shewring (Oxford University Press, 1980).
54 XI, 409: 'habitet tecum et sit pectore in isto'.
55 IV, 285-6: 'animum nunc huc celerem nunc dividit illuc / in partisque rapit varias perque omnia versat'. Cf. XII, 486-7, when Juturnus 'tosses on a shifting tide and conflicting cares call his mind this way and that'.
56 Onians, *The Origins of European Thought*, p. 129.

57 Jean Granarolo, *L'œuvre de Catulle* (Paris: Belles Lettres, 1967).
58 'Odi et amo. Quare id faciam, fortasse requiris, / Nescio:sed fieri sentio et excrucior' (*Carmen* 85).
59 'sic ego nec sine te nec tecum vivere possum, / et videor voti nescius esse mei' (*Amores* III, xi b).
60 Jean Granarolo, 'Catulle ou la hantise du *moi*', *Latomus*, 37:2 (April–June 1978), p. 37.
61 J. Evrard-Gillis, 'Jeu sur la personne grammaticale chez Catulle', *Latomus*, 36 (1977), pp. 114–22.
62 See *Essays* I, ii, 9A, II, xii, 638 B, etc. Olivier Guerrier, *Quand 'les poètes feignent': 'fantasies' et fiction dans les Essais de Montaigne* (Paris: Champion, 2002), stresses the influence of Catullus (pp. 330, 347–8) and Propertius (pp. 319, 341, 347). See also *supra*, pp. 26–8.
63 The representation of emotions by physical signs is also constant in Ovid's *Tristia*: I.3, 43–4; I.4, 11; IV.1, 95–6; IV.3, 25–6; V.1, 51–2.
64 Propertius, *The Poems*, trans. G. Lee (Oxford University Press, 1994), I, 5, p. 8.
65 *Ibid.*, I, 22, p. 26; *De se* is the Latin title.
66 Ellrodt, *L'inspiration personnelle*, vol. III, pp. 296–9.
67 Paul Veyne, *L'élégie érotique romaine* (Paris: Seuil, 1983), p. 41.
68 *Ibid.*, pp. 65, 66.
69 *Ibid.*, p. 62.
70 Ellrodt, *L'inspiration personnelle*, vol. III, pp. 292–9.
71 Veyne, *L'élégie poétique romaine*, p. 189.
72 Quotations are taken from *Horace: Letters and Epistles. Persius: Satires*, trans. Niall Rudd (London: Penguin, 2005).
73 Cf. *Epistles*, I, i, 16–27; I, xiv, 31–6.
74 Juvenal, *The Satires*, trans. Niall Rudd (Oxford University Press, 1992).
75 Quotations are taken from *Persius Satires*, trans. John Connington (Bristol: Bristol Classical, 1983).
76 Martial, XIII, ii; quoted in *Essays*, II, xvii: 742 A; VS 653.
77 See Courcelle, *Connais-toi toi-même*, pp. 52–62.
78 Chevalier, *Histoire de la pensée antique, vol. II*, p. 136.
79 See Pierre Hadot, *Exercices spirituels et philosophie antique* (Paris: Études augustiniennes, 1981), pp. 135–72.
80 See *Meditations*, II, 17 and VIII, 45 in any edition.
81 *Meditations*, V, 11 (my translation).
82 Bernard Groethuysen, *Anthropologie philosophique* (Paris: Gallimard, 1953), p. 88.
83 On the influence of Seneca's style, see Ellrodt, *L'inspiration personnelle*, vol. III, pp. 388–91.
84 Notably in *Ep.* 13, 11; 24, 1. Foucault noted that Seneca often described the movement of the soul in the cosmos rather than a self-questioning: *L'herméneutique du sujet*, p. 270.
85 Courcelle, *Connais-toi toi-même*, pp. 219, 275, 291.
86 Groethuysen, *Anthropologie philosophique*, pp. 88–90.

87 Aristotle, *Magna moralia*, III, 15, 1213a, 14. Cf. Shakespeare, *Troilus and Cressida*, III, iii, 100–6.
88 Courcelle, *Connais-toi toi-même*, p. 21.
89 In a satire (I, iii) mentioned *supra*, p. 35. In I, iv, however, Horace sees his failings at once, 'thanks to the plain speaking of a friend and to his own reflections'.
90 Augustine, *Confessions*, VI, ii.
91 See the letter by D. M. Schenkevelt in the *Times Literary Supplement*, 22 March 1991, p. 13, and other letters in the *Times Literary Supplement*, of 8 February, 1 March, 19 April, 26 April and 24 May 1991. Bernard M. W. Knox, 'Silent reading in Antiquity', *Greek, Roman and Byzantine Studies*, 9:4 (1968), pp. 116–27, noted that Theseus in Euripides' *Hippolytus* (856–74) seems to read Phaedra's letter silently, as Demosthenes reads the oracle in the *Knights* of Aristophanes. According to Paul Saeger, silent reading in isolation became widespread only in the fourteenth and fifteenth centuries: 'Silent reading: its impact on late medieval script and society', *Viator*, 13 (1982), pp. 367–414. He gives no proof that the reader's lips did not move.
92 See the preface to *The Psalms of David and Others*, trans. A. Golding (London, 1571).
93 Stanley Toliver, *Poetry with a Purpose: Biblical Poetics and Interpretation* (Indiana University Press, 1988).
94 Groethuysen, *Anthropologie philosophique*, p. 129.
95 *St Augustine's Confessions, with an English Translation by William Watts 1633* (Oxford: Heinemann; and Harvard University Press, 1960), vol. I, p. 120. This translation (henceforth cited as 'Watts') is often closer to the Latin text than modern ones.
96 Pierre Hadot, *Problèmes et méthodes d'histoire des religions* (Presses Universitaires de France, 1968), p. 21.
97 *Confessions*, X, xvi; Watts, vol. II, p. 119.
98 X, 32; Watts, vol. II, p. 163–5.
99 VIII, x, 22; Watts, vol. I, p. 451.
100 VIII, 10; Watts, vol. I, pp. 453, 455.
101 Epictetus, *Dissertationes*, III, 22, 53; Courcelle, *Connais-toi toi-même*, p. 61.
102 IX, i; X, 6; Watts, vol. II, pp. 3, 89.
103 Ellrodt, 'Genèse et dilemme de la conscience moderne'; Taylor, *The Sources of the Self*, p. 131.
104 *Confessions*, VIII, ix; Watts, vol. I, p. 449.
105 *Confessions*, IV, iv; Watts, vol. I, p. 161.
106 *Confessions*, IV, v; IV, vi; X, xiv; Watts, vol. I, pp. 163, 167; vol. II, pp. 111–15.
107 *Confessions*, IV, vi; Watts, vol. I, p. 167.
108 Mathieu-Castellani, *Montaigne*; also Gisèle Mathieu-Castellani, 'Les *Confessions* de saint Augustin dans les *Essais* de Montaigne', in N. Peacock and J. J. Supple, *Lire les Essais de Montaigne* (Paris: Champion, 2001).
109 As Karl J. Weintraub argues in *The Value of the Individual: Self and Circumstance in Autobiography* (Chicago University Press, 1978).

110 Alfred de Vigny, *Journal d'un poète* (1843), 'du roman'; quoted by Georges Gusdorf, *La découverte de soi* (Presses Universitaires de France, 1948), p. 16.
111 See C. S. Lewis, *The Allegory of Love* (Oxford University Press, 1936, reprinted 1972), pp. 66–73. Another ritualized expression of feeling was found in the philosophical 'consolation' addressed to oneself which Boethius popularized, after Ambrose (489–524): 'De excessu fratri'. See Jacques-Paul Migne, *Patrologia Latina*, vol. XVI, col. 1290–354. Imitations multiplied up to Petrarch: *Epistolae de rebus familiaribus*, IV, 10.
112 *Psychomachia*, ll. 893–4, 904.
113 St Bernard in Migne, *Patrologia Latina*, vol. CLXXXIV, col. 485.
114 See Charles Trinkhaus, *In Our Image and Likeness: Humanity and Divinity in Italian Humanist Thought* (University of Notre Dame Press, 1995), p. 21.
115 See S. J. Day, *Intuitive Cognition: A Key to the Significance of the Later Scholastics* (New York: St Bonaventure, 1947).
116 Gregory Zilborg, *A History of Medical Psychology* (New York: W. W. Norton, 1941), p. 176. See also Ephreme Longpré, 'The psychology of Duns Scotus and its modernity', in Claude L. Vogel, ed., *Psychology and the Franciscan School: A Symposium of Essays* (New York: Bruce, 1932), pp. 19–77.
117 Antoine Compagnon, *Nous, Michel de Montaigne* (Paris: Seuil, 1980).
118 Migne, *Patrologia Latina*, vol. CLXXXIV, cols 485–90.
119 St Bernard, *Sermons*, II, 1, and *De diversis*, c. 542c. See St Bernard, *Œuvres*, trans. M.-M. Davy (Paris: Aubier, 1945), vol. I, pp. 87–94.
120 *Ibid.*, vol. I, p. 94.
121 *Traité 'De l'amour de Dieu'*, *ibid.*, vol. I, pp. 259–60.
122 Foucault, *L'herméneutique du sujet*, p. 240.
123 Sermon *Beati pauperes*, Matt. 5. 3, reproduced in Meister Eckhart, *Traités et sermons*, ed. Maurice de Gandillac (Paris: Aubier, 1942), p. 258.
124 *Ibid.*, p. 255 and introduction, p. 15.
125 *Ibid.*, p. 251.
126 Weintraub, *The Value of the Individual*, p. 87.
127 Michel Zink, *La subjectivité littéraire* (Presses Universitaires de France, 1985), p. 241.
128 *Ibid.*, p. 8. See also Leo Spitzer, 'Note on the poetic and the empirical "I" in mediaeval authors', *Traditio: Studies in Ancient and Medieval History, Thought, and Religion*, 4, (1946), pp. 414–22.
129 Zink, *La subjectivité littéraire*, p. 57.
130 Burt Kimmelman, *The Poetics of Authorship in the Later Middle Ages: The Emergence of the Literary Persona* (New York: Peter Lang, 1996), pp. 86–92. I have not explored the medieval romances in which Robert Hanning and Colin Morris discovered a sense of individuality, which does not seem to me to rest on introspection. R. W. Hanning, *The Individual in Twelfth Century Romance* (Yale University Press, 1977); C. Morris, *The Discovery of the Individual, 1050–1200* (London: SCPK, 1972; Toronto University Press, 1995).
131 Gregory Stone, *The Death of the Troubadour: The Late Medieval Resistance to the Renaissance* (University of Pennsylvania Press, 1994), p. 5.

132 Antoine Tavera, 'Hardiesse et conscience de soi chez les premiers troubadours', in *Actes du groupe de recherche sur la conscience de soi* (Publications de la Faculté des Lettres et Sciences Humaines de Nice, first series, vol. XVIII, 1980), pp. 31 and 46.
133 *Ibid.*, pp. 28, 34–5.
134 Cited by Maurice Valency, *In Praise of Love* (London: Macmillan, 1958), p. 137.
135 Paul Zumthor, *Essai de poétique médiévale* (Paris: Seuil, 1972). Notable critics are Sarah Kay and Sylvia Huot: Sarah Kay, *Subjectivity in Troubadour Poetry* (Cambridge University Press, 1990); Sylvia Huot, *From Song to Book: The Poetry of Writing in Old French Lyric and Lyrical Narrative Poetry* (Cornell University Press, 1987).
136 Olivia Holmes, *Assembling the Lyric Self: Authorship from Troubadour Song to Italian Poetry Books* (University of Minnesota Press, 2000), p. 8.
137 Figurelli speaks of their effort to 'express the obscure, intricate, and sometimes indefinable events of individual consciousness with a scholastic precision'. Fernando Figurelli, *Il dolce stil novo* (Naples: Riccardo Riccciardi, 1933), p. 13. This is an old book, but Figurelli conveniently assembles a large number of texts which he comments on judiciously.
138 Ellrodt, *L'inspiration personnelle* , vol. III, pp. 197–205.
139 N. Sapegno, *Il trecento* (Milan: Vallardi, 1934), p. 29.
140 In Tommaso Casini, ed., *Le rime dei poeti bolognesi del sec. XIII* (Bologna: Romagnoli, 1881). Quoted by Figurelli, *Il dolce stil novo*, p. 130.
141 'Io vo come colui ch'e fuor di vita / che pare, a chi lo sguarda, come sia / fatto di rame o di pietra o di legno'. Figurelli, *Il dolce stil novo*, p. 290, gives other examples.
142 See the extracts given by Figurelli, *ibid.*, pp. 370–1.
143 Quoted by Figurelli, *ibid.*, p. 371.
144 See the examples given by Figurelli, *ibid.*: pp. 280–2 for Cavalcanti; p. 316 for Lapo Gianni; pp. 365–6 for Cino da Pistoia; pp. 396–7 for Frescobaldi.
145 Dante, *Vita nuova*, sonnet 'Cio che m'incontra' and §XII and §XVI.
146 Quoted by Weintraub, *The Value of the Individual*, pp. 106–11. From another point of view, Thomas Greene noted that Petrarch called into question 'the radical stasis of the medieval personality'. Thomas Greene, 'The flexibility of the self in Renaissance literature', in P. Demetz, T. Greene and L. Nelson Jr, eds, *The Disciplines of Criticism* (Yale University Press, 1968).
147 Petrarch, *Canzoniere*, LXXIII, 91–2 (my translation); cf. LXXI, 106–8; LXXII, 76–8.
148 See Ellrodt, *L'inspiration personnelle*, vol. III, pp. 206–14.
149 I have not extended my research to Spanish literature, for instance. My comparison of Hispanic poets of the Renaissance with Donne in *L'inspiration personnelle* (vol. III, pp. 224–41) had not disclosed in them his characteristic modes of self-consciousness, even in Pedro de Padlila's emphasis on *contrarios effectos amorosos* (p. 234), nor any irony directed at oneself in their generally burlesque humour (pp. 238–9). The other European literatures, further still from my competence, were only briefly evoked (pp. 270–1).

150 Georg Misch, *Studien zur Geschichte der Autobiographie* (Göttingen: Vandenhoeck and Ruprecht, 1954–60), vols I–IV.
151 Zink, *Subjectivité littéraire*, p. 193.
152 *Ibid.*, pp. 171–264.
153 See Friedrich, *Montaigne*, pp. 191, 221, 416, n. 278.
154 Weintraub, *The Value of the Individual*, pp. 161, 148, 151.
155 *Benvenuto Cellini: Memoirs* (Oxford University Press, 1927).
156 Agrippa d'Aubigné, *Vie à ses enfants*, ed. Gilbert Schrenck (Paris: Paris 4, 1983). Agrippa practises the 'anatomy' prescribed by Calvin, but in a different spirit.
157 Alain Renaut, in *L'ère de l'individu*, relies on Ernst Cassirer's *L'individu et le cosmos dans la philosophie de la Renaissance* (Paris: Éditions de Minuit, 1927) to assert that 'modernity appeared in culture with the irruption of humanism' (p. 57), but his intention is to demonstrate that 'the ideal of autonomy which characterizes humanism requires the definition within my self of an element of common humanity, irreducible to the bare assertion of my own singularity' (p. 59; my translation). Montaigne would not have denied it, but it is not the aspect of self-consciousness I seek to analyse.
158 François Rabelais, *Gargantua*, ch. 55; quotations from François Rabelais, *Gargantua and Pantagruel*, ed. and trans. M. A. Screech (London: Penguin, 2006), p. 373.
159 See *Essays*, II, x: 460 A; VS 410. See also Screech, *Montaigne and Melancholy*, p. 50.
160 On spiritual autobiography in England see chapter 3.
161 Jean-Claude Margolin, in M. T. Jones-Davies, ed., *L'intériorité au temps de la Renaissance* (Paris: Champion, 2005), p. 64.
162 Groethuysen, *Anthropologie philosophique*, ch. 10.
163 *Opus Epistolarum*, V 227, letter of 1 February 1523.
164 Erasmus, *Ecclesiastes*, 708.
165 Erasmus, *Cicerionianus*, 165; quoted by Jean Lecointe, *L'idéal et la différence: la perception de la personnalité littéraire à la Renaissance* (Geneva: Droz, 1993), pp. 439, 451.
166 Nathalie Dauvois, 'La représentation de la passion entre prose et vers chez les derniers rhétoriqueurs', in François Lecercle and Simone Perrier, eds, *La poétique des passions à la Renaissance* (Paris: Champion, 2001), pp. 308, 312.
167 As Alice Planche points out in 'Charles d'Orléans et le théâtre allégorique de la conscience', in *Actes du groupe de recherche sur la conscience de soi* (Publications de la Faculté des Lettres et Sciences Humaines de Nice, first series, vol. XVIII, 1980), p. 64.
168 François Villon, *Œuvres*, ed. A. Longeon (Paris: Champion, 1992), pp. 1, 13, 73, 96.
169 Nathalie Dauvois, *Le sujet lyrique à la Renaissance* (Presses Universitaires de France, 2000), pp. 5–6.
170 *Ibid.*, pp. 86–8, 108.
171 *Ibid.*, pp. 53, 25, 62.

172 *Ibid.*, p. 39.
173 Philippe Desan, 'Montaigne paysagiste', in Dominique de Courcelles, ed., *Nature et paysages: l'émergence d'une nouvelle subjectivité à la Renaissance*. (Paris: École des Chartes, 2006), pp. 44–5.
174 Cathy Yandell, 'Les roses de Ronsard. Humanisme et subjectivité', in Dominique de Courcelles, ed., *Nature et paysages: l'émergence d'une nouvelle subjectivité à la Renaissance* (Paris: École des Chartes, 2006), p. 31. Yandell quotes Terence Cave's 'Ronsard as Apollo', *Yale French Studies*, 4 (1972), p. 79.
175 Yandell, *ibid.*, p. 37. One should also notice that Ronsard, like the poets of Antiquity, tends to express his emotions through physical signs: 'The hairs on my head shiver, stand upright; / With cold ice a fever sets me on fire' (my translation). *Second livre des amours*, XXXV. See Pierre de Ronsard, *Œuvres complètes*, ed. Gustave Cohen (Paris: Pléiade, 1958), vol. I, p. 138.
176 Montaigne does not mention Scève, whose emblematic and 'expressionistic' rendering of passion was very different from the self-analysis practised in the *Essays*, as I briefly show in the French version of this book (p. 78).

Chapter 3

Shakespeare and the new aspects of subjectivity

1. The medieval heritage in England

The evolution of subjectivity discernible in several Continental literatures before Montaigne, discussed in the preceding chapters, does not appear to have been markedly different in England. Given that it is unlikely that Shakespeare had access to it, to plot its trajectory all the way back to the Anglo-Saxon canon is unnecessary. However, it may be noted that when invited to define self-consciousness in *Beowulf*, a medievalist limited his analysis to the 'heroic consciousness' which asserts itself in action or in the imitation of a model.[1] The earlier medieval ballads attained a popularity and influence that persisted for several centuries. At once lyrical, narrative and dramatic, and often proceeding from real incidents, it is possible that some of them could have had an autobiographical foundation and yet remained impersonal insofar as the emotions were stirred only to give more importance to the action.[2]

One may grant the same elemental authenticity to many poems of the medieval period without discovering a trace or evolving sense of subjectivity in any of them. For example, *Pearl* (1250–1380?), an anonymous work presented as a 'vision', is filled with miniature allegories that may have been born from a desire to express a genuine grief and yet it leads to a traditional *consolatio* without any resort to a genuine introspection.[3] In Langland's *Piers Plowman*, *The Book of Margery Kempe*, Chaucer's *Troilus and Criseyde*, and *Sir Gawain and the Green Knight*, works composed between 1360 and 1430, David Aers has called attention to a progress in the building of a private identity distinguished from the identity of the community.[4] It is possible to agree with his analysis while failing to discover in these texts any notable deepening of interiority or any sustained or careful exploration of the self.[5] I would suggest, therefore, that it is sufficient to limit our enquiry to three poets: two of them at least inspired Shakespeare.

Although it has been argued that parallels between *Piers Plowman* and *Hamlet* exist, there is no firm evidence that Langland's poem was known to the Elizabethan dramatist.[6] In any case, the link between conscience and cowardice is universalized when an allegorical character – a knight – represents conscience. As such, it does not express the personal questionings and the inner conflicts of the Shakespearian character. Like the later *Canterbury Tales* of Chaucer, *Piers Plowman* is more concerned with drawing from all classes of society more than it is the individuation of the characters. It opens, for example, with a vision of a field filled by a crowd. When the inner journey does begin, it is much less an exploration of the self personally experienced in the Augustinian mode than an objective exposition, theologically oriented, of the prevalent psychological theories: the outer manifestations of the inner life are privileged.[7]

Shakespeare has a more obvious debt to John Gower (1330?–1408). Gower's *Confessio amantis* (1386–90) is the source of *Pericles*, describing the conflict in the soul between *Wit* (reason) and *Will* (desire) objectively, and with a scientific precision that mingles psychology and politics.[8] Self-consciousness allegorized is represented by the buckler of Pallas.[9] It must be noted, however, that from this poem Shakespeare borrowed plot elements, rather than its suggestions on the inner life.

Celebrated and imitated by Spenser, Geoffrey Chaucer was universally admired, according to the prologue of *The Two Noble Kinsmen*. It is apparent that Chaucer provided important elements of the plot for this comedy, composed by Shakespeare in collaboration with John Fletcher, and also elements within *Troilus and Cressida*.[10] But, again, his work does not appear to resonate with the inner conflicts that we can discern in Shakespeare's characters. In the *Canterbury Tales*, for example, the characters have well delineated personalities. But one does not notice in them anything 'fluctuating and diverse' after the manner of Montaigne. As Blake observed, each represents a category: 'as Newton numbered the stars, and Linnaeus numbered the plants, so Chaucer numbered the classes of men'.[11] Of course, Chaucer's humour, generally considered as the most notable before Shakespeare's, could be interpreted as denoting a progression in the development of subjectivity. It can certainly be conceded that in the creation of his characters he displays the capacity for the critical detachment humour requires, especially when he himself is on stage.[12] Yet this humour is manifested only through sly insinuation, an amused tolerance, an apparent admission of his own lack of intelligence, confessing 'my wit is short' in the prologue. Such shows of modesty are not unprecedented among the minstrels, whether troubadors or *trouvères*.[13]

2. The Shakespearean moment: the English Renaissance at the turn of the century

A call to self-knowledge was a common theme in England throughout the sixteenth century. Yet its alignment followed the traditions of Christian Socratism, notably when the *Grammar* of William Lily (who died in 1522), revised by Erasmus, taught children that the beginning of wisdom is to know oneself. Sir Thomas Elyot, a humanist, wrote in *The Governor* in 1532 that it is necessary to know oneself in order to love one's neighbour and practise justice, an argument perhaps inspired by St Bernard but applied to the active life.[14] Another humanist, Roger Ascham, recovered the true meaning of the Socratic injunction when he advised readers in *Toxophilus* to study their capacities according to the wise injunction of Apollo, 'know thyself', that is, know what you are apt to and conform your actions to this knowledge.[15] What is striking in these injunctions is that self-knowledge is no longer a means of attaining knowledge of God, as with St Bernard, but an acquirement required for the conduct of life in society. Towards the end of the century, Spenser and Sidney in their conception of the perfect gentleman will consider self-knowledge essential for self-mastery and virtuous action in the ethical and political sphere.[16]

Thus the Renaissance progressively secularized Christian Socratism, but without any interventions of the kind of self-consciousness displayed in Montaigne's *Essays*. The long philosophical poem of Sir John Davies, *Nosce teipsum* (1600), brought nothing new in the way of introspection. Self-knowledge for Francis Bacon was the end and consummation of natural philosophy concerning man, but he also insisted that it was only a portion of natural philosophy in the realm of nature. When he invited man to 'descend into himself', he thought it a possibility offered only to the 'learned man' and spoke from an ethical point of view when extolling 'the pleasure of that *suavissima vita, indies sentire se fieri meliorem*'.[17]

It is generally agreed that a keener awareness of individual identity manifested itself in England than on the Continent.[18] But it must not, however, conceal the fact that, in the eyes of the contemporaries of this evolution, especially from a religious point of view, this 'identity' was still essentially constituted of a tissue of obligations resulting from a social position. William Perkins reminds his congregation that each man is *a person in relation with another one*; he is a spouse, a father or a mother and must act in accordance with his function.[19] Furthermore, in his *Institutes* (I, i, 12) Calvin had firmly maintained that a perfect knowledge of oneself could be attained only through knowledge of God, an undisputed position. These perspectives indicate that Margreta de Grazia's assertion that the theology of the Reformation was an instrument for the development of self-consciousness and interiority must be tempered.[20] In the early years of the seventeenth century, the treatises on conscience published in England tackled this problem only from a religious and ethical point of view.[21] When William Ames defined conscience as 'a reflexive act of the Understanding', he supported this assertion by citing a series of biblical texts, mainly the Psalms.[22] The Reformation brought about a proliferation of so-called 'private diaries', but before the seventeenth century the effort of introspection of their authors never went beyond commonplace religious self-examinations.[23]

This should not lead us to ignore the progress of individualism in profane literature. An arrogant self-assertion and a search for singularity in one's behaviour were overtly manifested.[24] Contemporary moralists condemned this rampant individualism, often associating it with Machiavellianism. Gabriel Harvey made the author of *The Prince* profess: 'I alone am wise; I alone live and triumph for myself'.[25] The individual expression of will was made lyrical in the central characters of Marlowe, from Tamburlaine to Faustus, albeit tempered with stoicism with Mortimer in *Edward II*. At the beginning of the seventeenth century the Machiavellian and Stoic characters of Webster in their proud isolation scorned any attempt at imitating other heroes (as the Renaissance moralists urged) and sought to maintain their individuality in the throes of death. Before killing the Cardinal in *The Duchess of Malfi*, Bosola asserted: 'I will not imitate things glorious / No more than base; I'll be mine own example' (V, iv, 81–2). And in *The White Devil* (V, vi, 253–5) Flamineo's last words before his death are: 'I do not look / Who went before, nor who shall follow me; / No, at myself I will begin and end'.

In a different way, Elizabethan satire offers similar examples of the emphasis on subjectivity already noted in Roman satire.[26] In 1599, Marston dedicated 'To his most esteemed and beloved Selfe' *The Scourge of Villanie*, in which he proclaimed: 'I am my selfe, so is my poesie'.[27] Accordingly, a search for individual originality in thought and style became a characteristic feature of literary creation, and was a reaction against the previous doctrine and practice of imitation.[28] Yet this self-assertion was not necessarily attended by a similar urge for self-examination, nor an interest in the inner life, and it was far removed from the irony directed at oneself which stems from a phenomenon of auto-reflexivity.

In lyrical poetry, from the reign of Henry VIII, Sir Thomas Wyatt, when he did not imitate the Italians, had expressed desire, revolt or indignation in dissonant accents; but these moods, which found few echoes, were projected out of his sensitive self without any introspective analysis.[29] 'My mind to me a kingdom is', the widely popular song of Edward Dyer, expressed only the contentment one could find in a simple and decent life.[30] The vogue of the complaint favoured an outpouring of emotion which somehow revealed the subjectivity of the afflicted person, but this can hardly be seen as a sustained exploration of his or her inner mind. When Samuel Daniel's Rosamond declares 'into my selfe my waking thoughts retire', it leads only to a review of her sins, not a review of her essential inner nature.[31] An undeniable autobiographical inspiration is present in Spenser's poems, but it is camouflaged under the pastoral convention in *Colin Clout Come Home Again*, under the Petrarchan convention in his *Amoretti*. Sir Philip Sidney alone, in *Astrophel and Stella* (sonnet 94), shows himself keenly attentive to the ebb and flow of his stream of consciousness, and is sometimes perplexed by the elusiveness of his own feelings:

> GRIEF, find the words, for thou hast made my brain
> So dark with misty vapours which arise
> From out thy heavy mould that in-bent eyes
> Can scarce discern the shape of mine own pain.

Yet, when the sonneteer stages his own self, it is usually his outer social self, the knight or the courtier.[32] In the Elizabethan age, John Donne was the only author whose work was deeply affected or characterized by the acuity of its introspective self-observation.

As early as 1960 I had already pointed out affinities between Donne and Montaigne from this point of view in my main book on the Metaphysical poets, despite major differences in other respects. But this observation was not dictated by any sign of influence. Unlike Shakespeare, Donne does not seem to have taken an interest in the *Essays*, although he briefly alludes to them in a letter.[33] The affinities spotted thus proceed from a combination of psychological phenomena: a constant attention to his own states of mind coupled with a spontaneous auto-reflexivity. These lines written 'To the Countess of Bedford, on New-Year's day', are characteristic of Donne:

> This twilight of two yeares, not past nor next,
> Some emblem is of mee or I of this,
> Who Meteor-like, of stuffe and forme perplext,
> Whose what, and where in disputation is,
> If I should call mee any thing, should misse.[34]

As with Montaigne, self-analysis placing the observer at a distance from himself creates a void, blurs his gaze and breeds a deep perplexity. It was,

I admit, traditional to present self-knowledge as either neglected or hard to attain. Yet it is significant that this idea should so often recur in the mind of the poet, sometimes incidentally, as in 'Obsequies to the Lord Harrington', when he says: 'And I discerne by favour of this light / My selfe, the hardest object of the sight' (ll. 29–30).

'Negative love' does not merely express his sense that love is always felt as an experience of deprivation, a desire for an unknown object – an impression also expressed in 'Love's alchymie' and 'To the Countesse of Huntingdon'. This ignorance, for which Montaigne created the term 'inscience', extends to the mystery of personality: 'If any who deciphers best, / What we know not, our selves, can know, / Let him teach mee that nothing'. To define himself was Donne's essential and repeated effort. Like Montaigne, the repetition occurs because he always failed to attain this ambition. In both minds, the effort of analysis deepened their perplexity and failure was the consequence of their clear-sightedness.

Donne has described his changes of mood in a letter in which he showed how he could make himself in quick succession sad or cheerful.[35] He seems never to be committed to an emotion, because he feels its transitory nature and finds himself always prone to experience a different state of mind. This changeableness is felt as a flexibility or even an insubstantiality. This, too, is what Montaigne also constantly observed in his self-scrutiny. Donne, like Montaigne, also shows a peculiar ability to set himself spontaneously at a distance from an emotion at the very moment of experience. Donne's preacher tells his audience:

> I am not all here, I am here now preaching upon the text, and I am at home in my Library considering whether S. Gregory, or S. Hierome, have said best of this text before. I am here speaking to you, and yet I consider by the way, *in the same instant*, what it is likely you will say to one another, when I have done.[36]

This is the inner distance which makes the concomitance of emotion and irony possible in his poetry, a conjunction which may be thought eminently modern.

I have dwelt on Donne because he illustrates even more distinctly than Shakespeare an evolution in our modes of consciousness which many critics have traced in *Hamlet*.[37] This should not be taken as implying that the author of the *Songs and Sonnets* was influenced by Shakespeare in this respect, even though this 'great frequenter of plays' may partly owe the dramatic vivacity of his style to the influence of the London stage.[38]

This short, precise survey of the growth of individualism in Elizabethan literature invites a general conclusion. As Alain Renaut accurately observed, 'the ideal of autonomy which characterizes humanism requires the definition and presence within myself of a part of humanity irreducible to the bare assertion of my singularity'.[39] Ascham, Sidney and Spenser were humanists in whom this balance was attained. Yet by the end of the century some satirists and some characters on the late Elizabethan and early Jacobean stage offered illustrations of the 'individualistic drift' which, at least in philosophy, began in France only with Descartes, according to Renaut.[40] What made the originality of Montaigne and Donne was an association of intense egotism and a full consciousness of their 'part of humanity', a balance perhaps achieved through their constant ability to dissociate themselves from themselves in a spontaneous self-examination. I have shown elsewhere how Donne's egotistic consciousness could thus transcend individualism and bypass egotism without any change in its fundamental structure.[41] What about Shakespeare?

3. The self in Shakespeare's *Sonnets*

As a dramatist, Shakespeare must be considered a protean author, one who cannot be identified with any of the characters he sets on stage. One could be tempted to explore his personality in his sonnets. But should this temptation be rejected?

One generally considers Wordsworth's assertion naïve when he claims that 'with this key / Shakespeare unlocked his heart'.[42] Furthermore, a Lacanian critic, Joel Fineman, thought he had found in them the proof of a change of episteme and the emergence of a new type of subjectivity. Shakespeare would have transformed the traditional type of 'specular' description in earlier sonnets by discovering before Saussure an irremediable disjunction between language and the world. The sonnets to the dark lady are a discourse of the tongue, not of the eye: the words are essentially or ontologically in disagreement with what they talk about. As the play on 'I' and 'eye' in sonnet 152 suggests, the eye is bound to perjure itself. A new awareness of a radical disjunction of the signifier and the referent opened the way to the 'modern poetic subjectivity' which dictated the course of literary history and culminated in the present 'post-modernism'. Colin Burrow rightly finds this argument unconvincing in his edition of the *Sonnets*.[43] There may be some justification for the different attitudes. No one can deny that Elizabethan sonnets, in the tradition of Petrarch, obey conventions; yet those of Shakespeare profess to be in opposition to these conventions, from which Sidney himself had occasionally departed in the frank confession of his 'desire'.[44] Of course, one may argue that he was only seeking novelty at a time when Donne and other poets of his generation, discarding the principle of imitation, were in quest of originality.[45] But if the situation he evoked, or invented, was purely imaginary, one wonders why a dramatist did not make it more evident and plausible. Why introduce so many obscure allusions which could be deciphered only by the initiate? When it is not a mere rhetorical exercise, a poem, whether autobiographical or not, reveals the author's personality. Though some critics invite us to read Shakespeare's sonnets without seeking any coherence in them, the voice we hear in the poems is always the same and is as recognizable as a musical tone is recognizable. I agree with Janine Chassenet-Smirgel when she claims:

> any fragment of a work of Rembrandt or Bonnard, a single sentence of Proust or Chateaubriand, a line of Mozart or Debussy, are – at least virtually – recognizable, just as a fragment of bone allows a naturalist to discover the animal it comes from; or as a stroke of the pen allows a graphologist to identify the writer. Whether an individual creates his language or whether language passes through him, this language, when traversing the thinking mind and the speaking mouth must needs take on a particular turn, tone or sound whenever it is not reduced to mere repetition or parody.[46]

As Ben Jonson, echoing Juan Vivès, had asserted in the Renaissance, language issues from our innermost depths (psychoanalysts would agree) and best reveals a man: 'Speak and I shall know thee'.[47]

Even if we agreed that Shakespeare's *Sonnets* had no autobiographical origin it would remain interesting to notice that the pre-eminent theme of the sonnets to the dark lady is self-deception in various forms. Of course, when the poet proclaims an unattractive woman fair, he takes up the classical theme of the illusions of lovers (orchestrated by the dramatist in *A Midsummer Night's Dream*) and handles it with crude exaggeration in the Berninesque mode.[48] Yet, since he remains clear-sighted at the very moment when he entertains this illusion, like Berowne in love with Rosalind in *Love's Labour's Lost*, this complex play of illusion and awareness reveals Shakespeare's capacity for an ironical self-consciousness.[49]

In its terrible intensity, the impersonal record of violent and contradictory impulses in sonnet 129 encompasses in a single sentence the successive stages of a passion spent in a waste of shame:

> Th'expense of Spirit in a waste of shame
> Is lust in action; and till action, lust
> Is perjured, murd'rous, bloody, full of blame,
> Savage, extreme, rude, cruel, not to trust,
> Enjoyed no sooner but despisèd straight,
> Past reason hunted, and no sooner had

> Past reason hated, as a swallowed bait
> On purpose laid to make the taker mad;
> Mad in pursuit, and in possession so;
> Had, having, and in quest to have, extreme,
> A bliss in proof, and proved, a very woe;
> Before, a joy proposed, behind, a dream.
> All this the world well knows; yet none knows well
> To shun the heav'n that leads men to this hell.

Yet, through this apparent impersonality, the paradoxes of desire, through the clash of consonants and contraries, convey to the reader the fits and starts of a strained subjectivity.

In his denunciation of self-love (sonnet 62) the poet does not anticipate the subtleties of La Rochefoucaud, as Daniel Dyke will do in his Augustinian *Mystery of Self-deceiving*, published only in 1615.[50] More complex is sonnet 138, in which, while lying about his age and yet admitting he still entertains the illusion that his mistress may be deceived, the poet is still willing to believe her, though he knows that she lies when swearing she is made of truth:

> When my love swears that she is made of truth
> I do believe her, though I know she lies,
> That she might think me some untutor'd youth,
> Unlearnèd in the world's false subtleties.
> Thus vainly thinking that she thinks me young,
> Although she knows my days are past the best,
> Simply I credit her false-speaking tongue;
> On both sides thus is simple truth suppress'd.
> But wherefore says she not she is unjust?
> And wherefore say not I that I am old?
> O, love's best habit is in seeming trust,
> And age in love, loves not to have years told.
> Therefore I lie with her and she with me,
> And in our faults by lies we flatter'd be.

'On both sides thus is simple truth suppress'd', yet the illusion here seems invested with a reality which surpasses simple truth. The coexistence of a belief accepted though it is known to be false and of a clear realization of an illusion requires a simultaneous perception of an experience and of the experiencing subject. The 'self' is observed by an overarching 'I', a phenomenon observed in experiences recorded by Montaigne and by Donne.

The sonnets written for the young man have a certain continuity.[51] The succession of contrasting attitudes and feelings proceeds from changing circumstances. What concerns me here, however, is the poet's ability to keep different emotions, different judgements in balance within the same poem. The complexity of an experience or a character may sometimes be presented objectively, as in sonnet 94:

> They that have power to hurt and will do none,
> That do not do the thing they most do show,
> Who, moving others, are themselves as stone,
> Unmovèd, cold, and to temptation slow –
> They rightly do inherit Heaven's graces
> And husband Nature's riches from expense;
> They are the Lords and owners of their faces,
> Others but stewards of their excellence.
> The summer's flower is to the summer sweet,
> Though to itself it only live and die,
> But if that flower with base infection meet,
> The basest weed outbraves his dignity;
> For sweetest things turn sourest by their deeds;
> Lilies that fester smell far worse than weeds.

Each assertion associates a quality and a defect, praise and blame, thus maintaining the mind of the reader in a state of perplexity up to the final statement, an unequivocal condemnation which does not suppress admiration. Read in isolation the sonnet would leave us in doubt; its significance as a genuine experience and its special intensity would be perceived only through its structure, its antithetical shapeliness. The opening word 'They' points to a plurality of representatives of a social class, but the closing evocation of a single flower implies that the poet is thinking of the beloved young man whose narcissistic tendencies he has already exposed in other sonnets. The succession of positive and negative attributes illustrates the ambivalence of his feelings for this puzzling individual. The power to hurt is disquieting; its control and restraint are reassuring, but the unexplained divorce between appearance and action implies a duality, perhaps a secret duplicity. To provoke a movement of attraction to oneself as a beloved or admired person while remaining 'Unmovèd, cold' is the privilege of a young man of fascinating beauty. But why is he 'to temptation slow'? Is he virtuous or incapable of loving? After inheriting all the gifts of nature, why refrain from spending them? Is it out of wisdom or because he is incapable of any gratuitous action or self-surrender? Lord and owner of his face, he maintains his admirers, his friend in the position of 'stewards'. A solitary flower which would live only for itself and die without yielding any fruit would at least lavish its sweetness on the summer. Yet, despite a semblance of exquisite perfection, corruption is present and *optima corrupta pessima*. The character and the situation may have been wholly invented (I think it unlikely), but the full suggestiveness of the sonnet cannot be felt by a reader unacquainted with the other sonnets in the sequence, which gradually reveals the personality of a man capable at once of base submission and clear-sighted indignation: which implies self-awareness and introspective self-consciousness.

In the sonnets to the young man which openly stage the poet's reactions and his judgement, praise or blame, trust or distrust, there is a clear control of the emotions, which also implies self-consciousness. This can be observed in sonnets 69 and 84, among others. The revelation of an unpleasant trait of character, calling for a warning, is delayed and emerges only in the closing couplet: accordingly, the contrasts are not simultaneously perceived when reading the poem, but they must have been prepared for in the process of composition, which implies that the author must have had a simultaneous consciousness of them.

The poet whose voice we hear in the *Sonnets* several times suggests the existence of a contrast between his real self and his 'social' self, the role he has to play or his character as seen by others. This contrast seems to me the more significant since, according to many critics, his contemporaries were essentially defined in their own eyes by their function in society and in the family. I do not think this would apply to Spenser and Sidney, yet I discern a difference between them and Shakespeare. For the authors of *Colin Clout* and *Astrophel and Stella* there is no divergence between the social self and the true self. When Sidney says 'Having this day my horse, my hand, my lance' (sonnet 41), he makes no distinction between his intimate self and his body or his equipment as a knight. When Shakespeare complains that his nature 'is subdued / To what it works in, like the Dyer's hand' (sonnet 111), he obviously feels a difference between his inner self and the player compelled by fortune: 'The guilty goddess of my harmful deeds, / That did not better for my life provide / Than public means which public manners breeds'.

If the self were reduced to the social self, would the poet dare answer censure and obloquy in the way of sonnet 121?

> 'Tis better to be vile than vile esteemed,
> When not to be receives reproach of being,
> And the just pleasure lost which is so deemed
> Not by our feeling but by others' seeing.
> For why should others false adulterate eyes
> Give salutation to my sportive blood?
> Or on my frailties why are frailer spies,
> Which in their wills count bad what I think good?

In his relationship with a young aristocrat he may, of course, play the part of a poet of humble origin bound to speak with a conventional humility. One may even admit that, in his moments of indignation, whether open or covert, in his flashes of irony, he does not really depart from his role. We must read him more closely.

The relation established between the poet and the young man was bound to make his self-consciousness more acute. 'Desire' in the sonnets to the dark lady apparently seeks only to capture a body, an object. Now 'love', as Sartre argued, seeks to capture a 'subject', a 'consciousness'.[52] Yet love may also be 'a going out of our selves', as Shelley defined it in his 'Essay on love'. In Shakespeare's sonnets there is more complexity. Curiously, we are never invited to penetrate the consciousness of the beloved, which is surprising when the poet is a dramatist.[53] This silence may be due to an imposed reserve or to the unresponsiveness of the beloved, evoked in other sonnets. I am, however, inclined to ascribe it to the fact that this love is essentially an aesthetic ecstasy provoked by the physical beauty of the young nobleman. This emotion does not call for a response of the beloved; it only requires his presence, actual or felt in a dream, as in sonnets 27, 28, 43 and 61. One should note that the word 'desire', in relation to the young man, is used either to express the poet's desire for his presence, without any evidence for closer intercourse (sonnet 51, l. 10), or to call for the perpetuation of the 'fairest creatures' (sonnet 1).

Intersubjectivity seems, then, absent in Shakespeare's *Sonnets*, though the pronoun 'I' is less frequent while 'thou' and 'you' are more frequent than in the sonnets of Petrarch or Sidney. An *I*, according to Ricoeur, places us in the field of language and tends to create an intersubjective situation: 'this *I* can designate, besides the speaker, the unique *I* which I myself am'.[54] In Shakespeare's *Sonnets*, the *I* fills this second function and claims to be the only *I*. Yet, generally, it is not egocentric, for the poet is lost in the contemplation or recollection of his friend in 'the sessions of sweet silent thought' (sonnet 30). That this solitary *I* should seek an identification with the lover might be a Neo-Platonic commonplace. Besides, the poet's argument in sonnet 42 is more ingenious than convincing:

> That thou hast her, it is not all my grief,
> And yet it may be said I loved her dearly;
> That she hath thee, is of my wailing chief,
> A loss in love that touches me more nearly.
> Loving offenders, thus I will excuse ye:
> Thou dost love her, because thou know'st I love her,
> And for my sake even so doth she abuse me,
> Suffering my friend for my sake to approve her.

> If I lose thee, my loss is my love's gain,
> And losing her, my friend hath found that loss;
> Both find each other, and I lose both twain,
> And both for my sake lay on me this cross:
> But here's the joy: my friend and I are one;
> Sweet flattery! then she loves but me alone.

The exclamation 'Sweet flattery!' pinpoints the fact that the speaker is consciously trying to deceive himself, as in sonnet 93. Because he wishes to preserve a sentimental link with the young man, he can be sincere when saying (sonnet 40): 'Take all my loves, my love, yea, take them all; / What hast thou then more than thou hadst before?' Self-consciousness may then become self-denial or self-effacement in several sonnets (57, 58, 88, 89). The poet even declares himself willing to be rejected by his friend and would even hasten so painful a separation: 'Then hate me when thou wilt; if ever, now; / [...] If thou wilt leave me, do not leave me last' (sonnet 90).

The poet's age and his social position are an obstacle to this identification with the friend and even disallow an open and constant propinquity. The difference in age was traditional but Shakespeare's insistence on it (sonnets 22, 62, 63, 73) and on the possible imminence of his own death (sonnets 32, 73) suggests an intense personal preoccupation with the subject which will be considered again in chapter 5, devoted to the subjective apprehension of time. Incidentally, and without suggesting a link, one may note that Montaigne incessantly evokes his 'decrepitude' and the end of his life in his *Essays*.[55]

Some of the most moving sonnets express the poet's consent to an estrangement or a secret relation with the friend (49, 87) and even an acceptance of oblivion after his own death: 'No longer mourn for me when I am dead [...] / Do not so much as my poor name rehearse. / But let your love ev'n with my life decay' (71). The lover (as well as the poet) ceaselessly discommends himself (sonnets 26, 32, 49, 57, 71, 80, 87–9, 96) and addresses to himself censures, which alternate with reactions of hurt pride and attempts at exculpation (sonnets 109, 110, 111, 119, 120, 121).

A contraction and an intensification of self-consciousness are suggested when 'my love' may refer at once to the beloved and to the poet's love for him. His most earnest wish is 'That in black ink my love may still shine bright' (sonnet 65). Yet the poet, I think, cares little for the immortality of the young man he never names, nor even for his own immortality (he has not the pride of a Ronsard); he seeks to convince himself of the immortality of love, a love able to create its own certainty (or consented illusion) of an unalterable constancy in the sonnet on 'the marriage of true minds' (sonnet 116). This precarious balance between a surrender of the imagination to what may be a mere deception and a genuine intuition of transcendence will appear also in the ultimate claim of Cleopatra, her 'immortal longings' (*Antony and Cleopatra*, V, ii, 276). In the poem as in the tragedy, what may be an illusion is apprehended as a reality, not because of the sheer power of the poet's rhetoric, as G. B. Shaw unjustly claimed, but through a genuine poetic 'intensity' (in the Keatsian sense), able to combine the intuition of essence and the apprehension of time's 'millioned accidents' (sonnet 115).

In Shakespeare's sonnets, the inner life of the poet has moments of fullness, periods of frustration and deprivation. Despite occasional proclamations of faithfulness, inconstancy is present. Yet we do not find in these poems what we noted in Montaigne and in Donne: the impression, albeit it fleeting, of a dissolution of the self. When the poet asserts in sonnet 121 'I am that I am', he confronts those who disparage him and, as do several of his heroes on stage,[56] asserts an identity which even the influence of the stars could not change. Edmund in *Lear* (I, ii, 128–30) asserts: 'I should have been that I am, had the maidenliest star in the firmament twinkled on my bastardizing'. Coriolanus proclaims 'I play the man I am' (III, ii, 14–15), which is true, in a sense, of all the Shakespearian heroes. Iago alone, the great dissembler, can truly say: 'I am not what I am' (*Othello*, I, i, 65).

It seems to be sometimes assumed that men in the Renaissance were conscious only of their social self; it may be true of some of them, but certainly not of all of them. It is even sometimes assumed that the word *self* had only a grammatical function in the language of the Elizabethans. I wish to point out, first, that Shakespeare seems to have used this word more often than his contemporaries and apparently created many compounds, such as self-affected, self-neglecting, self-reproving.[57] This creation seems to enhance a sense of identity. The *Oxford English Dictionary* records no example of 'self' used to designate 'what in a person is really and intrinsically he' before Hume and Berkeley, whose interest in self-consciousness is well known. Yet the notion of personal identity seems to be present in such phrases as 'make thee another self', 'Self so self-loving' (sonnets 10, 62), 'banish'd from her / Is self from self' (*Two Gentlemen of Verona*, III, i, 172–3), 'To thine own self be true' (*Hamlet*, I, iii, 78), 'I have a kind of self resides with me, / But an unkind self, that itself will leave' (*Troilus and Cressida*, III, ii, 144–7) and many others.

The sonnets were mostly written before *Hamlet* and before Shakespeare had read the *Essays* of Montaigne. We must now turn to the dramatic works to find more convincing evidence of new forms of self-consciousness in early modern literature.

4. The dramatic self: from the medieval monologue to the Shakespearean soliloquy

On a stage, the subjectivity of a character can be best disclosed in a monologue. James Hirsch has proposed a distinction between the interior monologue as we conceive it nowadays and the self-addressed speech, which he considers as the usual form in Shakespeare's age.[58] The interior monologue is supposed to open a window into the mind of a character. Yet it cannot be a 'direct representation of the character's thought': it is only 'the author's representation of the character's representation in speech of his or her thought'. I think this distinction too radical, for such a representation can be achieved only as if it were a genuine experience: it is bound to reflect a particular way of thinking. It is also excessive to claim that all the soliloquies in the plays of Shakespeare represent speeches which characters address to themselves. One may distinguish three types: (1) a speech which a character on stage addresses to an audience; (2) a speech which he addresses to himself; (3) a speech which is supposed to form itself in his mind without any interlocutor. Generally, the first type expresses premeditated thoughts; it is only in the second type, and chiefly in the third, that the *pensée pensante* can be displayed in its spontaneous generation, or at least with an apparent unpremeditation.[59]

Historically, the evolution of the monologue from the Middle Ages to Shakespeare's plays discloses the late appearance of an intensified attention to the inner life, characterized by the spontaneous reflexivity I have analysed in the *Essays* of Montaigne. A monologue of Brutus in *Julius Caesar* is a turning-point and Hamlet nowadays is often hailed as the hero, or herald, of the early modern age.[60] It is through the evolution of the Shakespearean soliloquy that the evolution of subjectivity is best grasped. Attention is best focused first on the most significant monologue, not the celebrated 'To be or not to be', but the outburst of feeling which follows the evocation by a player of Hecuba's distress after the murder of Priam (*Hamlet*, II, ii, 505–22). Hamlet flies into a passion because he is unable to vent his own grief with the same vehemence. He lashes himself with words and berates Claudius in terms of increasing violence:

> Bloody, bawdy villain,
> Remorseless, treacherous, lecherous, kindless villain!
> O, vengeance!

Then he suddenly breaks off and speaks to himself in a very different tone:

> Why, what an ass am I! Ay, sure, this is most brave
> That I, the son of a dear father murderèd,

> Prompted to my revenge by heaven and hell,
> Must, like a whore, unpack my heart with words,
> And fall a-cursing like a very drab,
> A scallion! Fie upon't, foh!
> (II, ii, 580–8)

Though the differences should not be forgotten, I am inclined to think that Hamlet suddenly discovers he has been acting for himself the comedy of indignation, much as the hero of Sartre in his *Les mains sales* discovers he 'acts the comedy of despair'. What moves him to admire and envy the deep tragedian is not the player's capacity for action but his ability to act so as to 'force his soul so to his own conceit'. A dream of passion – grief for Hecuba – acquires, through his acting, the fullness, roundness and reality of grief in itself, grief self-subsistent and aesthetically satisfying, not the kind of grief Hamlet can feel for his father, in shreds and patches of intermittent passion. Are words used by him to lash himself into action, or mainly to whip up his own emotions? Did he earlier reject 'the trappings and the suits of woe' (I, ii, 86), will he later parody the ranting of Laertes over Ophelia's grave (V, i, 266–74) because his own emotions are too deep for words, or out of an intuition that no self-conscious emotion is truly genuine? He himself seems capable of feeling only in fits and outbursts; like Sartre's Hugo, but also like Montaigne, he cannot 'engage himself' deliberately.[61] When addressing the players, Hamlet advises them to temper the expression of fictive passion by retaining their self-control (III, ii, 1–14). In (supposedly) real life he himself can momentarily achieve this composure through his own, spontaneous self-consciousness.

One may now trace the evolution which led from premeditated monologues structured in accordance with the rules of rhetoric to the spontaneous expression of what will (much later) be called the 'stream of consciousness'.

A monologue on stage may fulfil various functions. It may be a direct address to the audience (after the manner of a prologue) in order to introduce a character, outline a situation, announce an intention and so on. It is only in particular circumstances that the analysis of a state of mind, the exposition of a motive, the expression of a feeling will create some psychological complexity. This type of speech may also be uttered by an actor watched by other actors to meet the requirements of the dramatic action; and he may know whether he is watched or not, which will affect the sincerity of his speech.

'Monologue' and 'soliloquy' are interchangeable terms. One may, however, decide to use 'monologue' as the more general term, applicable equally to a scene with one character only on stage and to a speech uttered by an actor who is not speaking to absent, hidden or imaginary hearers. The term 'soliloquy' may be preferably used if a character addresses himself when wholly rapt in his own thoughts, in utter forgetfulness of any other presence; this may be the case even in short asides.[62] This distinction, however, cannot be systematic.

On a medieval or Renaissance stage, monologues were not conceived as the voicing of mute thought: the characters spoke to themselves aloud quite naturally. This was an age when silent reading was still exceptional and even prayers called *preces privatae* were commonly spoken audibly.[63] According to some historians, the difference between a true 'inner soliloquy', that is, the silent engendering of mute thoughts in a mind, and their oral expression in a more or less deliberately ordered speech would have been perceived only by the end of the seventeenth century.[64] This assertion, however, must be qualified.

The kind of medieval theatre Shakespeare himself may have watched in his youth resorted to the monologue for the sake of exposition and information, functions it retained on the Elizabethan and Jacobean stage. Systematic enquiries reveal that from the twelfth to the fifteenth century, from the mysteries and moralities to the interludes, the monologue grew more psychological, but most often under the influence of a time-honoured psychomachia.[65] This evolution may be considered a prelude to the Elizabethan dramatic monologue. Richard Hillman even thinks one may discover in medieval texts a representation of subjectivity in harmony with Lacanian psychoanalysis. God's speech in *Everyman* (ll. 22–63) is assumed to create 'the impression of a thought and an emotion set forth in our human time without the support of a fixed and stable identity'.[66]

A reader conversant with the Lacanian theory of the subject may have had this impression, but to the common reader nothing in the divine monologue, nor in the other passages quoted, suggests that the speaker (in fact the author who makes him speak) is conscious of a split personality, unstable after the manner of Shakespeare's Hamlet or Montaigne in his *Essays*, though Hillman mentions them.[67] The absence of any auto-reflexivity in God's speech seems to me obvious, as a close reading of this monologue, which is too long to quote, will, I think, convince the reader.

In the three monologues of the hero in *Everyman* one may, indeed, admit the presence of introspection, provided its extent and effect are limited to the traditional review of one's sins, which breeds a momentary despair and the temptation of suicide, a theme which will reappear with Spenser's Guyon and Marlowe's Faustus.[68] To speak of an immersion in the depth of consciousness as a French critic did is, however, excessive, as this quotation from the first monologue shows:[69]

> Alas, I well may weep with sighs deep!
> Now have I no manner of company
> To help me in my journey, and me to keep:
> And also my writing is full unready.
> How shall I do now for to excuse me?
> I would to God I had never be get!
> To my soul a very great profit it had be;
> For now I fear pains huge and great.
> The time passeth. Lord, help that all wrought
> For though I mourn it availeth nought.[70]

Vice appeared early in the morality plays and had various embodiments, human or devilish. In John Skelton's *Magnificence* (c.1513), an elaborate composition, Belial is the first protean character seen on stage, displaying his *Schadenfreude* and his art of dissembling. His persistence in Elizabethan drama is well known. Shakespeare's Richard III and Iago are often said to derive from Vice, but we shall see how much the type has been enriched and individualized.

From the medieval theatre to the theatre of the Renaissance the main development was the replacement of the address to the audience by the self-address as the dominant convention. As Hirsch points out, 'a Renaissance character who talks *himself* into an action that violates his conscience is significantly different from a medieval character who justifies his immorality to the audience'.[71]

The latest moralities were influenced by an emerging taste for Senecan rhetoric and in the anonymous morality play *Appius and Virginia*,[72] the traditional psychomachia seems to be moving towards a new interiority in the expression of a 'divided' personality by the hero himself. Yet Conscience and Judgment on stage are still embodied allegorical figures:

> But out, I am wounded: how am I divided!
> Two states of my life from me are now glided;
> For Conscience he pricketh me condemned,
> And Justice saith, Judgment would have me condemned:[73]

To assume, as Spivack does, that this soliloquy, in a more elaborate style, might be spoken by Angelo or Macbeth, or by Richard III in his debate with his conscience on the eve of the battle of Bosworth, masks an evolution in the expression of subjectivity.[74]

From the beginning of the sixteenth century, one notices a multiplication of monologues, on stage and in narrative poems, in which a character not only introduces himself and vents his thoughts and feelings but distinctly speaks to himself. There may have been a reciprocal influence between the theatre and the immensely popular *Mirror for Magistrate* (1559), published by George Ferrar with the participation of Thomas Sackville. However, these historical figures, when they lament their errors and misfortunes, describe themselves as tragic illustrations of a universal principle, as Richard Hillman admits.[75]

The translation of the tragedies of Seneca, begun in 1559 and completed with the publication of *Tenne Tragedies* in 1589, had made his rhetoric fashionable. In the *Gordobuc* (1560-1) of Thomas Sackville, the traditional medieval debate is conducted in Senecan declamatory speeches and choruses, without any exploration of the depths of interiority, even in monologues.[76] Like Seneca's sentences in his soliloquies, they never contain the broken expressions which one encounters in Shakespeare: we always hear a discourse; we are not immersed in the stream of consciousness of a character.[77]

A progress in the expression of subjectivity is still hardly perceptible in the numerous monologues with which Thomas Kyd's *Spanish Tragedy* was interspersed in 1592. They are essentially lamentations meant to inform the audience of the schemes of the avenger, Hieronimo. No subtlety can be discovered in them, despite a presumed influence on *Hamlet*.

Whether in self-address or when speaking to someone else, the characters resort to the third person. This use of the third person to designate oneself, observable in the young child, is in line with a primal state of subjectivity, though writers, of course, can use it for various reasons: rhetorical emphasis, the speaker's rank, his sense of his own importance. Shakespeare himself will resort to it, notably in *Julius Caesar* (II, ii), but with more subtlety.

In the years which preceded the first plays of Shakespeare, the monologue, frequent in the 'histories', made little progress in dramatic liveliness and interiority. In Robert Greene's *Alphonsus, King of Aragon* (1591), the monarch almost constantly speaks in the third person, and so do many other characters.[78] It is only in *James IV*, probably Greene's last play (1594), that this rhetorical use becomes less conspicuous.

Marlowe himself will often resort to the third-person self-address. He will invest some soliloquies of *Tamburlaine* and the *Jew of Malta* with unrivalled eloquence and splendour, but the heroes project their desires – and probably those of their creator – on the world without truly revealing inner depths. In *Doctor Faustus*, after the Chorus, the action opens *in medias res* and the character addresses himself, not the audience. The opening monologue 'dramatizes' a disenchantment after long years of study, but we do not find in it the sudden and surprising turns which characterize the movement of thought in the soliloquies of Hamlet. The meditation progresses in a premeditated order within a dictated structure, leading from theology to logic, medicine and law before reverting to theology. Symmetry prevails: a Latin quotation which defines the aim of a science is followed by a disparaging evaluation and a rejection. The seduction of magic, announced by the opening Chorus, is then suddenly proclaimed in a lyrical outburst: 'O what a world of profit and delight, / Of power, of honour, and omnipotence / Is promised to the studious artisan!' (I, i, 54–6). The first cause of the hero's fall must be the tragic *hubris*, but the aspiration to knowledge is only an instrument for a will of domination like Tamburlaine's, a desire of wealth like the Jew's. And when the Good Angel and the Bad Angel enter the stage we are again in a morality play.

The later oscillation between despair and an unavailing effort at repentance seems to a critic the most penetrating 'religious self-scrutiny' in Renaissance drama, illustrating a conflict between the 'two rival formations of selfhood that struggle for acceptance in the mind of Faustus', humanistic tendencies restrained by traditional religious fears. Faustus is divided, no doubt, but the conflict between the lust of the flesh and the fear of damnation does not constitute 'two identities'.[79]

The long final monologue of Faustus is so well known that it need not be quoted but its movements must be recalled. In contrast with his impatient call for the conclusion of the pact with Lucifer, 'Is't not midnight? Come, Mephistopheles!' (II, i, 28), the hero now prays that 'midnight never come!' and will implore 'Come not, Lucifer!' (V, iii, 140, 191). But all the action seems to be outward rather than inward. The speech opens with a cosmic vision, evokes a frustrated leap to heaven, a vain attempt at hiding under mountains or being drawn up into the entrails of a cloud, an agonized search for dissolution and a fall into the ocean. This scene of extreme anguish is punctuated by the strokes of a clock, heightening the sense of fate. The twenty-four years allotted by the pact come to a close.

This monologue is intensely dramatic and, unlike the first, it records an experience truly lived in the present moment, despite the contraction of one hour into some sixty lines. At no moment, however, does Faustus display, much less analyse, his inner life: his attention and ours are engrossed by a series of images.

Introspection did not appear spontaneously in the Shakespearean soliloquies. In the early comedies, *The Two Gentlemen of Verona*, *The Taming of the Shrew* and *The Comedy of Errors*, the monologues were numerous, but essentially used for information or comment.[80] In *The Two Gentlemen* (II, vi, 1–43) Proteus opens a debate on his perjury, but he does it after the manner of Tarquin in *The Rape of Lucrece*.

In the first tragedy, *Titus Andronicus* (1592), Aaron announces his intentions (II, i, 1–25; IV, ii, 171–9). Lucius, then Marcus, briefly disclose their plots (III, i, 287–99; IV, i, 122–8). In *Henry VI, Part 1*, probably composed in collaboration (c. 1591), several scenes end with brief informative monologues.[81] Were they written by Shakespeare? In *Henry VI, Part 2* (1591), York describes the situation and expounds his tactics in two long monologues (I, i, 214–59; III, i, 331–83). He exhorts himself 'to change misdoubt to resolution', but never ponders on his doubts after the manner of Hamlet.

In *Henry VI, Part 3* (composed in 1592, or by the end of 1591) three soliloquies are of greater interest. The first discloses the state of mind of the king, his weariness and his longing for a quiet bucolic life (II, v, 1–54). It is still in the tradition of the popular 'complaints' and an outward projection of a longing without any introspection. The inward movements of passion, however, are felt in the soliloquy in which Gloucester – the future Richard III – reveals he does 'but dream of sovereignty/Like one that stands upon a promontory/And spies a far-off shore where he would tread' (III, ii, 134–6). However, he still sees himself in an outward projection of himself, 'like one lost in a thorny wood,/That rends the thorns and is rent by the thorns,/Seeking a way and straying from the way,/Not knowing how to find the open air,/But toiling desperately to find it out –' (174–8). He gives an objective explanation for his quest: a physical deformity has disproportioned him and will not allow him to 'witch sweet ladies' (150–64). Like the medieval Vice, he complacently vents his devilish intentions (182–95).

Gloucester will proudly assert his solitary identity in his last monologue: 'I had no father, I am like no father;/I have no brother, I am like no brother [...]/I am myself alone' (V, vi, 79–84). This is an expression of Machiavellian individualism as interpreted by the Elizabethans, anticipated by his decision to 'set the murderous Machiavel to school' (III, ii, 193), but it is not an illustration of self-analysis, only the assertion of a desire of self-generation.[82]

The initial monologue in *Richard III* provides information about the motivations and intentions of Gloucester. Throughout the play the hero has a tendency see himself as an actor bound to play different parts. An alienation effect is achieved, but through a projection of the self rather than self-analysis, save in moments of irony. This irony, however, is directed at his physical appearance or displayed through his exultation when seducing the woman whose husband had died at his hands (I, ii, 215–50). His last monologue might have invited a closer self-analysis. Cursed in a dream by the ghosts of his victims, Richard, when waking up, seems at first to express his anguish in a series of spontaneous interrogations, but they are woven into a chain of argument which is an artificial construction rather than the expression of an experience inwardly felt, and it leads to an allegory of conscience and its 'thousand several tongues' (V, v, 131–60). The self is insistently obtruded, but with an occasional use of the speaker's name in the third person, which makes it external and will recur as a knell in the last word of the monologue:

> What do I fear? Myself? There's none else by.
> Richard loves Richard, that is, I am I.
> Is there a murderer here? No. Yes; I am?
> [...]
>   I myself
> Find in myself no pity for myself.
> Methought the souls of all I had murdered
> Came to my tent, and everyone did threat
> Tomorrow's vengeance on the head of Richard.

In *Richard II* (1595), the monarch is another player king who loves to take theatrical attitudes on all occasions and lyrically outpour the flood of emotion he is incapable of controlling. In a single soliloquy, he meditates upon his condition as a dethroned king and his imagination turns his cell into a world. He still allegorizes his inner life after the manner of the medieval and early Renaissance poets when he pretends to give birth to thoughts to which he ascribes various activities outside the conceiving mind (V, v, 6–9):

> My brain I'll prove the female to my soul,
> My soul the father, and these two beget
> A generation of still-breeding thoughts,
> And these same thoughts people this little world.

He can therefore assert 'thus play I in one person many people' (V, v, 31) and yet, being conscious of their unreality, confess: 'straight [I] am nothing'. He accepts this nothingness, since 'Nor I, nor any man that but man is / With nothing will be pleased till he be eased / With being nothing' (39–41). This already heralds a yearning for annihilation which Hamlet will exemplify, but it is not yet the clear intuition of the possible inexistence of a stable self we have discovered in the *Essays* of Montaigne. In his confrontation with Bolingbroke, Richard has only evoked the loss of his royal identity, of his 'name', his 'title', the dissolution of 'a mockery king of snow' melting into water drops (IV, i, 245–52).

In *Romeo and Juliet* (c. 1595), the heroine, about to give herself to her lover, is exulting in the expectation of this moment and her soliloquy is the lyrical expression of her desire (III, ii, 1–31). Her later deliberation before drinking the Friar's potion is more dramatic: she is conscious she has to 'act alone [her] dismal scene' (IV, iii, 19), but her perturbed mind only projects visions of horror: those 'hideous fears' (49) are not explored subjectively. Romeo, in his sumptuous meditation on death before the apparently lifeless body of Juliet (V, iii, 74–120), is entirely rapt in his contemplation of the beloved and speaks of his 'world-wearied flesh' without exploring his own mind.

The tone changes radically when the Bastard in *King John* wryly comments upon events or his own career. The date of composition of the play is uncertain (c. 1596), but we are assuredly far from the lyrical tone of *Richard II* and *Romeo and Juliet*. It has been wrongly assumed, I think, that the Bastard is a descendant of Vice for, unlike Richard III, he exhibits no devilish traits and 'will not practise to deceive' (I, i, 214). He clearly has characteristics in common with the satirists of the end of the century, adopting their realism, their addiction to railing, the prosaic tone of spoken language. Like them, he strongly asserts his individuality: 'And I am I, howe'er I was begot' (I, i, 175). After railing on 'Commodity, the bias of the world' (II, i, 575), he ironically chooses to 'worship' it in his own interest. Yet his vivacity, his ability to unmask illusions, does not lead to a deeper penetration into his inner life.

This observation can apply to the monologues in which Henry IV addresses sleep (*Henry IV, Part 2*, III, i, 5–31) and Henry V denounces the 'idol Ceremony' (IV, i, 228–81), speeches written between the end of 1596 and the beginning of 1599. However, a comic hero, Falstaff, displays an irony directed at himself which seems to require an acute self-consciousness.

The particular conditions required for the apparition of humour have been touched upon when speaking of Chaucer.[83] In his wide study on English humour, Louis Cazamian extended the notion more than I would.[84] He suspected its presence when Launce in *The Two Gentlemen of Verona* or Bottom in *A Midsummer Night's Dream* seemed conscious of their own absurdity: or when Mercutio displayed an aggressive irony towards other characters in *Romeo and Juliet*; or again when Jaques illustrated the satiric mood of the 'malcontent', whose egotistic origin is unmasked by Rosalind and Orlando in *As You Like It*.[85] The subjectivity I am looking for need not be present in any 'jest with a sad brow' (*Henry IV, Part 2*, V, i, 75), though this is the usual attitude of the humourist. And when Shakespearean fools exemplify Touchstone's distinction 'The fool does think he is wise, but the wise man knows himself to be a fool' (*As You

Like It, V, i, 30–2), a certain ability to stand at a distance from oneself may be present, but it was not unprecedented in jesters. Feste, as Viola describes him in *Twelfth Night* (III, i, 59–67), would be the best illustration of it and Cazamian rightly observed that he seemed to be the spokesman of his creator and reflect his subjectivity. More obvious, however, is the presence in the jests of Falstaff of new forms of self-consciousness. His cynical lucidity about himself, his way of playing with his personality and his own lies disclose a kind of auto-reflexivity which has some analogy with Montaigne's, despite obvious differences in other respects.[86] Yet when Falstaff reappeared in the *Merry Wives of Windsor* (1597) to satisfy the queen, the diminished hero could only jest about his corpulence and his concupiscence (III, v, 4–14; V, v, 1–14).

Before Falstaff, instances of an irony directed at oneself had been offered by the Biron of *Love's Labour's Lost* (1593–4), the clearer-sighted of the young noblemen who sought to disenthrall themselves from the passion of love. He is, with Hamlet, a Shakespearean character whom we are tempted to identify with his creator, for he combines intellectual acuity and irony with a capacity for intense emotion. Like the poet of the *Sonnets* speaking of his love for the dark lady, he can deride the illusions of lovers and entertain them himself, and he can acknowledge he deceives himself without being deceived, since he is conscious of so doing:

> And I, forsooth, in love –; I that have been love's whip,
> A very beadle to a humorous sigh,
> [...]
> Nay, to be perjured, which is worst of all:
> And among three to love the worst of all –
> A whitely wanton with a velvet brow,
> With two pitch-balls stuck in her face for eyes –
> Ay, and, by heaven, one that will do the deed
> Though Argus were her eunuch and her guard.
> (III, i, 169–196)

> The King, he is hunting the deer. I am coursing
> myself. They have pitched a toil, I am toiling in
> a pitch [...]
>   By the Lord, this love is as mad as
> Ajax [...]
>   By
> heaven, I do love, and it has taught me to rhyme
> and to be melancholy;
> (IV, iii, 1–18; cf. 230–46)

This irony directed at oneself implies an ever-waking self-consciousness and it will appear again in other comedies, particularly among mocking heroines. To poke fun at those whom we love and keep our love for them unabated is the touchstone of a clear-sighted love – and of the presence of humour. Shakespeare's originality was to unite in a single character the waggish young woman and the passionate lover. Hence the absence of sentimentality, of the attitudes which make the Shakespearean heroine modern in our eyes.[87] This does not mean, of course, that he has conferred on them an interiority comparable to Hamlet's and the demonstration may be limited to one exemplary case. In *As You Like It* (1599), Rosalind is endowed with this disposition. Disguised as a boy, she does not only mock her lover, Orlando, but ridicules love, her own love, without ceasing to love. She claims she will cure Orlando of his love sickness as she had formerly cured another lover:

> He was to imagine me his love, his mistress, and I set him every day to woo me. At which time would I, being but a moonish youth, grieve, be effeminate, changeable, longing and liking, proud, fantastical, apish, shallow, inconstant, full of tears, full of smiles; for every passion something, and for no passion truly anything, as boys and women are for the most part cattle of this colour – would now like him, now loathe him. (III, ii, 391–408)

Orlando agrees, and this comedy is for Rosalind a delightful opportunity to hear words of love addressed to her. Despite her ironic comment on them, the presence of her true feeling is felt, especially in the imaginary marriage scene in which she enjoys the illusion of giving herself to the man she loves. Her satirical vein is a means of expressing her inner delight in the presence of her lover, the youthful intoxication of a passion so assured of its reality and permanence that it can safely be held up to ridicule before this ambiguous confession of true feeling: 'Alas, dear love, I cannot lack thee two hours' (IV, i, 169). When Orlando is gone, Rosalind will freely give vent to her true sentiment without any change of tone in her ironic outpouring of passion:

> O coz, coz, coz, my pretty little coz, that thou
> didst know how many fathom deep I am in love! But
> it cannot be sounded. My affection hath an unknown
> bottom, like the bay of Portugal.
> (IV, i, 195–8)

In this comedy the monologue is unnecessary for a brief revelation of an inner truth. There is no introspective use of it either in four preceding comedies: *A Midsummer Night's Dream* (1594–5), *The Merchant of*

Venice (1596–7), *The Merry Wives of Windsor* (1597) and *Much Ado About Nothing* (1598–9).[88] In *Twelfth Night*, composed shortly after *Hamlet*, Viola describes her paradoxical situation in objective terms (II, ii, 17–41) and Olivia submits to her fate in four lines (298–301).

One may wonder whether Shakespeare deliberately confined the soliloquy to his tragedies or to tragic moments in his tragicomedies. This mode of expression regained its psychological importance in *Julius Caesar* (1599). Before reaching a decision and acting, Brutus plunges into a deliberation which opens dramatically, but is followed by an argument built on a classical model, a model earlier illustrated by the inner speech of Tarquin in *The Rape of Lucrece* (ll. 190–220):

> It must be by his death. And for my part
> I have no personal cause to spurn at him,
> But for the general. He would be crowned
> (II, i, 10–12)

There is originality in the brusque elliptic opening, the irregular inflexions of spoken language, the absence of rhetorical construction, the rumination along a chain of hesitating thoughts. Yet the point of view becomes subjective only when Brutus, having taken his decision, turns his attention to himself and ruminates on his inner debates and his sleeplessness (63–8):

> Between the acting of a dreadful thing
> And the first motion all the interim is
> Like a phantasma or a hideous dream.
> The genius and the mortal instruments
> Are then in counsel, and the state of man,
> Like to a little kingdom, suffers then
> The nature of an insurrection.

However, there is as yet no evidence of the capacity for instantaneous, self-conscious analysis evidenced in the soliloquy of Hamlet analysed at the beginning of this section.

Though the soliloquy may retain at times its traditional functions of information and deliberation even in *Hamlet* (1600–1), more than 200 lines of monologue in this tragedy are spoken by the hero with a dominant subjective orientation. Moreover, the prince sometimes reveals his inner life in a dialogue or an aside.[89] Yet the question 'To be or not to be' in the most famous soliloquy (III, i, 58–90) leads only to an evocation of the fears aroused by the prospect of a life after death, and this projection towards the hereafter provokes no effort of introspection.

The experience is generalized by the use of 'we' instead of 'I'. Further on, Hamlet will even revert to the former type of monologue and indulge in a grandiloquent style when he declares himself ready to 'drink hot blood', yet, when thinking of his mother, will not allow the soul of Nero to enter his bosom (III, ii, 377–88). What is most original in *Hamlet* is not the frequency of the soliloquies and their dramatic vivacity, anticipated in other plays, but the impression we have, when reading or watching the play, of entering the stream of consciousness of the speaker at the very moment of experience:

> O that this too solid flesh would melt,
> Thaw, and resolve itself into a dew,
> Or that the Everlasting had not fixed
> His canon against self-slaughter. O God, O God,
> How weary, stale, flat, and unprofitable
> Seem to me the uses of this world!
> Fie on't, ah, fie, fie!
> (I, ii, 129–35)

We have seen that the intensity of his emotion can lead Hamlet to call into question its reality in an ironic contemplation of himself. He seems to be moved by fits and starts. His introspection does not lead him to a better understanding of himself. He is uncertain about his own motives and cannot find the cause of his irresolution:

> Now whether it be
> Bestial oblivion, or some craven scruple
> Of thinking too precisely on th'event –
> A thought which, quarter'd, hath but one part wisdom,
> And ever three parts coward – I do not know
> Why yet I live to say 'This thing's to do',
> Sith I have cause, and will, and strength, and means
> To do't.
> (IV, iv, 30–7; additional passage)

There is, as Montaigne would have said, 'too much subtleness and inquisitiveness' in his mind. 'That is why the more commonplace and less tense of wits are more appropriate to the conduct of affairs' (*Essays*, II, xx: 766 B; VS 675).

An author cannot endow a character with a mode of consciousness of which he himself has no experience. Hamlet is therefore the best representative of Shakespearean subjectivity.[90] The characters the dramatist created after Hamlet do not offer the same range of possibilities and it is not surprising. On Troilus or Angelo, Othello and Iago, on Lear or Macbeth, Timon or Antony, he had to confer modes of consciousness in keeping with the plot and their personality. In most cases, self-knowledge is attained only through trials.

The gradual working of introspection is best illustrated by the so-called 'problem plays' composed shortly after *Hamlet*. In *Troilus and Cressida* (1602), the hero, rapt in the anticipation of an imaginary relish, analyses the physical effects of his desire (III, ii, 16–27, 32–6). Cressida is puzzled by the hesitations of a curiously divided self (III, ii, 144–7):

> I have a kind of self resides with you –
> But an unkind self, that itself will leave
> To be another's fool. Where is my wit?
> I would be gone. I speak I know not what.

Troilus understands and shares this view: 'Well know they what they speak that speak so wisely' (148). Yet he may be trying to dispel some doubts when he urges her to take the oath that will make each lover 'truth's authentic author' (177). The use of the third person may here indicate a projection of the self into an exemplary identity: 'True swains in love shall in the world to come / Approve their truth by Troilus' (168–9). Witnessing Cressida's breach of loyalty, the betrayed lover, startled and shocked, seems to forget the presence of Ulysses for a while and one may consider as a soliloquy this immersion in his inner life in which the conflict felt by Brutus in *Julius Caesar* deepens, becomes mysterious and seems to suggest the impenetrability of the unconscious:

> This is and is not Cressid.
> Within my soul there doth conduce a fight
> Of this strange nature, that a thing inseparate
> Divides more wider than the sky and earth,
> And yet the spacious breadth of this division
> Admits no orifex for a point as subtle
> As Ariachne's broken woof to enter.
> (V, ii, 149–55)

In *Measure for Measure* (1603), the Duke of Vienna, Vincentio, whose indulgence had allowed licentiousness to run riot in his city, entrusts its government to a man known for his austerity and charges him with the eradication of vice. A young man, Claudio, who has had sexual relations with his betrothed before marrying her, is sentenced to death. His sister, Isabella, a novice in a convent, sues Angelo for his reprieve. He rejects her plea, but feels suddenly assailed by a temptation as yet unknown.

Fascinated and seduced by the very purity of the nun, he abruptly allows us to enter his inner discourse: 'From thee, even from thy virtue'. He urgently probes his mind to find an explanation:

> What's this? What's this? Is it her fault or mine?
> The tempter or the tempted, who sins most?
> Ha!
> Not she; nor does she tempt; but it is I
> That, lying by the violet in the sun,
> Do, as the carrion does, not as the flower,
> Corrupt with virtuous season. Can it be
> That modesty can more betray our sense
> Than woman's lightness? Having waste ground enough,
> Shall we desire to raze the sanctuary,
> And pitch our evils there? O, fie, fie, fie!

Then bursts the interrogation about his deeper self, calling into question his identity: 'What dost thou, or what art thou, Angelo?' (II, ii, 168–78). It is the confirmation of a psychological truth glimpsed by Isabella when she describes how 'man, proud man, / Dressed in a little brief authority / Most ignorant of what he's most assured, / His glassy essence, like an angry ape / Plays such fantastic tricks before high Heaven / As makes the angels weep' (II, ii, 122–7). For Angelo, it is the disintegration of a self he had artificially constructed.

After Hamlet, Troilus and Angelo, curiously this new acuity of self-consciousness becomes less evident in the Shakespearean characters. The main reason – perhaps the only one – is the choice of the subjects and the plots. In *Othello* (end 1603–4), the Moor of Venice had to be deceived by Iago and unhesitatingly kill a wife he dearly loved; he had therefore to be incapable of 'thinking too precisely on th'event' (*Hamlet*, IV, iv, add. 32). And when he leans over his sleeping wife before strangling her (V, ii), he is too much engrossed in his contemplation and too deeply moved by it to engage in a self-examination.

The soliloquies of Iago, when compared with the monologues of other villains, are sometimes said to disclose a greater interiority. This tendency is not noticeable in the last three soliloquies, two of which are asides (III, iii, 325–37; IV, i, 92–8; V, i, 11–22). The first three inform the audience of the evil designs of the speaker and are not introspective. What is new in comparison with Richard III is the effort of the villain to justify his behaviour: 'How am I then a villain?' (II, iii, 339). He offers repeated explanations of his detestation of the Moor, whom he supposes to have 'leapt into [his] seat' (II, i, 295), and to have done his office betwixt his sheets (I, iii, 378–80), a thought which 'doth like a poisonous mineral gnaw [his] inwards' (II, i, 296). Yet he seems to add another motive, later unexplored, when speaking of Desdemona: 'Now I do love her too / Not of absolute lust' (II, i, 290–1). Since Coleridge, his suspicions have been considered as 'the motive hunting of motiveless malignity'.[91] Iago, however, has a real motive for his hatred of the Moor, and he insists on it in the opening lines of the tragedy: Othelllo's choice of Cassio as his lieutenant instead of him (I, i, 7–32). He may be supposed to have been conscious that it was a slim motive for such dark designs and therefore anxious to justify them in his own eyes and legitimize his hypocrisy. Yet his 'I am not what I am' (I, i, 65) is only the dramatist's warning to the audience, not a calling into question of his identity.

One may attempt to go further in the search for a psychological explanation of Iago's malignity. W. H. Auden compared it to St Augustine's love of evil for the sake of evil in a youthful episode of the *Confessions*.[92] One can also suspect an inferiority complex when he compares himself with Cassio: 'He hath a daily beauty in his life / That makes me ugly' (V, i, 19–20). Yet he never seems to retreat into his own mind – as Augustine did and Hamlet would – to detect the origin of this propensity to evil and analyse it. He ultimately chooses an impenetrable silence: 'From this time forth, I never will speak word' (V, ii, 310). It may have been inspired by the perplexity of his creator before the mystery of evil, but it does not disclose the presence of any interiority. Had Shakespeare wished to ascribe obscure motivations to Iago, it would be contrary to Elizabethan usage not to make them clear for the audience.

Timon of Athens may have been written in collaboration with Middleton, in 1604 or later. A singular feature is the recurrence of the third-person address, after the manner of Tamburlaine. This use becomes constant when the hero spouts his contempt, hatred and resentment: 'grant, as Timon grows, his hate may grow / To the whole race of mankind' (IV, i, 39–40); 'yea, himself Timon disdains' (IV, iii, 22); 'Then, Timon, presently prepare thy grave' (IV, iii, 380); 'Of none but such as you, and you of Timon' (V, ii, 20); 'Let Alcibiades know this of Timon' (V, ii, 55); 'Timon hath made his everlasting mansion' and 'Timon hath done his reign' (V, ii, 100, 108). Is it a way of enclosing himself forever in his imprecatory role?[93]

In *The Tragedy of King Lear* (1605–6), we are immediately warned that this imperious old man 'hath ever but slender known himself' (I, i, 293). His identity has been spontaneously and unconsciously structured by the identification of his real self and his social self, his kingly role. When he decided to retain only the appearance of sovereignty, Lear lost his identity and became conscious of this loss. Hence his anguished interrogation, 'Who is it that can tell me who I am?' (I, iv, 212). One must note that Lear's acquisition of self-knowledge through his trials are evoked differently from Angelo's through the discovery of his latent desires. Initially, Lear can only ask someone else to tell him who he is, whereas Angelo questions himself: 'what art thou, Angelo?' (*Measure for Measure*, II, ii, 178). Furthermore, Lear's question still concerns his outer self, not the deeper self. His apostrophe to the storm is an egotistic imprecation: it places the dispossessed sovereign at the centre of a universal cataclysm, but without any self-questioning. After the experience of forlornness and madness, a kind of elementary self-knowledge is attained in his humble admission that he is 'a very foolish fond old man' (V, i, 53). Yet Lear will again lose clear-sightedness, in a kind of reverie.[94]

Edgar, the legitimate son, when obliged to hide himself, declares he gives up his identity to 'take the basest and most poorest shape', that of a mad beggar: 'Poor Tom! That's something yet. Edgar, I nothing am' (II, ii, 183–4). He will later play the part of a peasant, then of an anonymous knight, according to the requirements of the plot.

A kind of progress is even suggested, since he identifies himself with the most destitute, then with the lowly, before reappearing as a knight and being invited to 'Rule in this realm, and the gored state sustain' (V, iii, 295). Yet the momentary loss of his identity is never due to a calling into question of his real self. Nor does it imply, as Hirsch suggests, that we are the parts we play, that we have more than one self.[95] As to Edmond, the natural son, his vindication of his rights in a superb soliloquy (I, ii, 1–22) is the assertion of an individualism of a Machiavellian type, not the illustration of a Montaignean self-consciousness.

Only with *Macbeth* (1606) shall we have again the impression of entering the consciousness of the hero in the very moment of self-observation. But the Thane, unlike Hamlet, is no intellectual. It is not thoughts that he sees growing in his mind, but images; not intellectual interrogations, but hallucinations. His consciousness is so absorbed in them that he seems to forget those present by his side. An aside may then take on the character and the intensity of a soliloquy. Banquo invites us to notice that his companion is 'rapt' (I, iii, 55) in a kind of ecstatic fit:

> why do I yield to that suggestion,
> Whose horrid image doth unfix my hair,
> And makes my seated heart knock at my ribs
> Against the use of nature? present fears
> Are less than horrible imaginings.

My thought, whose murder yet is but fantastical,
Shakes so my single state of man that function
Is smothered in surmise, and nothing is
But what is not.
(I, iii, 135–43)

Like Tarquin in *The Rape of Lucrece* and like Brutus in *Julius Caesar*, Macbeth can weigh arguments before a decision but his mind is still focused on an image: 'pity, like a naked new-born babe, / Striding the blast' (I, vii, 21–2). His ambition is felt like a 'spur' (25) without any introspective analysis. In another long soliloquy (II, i, 33–64), that which Hamlet would have apprehended inwardly[96] is projected outwardly: a 'dagger of the mind' shows him the way and when he sees blood on the blade, he realizes that 'it is the bloody business which informs / Thus to [his] eyes'. Once crowned, he keeps soliloquizing to voice his fears and take his decisions (III, i, 49–73). When his downfall is inevitable, he sums up his life in objective terms, without any inner probing (V, iii, 23–30), and ultimately, in one of his customary asides, offers his celebrated description of life as 'a walking shadow, a poor player / That frets and frets his hour upon the stage' (V, v, 18–27).

As to Lady Macbeth, her conjuring of the 'murd'ring ministers' (I, v, 39–53) is also a projection of her imagination into a future scene in which the very identity of the subject seems to be dispersed 'from the crown to the toe' between different subjects, her blood, her breasts, her milk, her knife, as in Ancient Greek tragedy.[97]

In *Antony and Cleopatra* (end 1606), the changes of mood and behaviour prominent in the Roman hero and the Egyptian queen are true to life in the dialogues but are never expressed or justified in monologues.[98] The proud assertion 'I am Antony yet' (III, xiii, 92) may express his sense of an inviolable identity.[99] Yet, after Cleopatra's flight, Antony describes his state to Eros in a metaphorical language which suggests a dissolution of the self. After describing the changing shapes of the clouds, which 'mock our eyes with air', he concludes: 'now thy captain is / Even such a body. Here I am Antony, / Yet cannot hold this visible shape' (IV, xv, 1–14). This is not a lamenting over an instability of the self, but merely a way of describing a change of fortune: 'There is left us / Ourselves to end ourselves' (21–2). In a brief soliloquy Antony expresses a resolution which did not call for inner questioning: 'Since the torch is out, / Lie down, and stray no farther' (46–7).

In a tragedy probably written in 1608, Coriolanus is endowed neither with the intellectual subtlety of Hamlet nor with the imagination of Antony. He is a hero as monolithic as Timon, but he does not indulge in spouting words. As a man of action, he asserts his self-reliance and takes pride in what he achieved alone: 'Alone I did it' (V, vi, 117). He immures himself in his isolation, but he is hardly apt to sound his own motives and practise self-examination. The brusqueness of his three short soliloquies suits a warrior (II, iii, 113–31; IV, iv, 1–6; IV, iv, 12–26).

Pericles, also played in 1608, was the first of the so-called romances. The hero's monologues, mainly designed to provide information, express only his melancholy, and Gower's interventions supply a narrative thread in the medieval fashion.[100] In *The Winter's Tale* (1609), Leontes ruminates over his cuckoldom as a general misfortune of husbands (I, ii, 187–208). The narrative monologue of Antigonus conveys only information. Autolycus sings his songs and congratulates himself on his own wiles (IV, iii, 1–28; IV, iv, 596–619, 670–83, 831–41). *The Tempest* (1610–11) offers three monologues: Caliban complains about being ill-treated (II, ii, 1–14); Ferdinand speaks of the hardships he gladly endures for the love of Miranda (III, i, 1–15); and Prospero announces he gives up magic (V, i, 33–57). His previous decision not to seek vengeance might have proceeded from an inner debate. Ferdinand, observing him from outside, notes he 'is in some passion / That works him strongly' (IV, ii, 143–4), but we are not allowed to enter his mind and discover how he was led to give his assent to a universal principle: 'The rarer action is / In virtue than in vengeance' (V, i, 27–8).

It appears that Shakespeare, though he opened the way to the modern interior monologue in *Hamlet*, did not privilege introspection in a majority of his plays. The various requirements of the plots, the different personalities of his characters did not allow it. The interest shown by the author for the outer world in its wealth of particular circumstances and diversity of men and women would not allow in his creation of characters the kind of narcissistic re-creation of his own self traceable in some heroes of Marlowe. Besides, the dramatist obviously did not have to explore the self of his characters in the same way as Montaigne observed his own self in his *Essays*.

In the eyes of many modern critics, Hamlet is assumed to be a landmark for a change of episteme in the whole of Western theatre and for the appearance of a new kind of literary subjectivity.[101] This claim seems to me excessive, even within the limits of Shakespearean drama. A global change is always slow and this type of evolution long remains incomplete. Shakespeare himself in the choice of his characters privileged the man of action rather than the intellectual or the introvert. He invested some of his heroes with a capacity for instantaneous self-scrutiny, which implies its presence in their creator. Yet, though the identity or the stability of the self is sometimes called into question, its reality is never denied. Despite the contradictions and evolutions noted in his characters, some essential features of their personality remain constant, as the next chapter will show.

The balance between the observation of the inner self and the interest for the outer world is even more obvious in Shakespeare than in Montaigne. Interiority and the intervention of self-consciousness in his plays are more prominent in the period which extends from *Julius Caesar* to *Measure for Measure* and *King Lear*. How far was an immersion in the *Essays* responsible for the dramatist's increased interest in the exploration of consciousness and its hidden depths?

5. A reassessment of the influence of Montaigne on Shakespeare

Was Shakespeare's attention called to self-consciousness by Montaigne? He is unlikely to have read the *Essays* in French, though he had at least a smattering of the language when he wrote two scenes of *Henry V* (III, iv and V, ii).[102] His close acquaintance with Florio's translation of Montaigne may have begun before its publication in 1603, since it circulated in manuscript as early as 1599. William Cornwallis mentioned it in his own *Essayes*, written at the latest in 1600, shortly before the composition of *Julius Caesar* and *Hamlet*. He stated that he liked nothing better in Montaigne than his desire to know the private actions of Brutus[103] – a desire obviously shared by the author of *Julius Caesar*. The interest of the dramatist in Plutarch's *The Lives of the Noble Grecians and Romans*, translated by T. North in 1579, may have been stimulated by his reading of Montaigne.

As many as 750 words used by Florio in his translation of the *Essays* appear only in *Hamlet* and the following plays of Shakespeare.[104] The correspondences with Montaigne pointed out in earlier plays by several critics are unconvincing: they concern general ideas easily found in Roman authors or in the Renaissance collections of *loci communes*. This rejection concerns *Henry IV* and *Henry V*, *Love's Labour's Lost*, *The Merchant of Venice* and *As You Like It*; it may even be extended to *Julius Caesar*.[105] On the contrary, after *Hamlet*, plausible parallels may be found in plays performed between 1601 and 1606, particularly in *Troilus and Cressida*, *Measure for Measure* and *King Lear*. The link between these plays and the scepticism of Montaigne will be explored in chapter 6. A clear borrowing from the *Essays* will emerge only much later, in *The Tempest*. The concentration of Montaigne's influence in a few years of Shakespeare's production is noteworthy; and this is the period when, among various echoes, one discovers parallels related to self-consciousness or self-knowledge.

Starting from Hamlet as a character, one may remember that sensitive readers have been persistently reminded of Montaigne, from John Sterling in 1838 to Harry Levin in 1959. I recorded the parallels in 1975 and I still find them far too general and unconvincing.[106] More recently, it has been assumed that the *Essays* were the book Hamlet holds in his hands when Polonius asks him 'What do you read my lord?' and he replies 'Words, words, words' (II, ii, 193–5). It could only have been a French edition, since Florio's translation was not yet in print. Besides the prince was hardly likely to describe Montaigne as a 'satirical slave' who only uttered commonplaces: 'that old men have grey beards', etc.[107] Shakespeare may rather have had in mind the contemporary English satirists who indulged in trite sayings like Jaques in *As You Like It*.

More than 100 parallels between *Hamlet* and the *Essays* have been suggested.[108] Half a dozen only seem to me pertinent, especially when similar ideas are expressed in phrases or words found in Florio, as in the following instance:

> To die, to sleep –
> No more, and by a sleep to say we end,
> The heartache, and the thousand natural shocks
> That flesh is heir to – 'tis a *consummation*
> Devoutly to be wished.
> (*Hamlet*, III, i, 62–6; my italics)

> Death may peradventure be a thing indifferent, happily a thing desirable. […] If it be a consummation of one's being, it is also an amendment and entrance into a long and quiet night.[109]

The direct influence of Montaigne is also suggested by the fact that two consecutive essays in book II (xx, xxi) may have suggested the contrast between the character of Hamlet and the character of Fortinbras. Shakespeare portrays a hero doomed to irresolution by an excess of subtlety elaborately described by Montaigne in the essay 'We taste nothing purely':

> It is likewise true, that for the use of life and service of publike society, there may be excesse in the purity and perspicuity of our spirits. This piercing brightnes hath overmuch subtility and curiositie. […] Therefore are vulgar and lesse-wire-drawne-wits found to be more fit and happy in the conduct of affaires. And the exquisite and high-raised opinions of Philosophy, unapt and unfit to exercise. […]. Humane enterprises should be managed more grossly and superficially, and have a good and great part of them left for the rights of fortune. (Florio, vol. II, p. 401; Screech, II, xx: 766 B)

When Hamlet, after recalling 'the capability and god-like reason of man', charges himself with 'thinking too precisely on th'event' (IV, iv, 27–32 in Q), which caused his inaction, we are reminded of Montaigne's Simonides, in the same essay, whose imagination 'presented sundry subtill and sharpe considerations unto him: doubting which might be the likeliest: he altogether dispaireth of the truth' (Florio, vol. II, p. 402; Screech, II, xx: 767 B). Hamlet followed Montaigne's advice, 'leaving a good and better share to the rights of Fortune' (*Essays*, II, xx: 766 B), or rather 'providence', in the fifth act (V, ii, 165–70).

When the same essay reminds us that 'Man, all in all, is but a botching and party-coloured worke' (Florio, vol. II, p. 401; Screech, II, xx: 766 C) we notice again an agreement with Hamlet's views on human nature, and the prince's awareness of his imperfections is in keeping with Montaigne's confession: 'the best of the goodness in me has some vicious stain' (Screech, II, xx: 766 B). This cluster of Hamlet-like ideas is the more remarkable since the following essay, 'Against idleness, or doing nothing', offered suggestions for the portrait of Fortinbras, a 'vertuous and coragious prince', who would not 'mannage his wars by others, then by himselfe' (Florio, vol. II, p. 403; Screech II, xxi: 768 C), a mode of '*imperium*' apparently commended by Hamlet (IV, iv, 38–47).[110]

Weighing the evidence, it is probable that Shakespeare had read Montaigne before writing *Hamlet*. There are fewer interesting parallels in the problem plays composed in the following years. Yet numerous and distinct echoes have been traced in *King Lear*, a tragedy arising from a lack of self-knowledge.[111] I think it certain that Shakespeare's acquaintance with the *Essays* increased his attention to the inner life and the necessity of self-knowledge in the period from *Hamlet* to *King Lear*. Why this influence is less apparent in the following plays and revived only in *The Tempest* by the colonial theme may be accounted for by the requirements of plot and characterization in each play. It is clear in the *Sonnets* that Shakespeare's attention to the self was not dictated by the egotistic inclination paraded in the *Essays* of Montaigne. The dramatist had no incentive to set on stage introspective characters such as Hamlet and Troilus. The balance between self-absorption and an interest in the outer world, noticeable to a lesser extent in Montaigne, was reinforced in Shakespeare. The *Essays* have probably suggested some of the sceptical interrogations of the dramatist concerning reliance on reason and respect for values: this will be debated in the last chapter. What may be rejected, more obviously in Shakespeare's case than in Montaigne's, is the modern and post-modern disowning of a self endowed with some permanent features; a study of some of his characters will prove it in the next chapter.

Notes

1 A. Crépin, 'La conscience de soi héroïque: l'exemple de Beowulf', in R. Ellrodt, ed., *Genèse de la conscience moderne* (Presses Universitaires de France, 1983), pp. 51–60.
2 See, for instance, 'The unquiet grave', 'Two sisters' and 'Thomas the rhymer', included in all anthologies.
3 The theme of the 'consolation' addressed to oneself can be traced back to Cicero (*Epistulae ad Atticum*, XII, 14, 3) and was Christianized by Ambrose in *De excessu fratris satyri* (Jacques-Paul Migne, *Patrologia Latina*, vol. XVI, cols 1290–354), then popularized by Boethius and taken up again by Petrarch (*Epistolae de rebus familiaribus*, IV, 10).
4 David Aers, *Community, Gender, and Individual Identity* (London: Routledge, 1988).
5 In *Troilus and Criseyde*, Aers (*ibid.*) ascribes to the heroine a new type of self-consciousness, apparently limited, however, to a keener perception of conflicts between the public and the private sphere. In the same way Troilus experiences a dissolution of his 'public identity', not a dissolution of a Montaignean self (pp. 145, 148). In *Sir Gawain* attention is focused on the social role and on a 'heroic identity' (pp. 159–60); there is no sign that the mind turns inwards, observing its own movements, no experience of a divorce between the outer action and the inner experience (p. 167).
6 See Peter R. Moore, '*Hamlet* and *Piers Plowman*: a matter of conscience', *Cahiers Elisabéthains*, 65 (spring 2004), pp. 11–24.
7 See Nicolette Zeeman, '*Piers Plowman*' *and the Medieval Discourse of Desire* (Cambridge University Press, 2006), especially pp. 19, 99–108, 176–8. Her Lacanian reinterpretation of this psychology (pp. 32–7) is less convincing.
8 See Robert S. Miola, *Shakespeare's Reading* (Oxford University Press, 2000), p. 12. An influence of Gower is probable in earlier plays, *The Comedy of Errors* and *The Merchant of Venice* (*ibid.*, pp. 73, 80). See also James Simpson, *Sciences and the Self in Medieval Poetry* (Cambridge University Press, 1995), especially pp. 185–97 and 252–63.
9 According to Patrick J. Gallacher, *Love, the Word, and Mercury: A Reading of John Gower's* Confessio amantis (University of New Mexico Press, 1975), p. 112. On the *Confessio*, see also Henk Dragstra, Sheila Otway and Helen Wilcox, eds, *Betraying Ourselves: Forms of Self-representation in Early Modern English Texts* (New York: Palgrave/St Martin's Press, 2000).
10 Miola, *Shakespeare's Reading*, pp. 133–8, points out important modifications.
11 G. Keynes, ed., 'A descriptive catalogue', in *Complete Writings of William Blake* (Oxford University Press, 1974), p. 567. H. Marshall Leicester not unjustly claims that '*The Canterbury Tales* is a collection of individually voiced texts': *The Disenchanted Self: Representing the Subject in the Canterbury Tales* (University of California Press, 1990), p. 9. One may agree, yet fail to discover in them the particular forms of self-consciousness discerned in the *Essays* of Montaigne.

12   On the appearance and the psychological characteristics of humour, Louis Cazamian's book *The Development of English Humor* (Duke University Press, 1951) is a suggestive survey.
13   Cazamian's attempt to discover germs of humour in Anglo-Saxon literature and among the predecessors of Chaucer is unconvincing to my mind, for the mockery is purely objective (pp. 8–20, 40–62), as in the fabliaux and the *Roman de la rose*, in which what he calls 'the French medieval humour' is characterized by the finesse of an analytical mind (pp. 21–39).
14   In a treatise entitled *Of the Knowledge Which Maketh a Wise Man* (1533), Elyot made self-knowledge a requirement to gain access to the knowledge of men and the world.
15   Roger Ascham, *English Works*, ed. W. A. Wright (Cambridge University Press, 1904), p. 120.
16   Edmund Spenser, 'A letter of the author's', in *Faerie Queene*; Philip Sidney, *An Apology for Poetry*, in G. G. Smith, ed., *Elizabethan Critical Essays* (Oxford University Press, 1904), vol. I, p. 161.
17   Francis Bacon, *The Advancement of Learning* (1605), II, ix, 1 and I, viii, 2; see also James Spedding, ed., *Philosophical Works of Francis Bacon* (London: Routledge, 1905), p. 598.
18   See Helen Wilcox, '"The birth day of my selfe": John Donne, Martha Moulsworth and the emergence of individual identity', in A. J. Pierre, ed., *Sixteenth Century Identities* (Manchester University Press, 2002), p. 155.
19   Ian Breward, ed., *The Work of William Perkins* (Appleford: Sutton Courtenay Press, 1970), p. 382; quoted by Miri Tashma-Baum, 'A shroud for the mind: Ralegh's poetic rewriting of the self', *Early Modern Literary Studies*, 10:1 (May 2004), pp. 1–34.
20   Margreta de Grazia, 'World pictures, modern periods, and the early stage', in John C. D. Cox and David Scott Kastan, eds, *A New History of Early English Drama* (Columbia University Press, 1997), p. 14. Cf. Alan Sinfield, *Faultlines: Cultural Materialism and the Politics of Dissident Reading* (Oxford: Clarendon Press, 1992), p. 159; Martha Tuck Rosett, *The Doctrine of Election and the Emergence of Elizabethan Tragedy* (Princeton University Press, 1984), pp. 65–72.
21   William Perkins, *A Discourse of Conscience* (London, 1608); William Ames, *Conscience with the Power and Cases Thereof*, trans. out of Latin (*De Conscientia*, 1630) (London, 1639).
22   Ames, *ibid.*, book II, 1.
23   See Ellrodt, *Seven Metaphysical Poets*, pp. 314–15.
24   I have studied this new trend in Ellrodt, *L'inspiration personnelle*, vol. III, ch. 3.
25   Epigram published in Gabriel Harvey, *Gratulationum Valdinensium libri quatuor* (1578). Cf. Gabriel Harvey, *The Writers Postscript* (1593), in which Harvey declared that Machiavelli '*nor dreaded Di'vill; / Nor ought admired, but his wondrous selfe*'.
26   See *supra*, chapter 2, pp. 34–5.

27 John Marston 'To detraction', *The Scourge of Villanie*, in G. B. Harrison, ed., *The Plays of John Marston* (London: Lane, 1925).
28 See Ellrodt, *L'inspiration personnelle*, vol. III, ch. 3, section 3.
29 See *Ibid.*, vol. III, Index, Wyatt.
30 Published in *Psalms, Sonnets, and Songs* of William Byrd in 1588; see N. Ault, ed., *Elizabethan Lyrics* (London: Longman, 1949), pp. 123–4.
31 Samuel Daniel, *The Complaint of Rosamond* (1592), l. 445. There is a richer and more complex self-examination in 'A lover's complaint', but this poem, which may be ascribed to Shakespeare, was published with his sonnets only in 1609. See my introduction in *William Shakespeare. Tragicomédies II — Poésies* (Paris, Robert Laffont 2002), pp. 923–49.
32 See *Astrophel and Stella*, sonnets 41, 49, 53. See also the courtier so enthralled by his love that he takes no interest in affairs of state: *ibid.*, sonnets 23, 30, 52.
33 For this allusion to Montaigne's essay XL, 'Reflections upon Cicero', see the 1651 edition of Donne's *Letters*, p. 106.
34 Donne, like Montaigne, and for the same reason, repeatedly confessed the impossibility of him defining himself and expressed this through his sense of 'nothingness': see Ellrodt, *L'inspiration personnelle*, vol. I, pp. 123–5.
35 See E. Gosse, *Life and Letters of John Donne* (London: William Heinemann, 1899), vol. I, p. 191.
36 John Donne, *Sermons*, III, iii, 110; my italics.
37 See Francis Barker, *The Tremulous Private Body* (London: Methuen, 1984), pp. 35–40; Catherine Belsey, *The Subject of Tragedy* (London: Methuen, 1984), pp. 40–2, 50–4; Colin McGinn, *Shakespeare's Philosophy* (New York: Harper/Collins, 2006), ch. 3, 'Hamlet'.
38 Sir Richard Baker, *Chronicles* (1649), p. 424 in the 1730 edition. See Ellrodt, *L'inspiration personnelle*, vol. III, pp. 187–92.
39 Renaut, *L'ère de l'individu*, p. 59.
40 *Ibid.*, p. 60.
41 Ellrodt, *L'inspiration personnelle*, vol. I, pp. 128–35.
42 'Scorn not the sonnet', in *Miscellaneous Sonnets* (1842).
43 Joel Fineman, *Shakespeare's Perjur'd Eye: The Invention of Poetic Subjectivity in the Sonnets* (University of California Press, 1986); Colin Burrow, ed., *The Oxford Shakespeare: The Complete Sonnets and Poems* (Oxford University Press, 2002), p. 133.
44 *Astrophel and Stella*, sonnet 71. See Robert Ellrodt, 'The inversion of cultural traditions in Shakespeare's sonnets', in T. Kishi, R. Pringle and S. Wells, eds, *Shakespeare and Cultural Traditions* (University of Delaware Press, 1994).
45 See Ellrodt, *L'inspiration personnelle*, vol. III, p. 3.
46 Janine Chassenet-Smirgel, *Pour une psychanalyse de l'art et de la créativité* (Paris: Payot, 1971), p. 46, my translation.
47 'Imago est animi parentis sui'. Juan Vivès, *Opera omnia*, ed. Gregorius Majansius (Valencia, 1782), vol. I, p. 103; Ben Jonson, *Discoveries*, in *Ben Jonson, Vol. VIII: The Poems; The Prose Works*, eds C. H. Herford, Percy Simpson and Evelyn Simpson (Oxford University Press, 1947), p. 625.

48 See Ellrodt, *L'inspiration personnelle*, vol. III, Index, Berni.
49 See *infra*, pp. 82–3.
50 See Ellrodt, *Seven Metaphysical Poets*, pp. 315–16.
51 This continuity, sometimes denied, is justified in my bilingual edition of the *Sonnets*: Robert Ellrodt, *William Shakespeare: Sonnets* (Paris: Actes Sud, 2007), pp. 29–30.
52 Sartre, *L'être et le néant*, p. 434.
53 It would be less surprising in the sonnets of Sidney and yet we are told at least what Stella says and does: *Astrophel and Stella*, sonnets 29, 36, 45, 62, 64, 69, fourth song, eighth song.
54 Lewis Edwin Hahn, ed., *The Philosophy of Paul Ricoeur* (Chicago: Open Court, 1995), p. 597.
55 Notably in II, xxviii, 797 C: 'I think only of bringing things to a close [...]'. See also I, lvii, 'On the length of life', and the end of III, xiii, 1269.
56 Lear's acquisition of self-knowledge through his trials is different from Angelo's discovery of himself through the revelation of his dormant impulses; the king, whose mind is still confused, can only ask 'Who is it that can tell me who I am?', whereas Angelo asks himself 'who art thou, Angelo?' (*Measure for Measure*, II, ii, 178).
57 The Spevack *Concordance* lists twenty-nine compounds of *self* for which the *Oxford English Dictionary* offers no precedents before Shakespeare: self-affected, self-affrighted, self-charity, self-applied, self-assumption, self-bounty, self-breath, self-comparisons, self-cover'd, self-danger, self-doing, self-drawing, self-endeared, self-example, self-figur'd, self-glorious, self-gracious, self-learning, self-killed, self-misus'd, self-neglecting, self-offence, self-reproving, self-slaughter(ed), self-sovereignty, self-subdued, self-substantial, self-unabled, self-wrong. It may be supposed that some at least of these compounds were created by Shakespeare. Marvin Spevack, *Complete and Systematic Concordance to the Works of Shakespeare* (Hildesheim: Georghe Olms, 1968–80).
58 James Hirsch, *Shakespeare and the History of Soliloquies* (Farleigh Dickinson University Press, 2003), p. 44.
59 I use the term *pensée pensante* without any necessary reference to its linguistic application in the theory of Gustave Guilaume nor to its philosophical use by Gabriel Marcel. See Ronald Lowe, ed., *Essais et mémoires de Gustave Guillaume: prolégomènes à la linguistique structurale* (Presses de l'Université Laval, 2007); Gabriel Marcel, *Essais de philosophie concrète* (Paris: Gallimard, 1999).
60 Richard Hillman presents *Hamlet* as 'the single text that virtually all writers on subjectivity agree to be paradigmatically Early Modern'. Richard Hillman, *Self-speaking in Medieval and Early Modern English Drama: Subjectivity, Discourse and the Stage* (London: Macmillan, 1993), p. 15.
61 See *supra*, chapter 1, pp. 4–5.
62 For instance Macbeth in I, iii, 129–41; V, iii, 21–30.
63 See Saenger, 'Silent reading'.

64 As Hirsch insistently repeats in *Shakespeare and the History of Soliloquies*, pp. 62, 83, 115–19, 174, 188.
65 See Liisa Dahl, *Nominal Style in the Shakespearean Soliloquy with Reference to the Early English Drama, Shakespeare's Immediate Predecessors and His Contemporaries* (Torsten: University of Turku, 1969), ch. 2; Lloyd A. Skiffington, *The History of English Soliloquy: Aeschylus to Shakespeare* (University Press of America, 1985), pp. 41, 51–5, 64, 72–84. Hirsh, *Shakespeare and the History of Soliloquies*, p. 115, admits a progress towards interiority when the monologue of 'self-address' superseded the address to the audience.
66 Hillman, *Self-speaking*, p. 42.
67 *Ibid.*, pp. 10, 15, 133–8, 154–6, etc.
68 *Faerie Queene*, I, ix, 33–54; *Doctor Faustus*, V, I, 47–52.
69 Paul Bacquet, *Théâtre élisabéthain* (Paris: Gallimard, 2009), vol. I, pp. 1762–3.
70 A. C. Cawley, ed., *Everyman and Medieval Miracle Plays* (London: Dent, 1979), ll. 184–93.
71 Hirsh, *Shakespeare and the History of Soliloquies*, p. 116.
72 1567, printed in 1575; this version preceded Webster's.
73 In J. S Farmer, ed., *Five Anonymous Plays* (London: Early English Drama Society, 1908), p. 21.
74 Quoted by Skiffington, *The History of English Soliloquy*, pp. 51–3; see also pp. 85–7.
75 Hillman, *Self-speaking*, p. 77.
76 See the monologue of Videna in IV, i.
77 Dahl's observation in *Nominal Style*, p. 161.
78 R. Greene, *Plays and Poems*, ed. J. Churton Collins (Oxford: Clarendon Press, 1905): Alphonsus, ll. 260, 266, 372, 421; Carinus, ll. 114, 167; Belinus, ll. 279, 470, 481, 517, 561; Albinius, ll. 186–207, 242, 258; Medea, ll. 854, 875, 1664. The same tendency in is evident in *Frier Bacon and Frier Bongay*: ll. 217, 221, 256, 316, 567–71.
79 P. W. White, 'Theatre and religious culture', in John D. Cox and David Scott, eds, *A New History of English Drama* (Columbia University Press, 1997), pp. 150–5.
80 In *The Two Gentlemen*, Julia comments on letters (I, ii, 105–30), on her relations with Proteus (IV, iv, 88–105), addresses his portrait (IV, iv, 195–202); Valentine identifies himself with Silvia in scholastic terms: 'Sylvia is my self [...] She is my essence' (III, i, 170–87), or addresses her while commenting on his situation (V, iv, 1–17). There is no interiority either in *The Taming of the Shrew* (IV, i, 174–97) or and in the very brief monologues of *The Comedy of Errors* (I, ii, 95–105; III, ii, 162–70; IV, iii, 1–11; IV, iii, 81–91).
81 *Henry VI, Part I* (II, v, 122–9; III, i, 191–205; V, iii, 24–9).
82 See *supra*, pp. 61–2.
83 See *supra*, p. 60.
84 Cazamian, *The Development of English Humor*.
85 *Ibid.*, pp. 197–8, 202.

86 Ibid., pp. 240–56.
87 This modernity was demonstrated in the annexe to my *Montaigne et Shakespeare* (pp. 249–64), not included in the present volume.
88 In *Midsummer*, Hermia expatiates on love (I, i, 226–51) and describes her dream (II, ii, 151–62); Bottom celebrates his own in objective terms (IV, i, 198–214). In *Merry Wives*, Mistress Page reads a letter (II, i, 1–30), Ford laments over his cuckoldom (II, ii, end; III, ii, 26–39) and Falstaff over his misadventure (IV, v, 87–96).
89 See *infra*, chapter 4, section 1, pp. 103–6.
90 The soliloquy of Claudius presents only basic, traditional elements (III, iii, 36–72). Yet it expresses a sense of failure, an inclination to self-destruction comparable to Hamlet's.
91 Note by Coleridge on his copy of the works of Shakespeare. See Samuel Taylor Coleridge, *Lectures 1808–1819 on Literature*, ed. R. A. Foakes (Princeton University Press, 1987), vol. II, p. 315.
92 W. H. Auden, *Lectures on Shakespeare* (Princeton University Press, 2000), p. 205.
93 The monologues of Alcibiades (III, vi, 102–15) and Favius (IV, ii, 30–51) contain no introspection.
94 See *infra*, chapter 4, section 3, p. 120.
95 Hirsh, *Shakespeare and the History of Soliloquie*, p. 230. Two other brief monologues of Edgar offer only an objective comment on his condition and his intentions: III, ii, 79–95; IV, i, 1–9.
96 Hamlet, of course, is also subject to a hallucination, when he sees his father's ghost, invisible to Gertrude, but he claims his pulse, as hers, 'doth temperately keep time' (III, iv, 131).
97 See *supra*, chapter 4, section 2.
98 Although Antony does briefly describes his reaction to the death of Fulvia (I, ii, 115–23).
99 According to Belsey, *The Subject of Tragedy*, p. 35. Hamlet had also evoked the changing shapes of the clouds: III, ii, 364–70.
100 *Pericles*, scene 1, 164–85; scene 2, 1–33; scene 5, 41–51.
101 See Belsey, *The Subject of Tragedy*, pp. 45–6, and Stephen Greenblatt's chapter '*Hamlet*: interiority and revenge', in Gilles Mathis and P. Sahel, eds, *Hamlet ou le texte en question* (Paris: Messène, 1996), p. 14. Freud had already opposed the 'period' of Oedipus and the 'period' of Hamlet: *La science des rêves* (Presses Universitaires de France, 1950 [first published 1926]), p. 199.
102 Shakespeare seems to have frequented Huguenot refugees in London as early as 1598. See Park Honan, *Shakespeare: A Life* (Oxford University Press, 1998), p. 325. See also Kathleen Lambley, *The Teaching and Cultivation of the French Language in England During Tudor and Stuart Times* (Manchester University Press, 1920).
103 William Cornwallis, *Essayes* (London, 1600), p. 92 (essay 46).
104 See G. C. Taylor, *Shakespeare's Debt to Montaigne* (Harvard University Press, 1925).

105 See Robert Ellrodt, 'Self-consciousness in Montaigne and Shakespeare', *Shakespeare Survey*, 28 (1975), p. 39, notes 2, 3, 4. F. R. Fripp's parallel between the melancholy Jaques of *As You Like It* and Montaigne is unfounded: *Shakespeare: Man and Artist* (Oxford University press, 1938; reprinted 1964, vol. II). A few parallels with sonnets of uncertain date bear on general ideas, such as inconstancy in human actions: Sacvan Bercovitch, 'Shakespeare's sonnet 124', *Explicator*, 27:3 (November 1968).
106 Ellrodt, 'Self-consciousness in Montaigne and Shakespeare', pp. 40–1.
107 I have shown that the identification of this book with the *De consolatione* of Cardan is hardly more convincing: *ibid.*, p. 40.
108 See E. E. Schmid, 'Shakespeare, Montaigne und die Schauspielerische Formel', *Shakespeare Jahrbuch*, 82–3 (1945–6).
109 *Essays*, III, xii. I use here Florio's translation, available to Shakespeare (Everyman's edition, London: Dent, 1965, vol. III, pp. 308–9). There are at least three more pertinent parallels:

Hamlet, IV, iii, 20–4, 'Your worm is your only emperor for diet' and *Essays*, II, iv, Florio, vol. II, p. 155: 'The heart and life of a mighty and triumphant Emperor, is but the breakfast of a seely little worm'.

Hamlet, V, ii, 10–1, a merely verbal parallel, 'There's a divinity that shapes our ends, / *Rough-hew* them how we will' and *Essays*, III, viii, Florio, vol. III, p. 171: 'My consultation doth somewhat *roughy hew* the matter'.

Hamlet, V, ii, 190–4, 'If it be now', and *Essays*, Florio, vol. I, xix, 89 (I, xx: 105 in Screech): 'No one dies before his time'.

110 See *infra*, chapter 4, p. 106.
111 See Kenneth Muir's edition (London: Methuen, 1952), pp. 249–53.

Chapter 4

Complexity and coherence of the Shakespearean characters

A few decades after the death of Shakespeare, one of his heirs, John Dryden, who was not only a great dramatist but also a generally wise critic, praised him for having preserved 'the constant conformity of each character to itself from its very first setting out in the Play quite to the End'.[1] In the eyes of modern critics, however, those characters often appear as 'various and wavering' ('divers et ondoyant') as his own self seemed to Montaigne (I, i: 5 A; VS 9). Colin McGinn ascribes to them 'fluid identities', noting that they are sometimes even denied a proper self.[2] I maintain a middle course between these two opposed perspectives. I acknowledge the complexity of the main characters, and at times recognize their distinct evolution, yet point out constant features in each of them. Of course, to do this across the immense gallery of Shakespeare's portraits would be wearisome, if not atomized to the point of fruitlessness. My position may be aptly illustrated by the exploration of the characters of a few key *personae*. First among them, the Prince of Denmark.

1. Hamlet

As early as 1838, John Sterling asserted that 'the Prince of Denmark is nearly a Montaigne, lifted to a higher eminence, and agitated by more striking circumstances and severer destiny, and altogether a somewhat more passionate structure of man'.[3] Sterling's opinion has been echoed by Harry Levin.[4] Montaigne's influence is possible, as Florio's translation was available to William Cornwallis when he wrote, at the latest in 1600, 'I like nothing better in Montaigne than his desire of knowing Brutus' *private actions*', a desire obviously shared by Shakespeare in *Julius Caesar*.[5] Incidentally, there is no trace of Plutarch in Shakespeare before *Julius Caesar*: reading Montaigne may have called Shakespeare's attention to North's translation.

Among the elements already discussed, the *Essays* are marked by variety and discontinuity. As Dr Johnson first pointed out, Hamlet is 'the most various of roles'[6] and Catherine Belsey declares him 'the most discontinuous' of Shakespeare's heroes.[7] Even Brian Vickers admits there are 'irreconcilable aspects' to his character.[8] Yet, in different ways, Harold Jenkins, Philip Edwards, G. R. Hibbard in their editions of the play, John Lee in his exhaustive analysis, as well as psychoanalytical critics, from Ernest Jones to Norman Holland, Arthur Kirsch and Janet Adelman, have offered complex but coherent interpretations.[9] Another type of consistent elucidation is offered in Alastair Fowler's British Academy lecture: 'Recognising such dispersed aspects of character, far from disintegrating Hamlet as an individual, helps to synthesize his Renaissance subjectivity'.[10] The enigma of Hamlet, according to Harold Bloom, is the enigma of Shakespeare himself: an individual who is, as Borgès suggested, at once everyone and no one.[11]

My commentary will be based on the text. As such, it adheres to Umberto Eco's dictum that 'between the mysterious history of a textual production and the uncontrollable drifts of its future readings, the text represents a comfortable presence, the point to which we can stick'.[12]

From the beginning of the play we hear that Hamlet is in a fit of melancholy, as Montaigne said he was when he started writing his essays (II, 8: 433 A; VS 385). I agree we should not explain the hero's melancholy *only* with reference to Timothy Bright's 1586 *Treatise on Melancholy*,[13] but the many parallels traced by Harold Jenkins are incontrovertible.[14] In their study of Montaigne, neither Starobinski nor Screech found it possible to leave out physiological considerations. With Montaigne as with Hamlet, the melancholy proclaimed is not supposed to be a constant and predominant humour. The prince says: 'I have *of late* [...] lost all mirth, forgone all custom of exercise' (II, ii, 297–8; my italics). In both, their mood can be traced to a definite cause: for Montaigne it is the death of a dear friend, for Hamlet it is his father's death and his mother's hasty and incestuous remarriage. Robert Burton's 1621 treatise on melancholy reported that the death of friends and relatives had been one of the chief causes of melancholy at least since Antiquity.[15] Melancholy may at least partly account for the hero's recurrent death wish: death was also a constant preoccupation for Montaigne, as the ultimate experience of identity.[16] Melancholy changes one's outlook upon the world and obscures the 'brave o'erhanging firmament'.[17] Hamlet's dark view of the world, of society and of human nature is the expression of a pessimism induced by special circumstances rather than an exposition of philosophical scepticism.

When Hamlet says 'there is nothing either good or bad, but thinking makes it so', he is not necessarily echoing the speculation of Montaigne 'that the taste of goods or evills doth greatly depend on the opinion we have of them' (I, xiv; Florio's translation). Rather, he is explaining why Denmark now is to him a prison (II, ii, 248–9).[18] That there are 'no self-evident truths' for Hamlet, as some claim,[19] is doubtful, since he does not call into question the qualities of his father as 'a goodly king' (186–7), believes in virtue in the abstract even when questioning its existence in women and denounces 'the oppressor's wrong' (III, i, 72), for example. The 'truths' he has to piece together, as Montaigne did, are pragmatic.[20] Like Montaigne, he will come to make a pragmatic use of religion when 'our dear plots do pall', an admission that relies on the operations of the divine providence, which Horatio, as a Christian Stoic, confirms: 'That is most certain' (V, ii, 9–12).

A melancholy man was expected to be given to 'contemplations' and to be 'not so apt for action'.[21] As Montaigne retired into his library, Hamlet intended to 'go back to school in Wittenberg' (I, ii, 113). After the ghost's revelation, he feels bound to avenge his father, but he also feels unfitted for the role he has to play: 'the time is out of joint', why should he be born to set it right? (I, v, 189–91). To carry out his mission, Hamlet adopts the common ruse of the avenger. His friends are warned of his decision to 'put an antic disposition on' (I, v, 173), which is the cause of the 'transformation' noticed by Claudius (II, ii, 5). It enables him to play many parts: the lunatic, the jester, the satirist. But these 'actions that he [can] play' do not imply any change in 'that within which passeth show' (I, ii, 85). The audience would know he was 'essentially [...] not in madness / But mad in craft' (III, iv, 171–2).[22]

The admission of a stratagem, I admit, cannot account for Hamlet's outrageous behaviour towards Ophelia. But it is at least clear that his son's love for his mother suffers a sea-change when he feels that she has become tainted with impurity 'in the rank sweat of an enseamèd bed' (III, iv, 82). Henceforth, as Davis notes, 'Hamlet cannot talk to [Ophelia] in particular without thinking of women in general'.[23] Even without resorting to an Oedipal interpretation,[24] it is clear that sex and the sullying of the mother figure now provoke the physical and mental nausea also conspicuous in the ravings of Lear, the jealousy of Othello, or the loathing of lust in sonnet 129, 'Th'expense of spirit in a waste of shame'.[25] Hamlet would genuinely like to see Ophelia retire into a 'nunnery',[26] just as he seeks to remake his mother 'in the image of the Virgin Mother', as Janet Adelman points out.[27] Yet, despite Stanley Cavell's claims that Montaigne's essay 'On some verses of Virgil's' influenced Shakespeare's views,[28] I fail to see any resemblance between a rabid revulsion from the physical aspects of sex and the temperate and tolerant views of the French essayist.[29] For Montaigne, 'male and female, are cast in the same mould' (III, v: 1016 B; VS 897) and a lack of chastity is found excusable in either sex; Hamlet, and Shakespeare himself in the *Sonnets*, apparently find it more intolerable in women. Hamlet is obsessed by the sexual act, seeing it as a breeding of 'sinners' (III, i, 124). By contrast, Montaigne mentions original sin only once and looks on it as a sin of pride and disobedience, unlinked to sensuality (II, xii: 543 B–C; VS 488).

Hamlet's constant self-criticism may be intensified by his melancholy, but it proceeds from his self-consciousness and the insistence on truthfulness he shares with Montaigne. In their self-examination they both find that 'the best of the goodness in me has some vicious stain' (*Essays*, II, xx: 766 B; VS 674).[30] They are both willing to 'condemn [their] universal form',[31] but with a difference: Hamlet is incapable of Montaigne's serene acceptance of being 'neither Angell nor *Cato*'.[32] The secret of happiness, according to Schopenhauer, is not to wish oneself different.[33] Hamlet kept wishing himself different and, unlike the Shakespeare of sonnet 29, could not find acquiescence in his own self through the love of another.

When Hamlet repeatedly charges himself with procrastination, we must temper his self-criticism by remembering that the melancholy man is 'doubtful before, and long in deliberation'.[34] Melancholy, however, is not the only cause of delay. Montaigne has confessed his 'inability to reach decision[s]' in a striking way and declared it 'a most inconvenient defect when transacting the world's business', quoting Petrarch: 'Ne si, ne no, nel cuor mi suona intiero'.[35] As a scholar 'thinking too precisely on the event' (IV, iv, 32, Q2, p. 689) and distrusting his 'imaginations' (III, ii, 81), Hamlet had to make sure that he was not abused by a 'goblin damned' (I, iv, 21) or his own 'melancholy' (II, ii, 603).

The famous 'delays', or Derridean 'deferrals', may be accounted for by what is given in the text. When Hamlet's doubts are lifted, he seems ready to act, as he does when killing the overhearer behind the arras. But why did he put up his sword when he could have killed Claudius in prayer a moment before? Again, he had been 'thinking too precisely': 'That would be scanned' (III, iii, 75).[36] In an age when many Christians thought that God wanted the reprobate to 'heap on himself damnation' (*Paradise Lost*, I, 215), the audience would not have been shocked, as we are, by Hamlet's wish to send the villain to hell. He is not seeking an excuse for a reluctance to kill a defenceless man at his prayers; he will have no excuse for sending his former friends to death 'no shriving-time allowed' (V, ii, 48). Hamlet himself has confessed he is 'revengeful' (III, I, 127). The ghost has called for revenge, but he has mainly urged his son to put an end to usurpation and 'damnèd incest' in the royal bed without tainting his own mind (I, v, 81–5), which Hamlet does. The prince has also declared himself 'proud' (III, I, 126), and he shows it when envenomed with envy of Laertes' fencing skill (IV, vii, 86; V, I, 155–6), as when he deplored leaving behind him 'a wounded name' and called upon Horatio to save his reputation (V, ii, 296–301).

Fortinbras is recast by Hamlet in his own image as a 'delicate and tender prince',[37] as if to unite in him his own qualities and those of his warlike father (IV, iv). Is Hamlet inconsistent in praising a soldier 'with divine ambition puffed'? The soliloquy was cut off in the folio and, if the revision was Shakespeare's, it could mean he had sought to remove an inconsistency. But in the whole suppressed scene there was a nice balance between the critical awareness that 20,000 men were sent to imminent death 'for a fantasy and trick of fame' and a genuine admiration for the man who will expose himself 'To all that fortune, death and danger dare' when 'honour's at the stake'.[38] As often happens with Shakespeare, we are not invited to pass judgement, but to see both sides. Irony, however, is perhaps present in a passage of the *Essays* he may have had in mind: Montaigne alluded to wars in which we see 'thousands of foreigners pledging for money their very life-blood in quarrels which are no concern of theirs' (II, xxiii: 778 A; VS 685), a fact he found 'strange', yet did not openly condemn.

That Hamlet should give Fortinbras his 'dying voice' to rule over Denmark (V, ii, 308) is not even 'strange'. Hamlet is a king's son, who had voiced his admiration for an almost godlike *father* figure, praised as a man, a ruler and a warrior. He himself expected to be king when his uncle 'Popped in between th'election and [his] hopes' (V, ii, 66). When he is described by Ophelia as 'the courtier's, *soldier's*, scholar's eye, tongue, sword' (III, i, 154; my italics), the scholar is not given precedence. James Supple notes that Montaigne himself 'frequently use[s] the prestige of the military ideal to highlight the weaknesses inherent in its literary counterpart, but rarely reverses the process'.[39] As Hibbard points out in his introduction to the play, Hamlet is not horrified at the shedding of blood; he 'has all the hauteur of the Renaissance monarch or aristocrat'.[40]

Nor is he 'a second Hamlet' on his return to Denmark, as some critics claim.[41] It is apparent that he is less anxious, but also evident that he shows the same inclination to discourse on death, and the same obsessions with the melting of 'this too, too solid flesh' now imagined in 'progress through the guts of a beggar'.[42] Likewise, he still declares himself 'splenetive and rash' (V, i, 258), and in parodying the emphasis of Laertes' grief he again ironically denounces the difference between the trappings of woe and 'that within which passeth show'.[43] He is no longer obsessed by his mother's guilt, although this is not surprising, given that he has vented his long-repressed feelings and may think her now repentant.[44] He hardly mentions his father, yet he alludes to his earlier 'dear plots' (V, ii, 9) and tells Horatio he is determined not 'to let this canker of our nature [Claudius] come/In further evil', promising 'It will be short' (V, ii, 68–74).[45] Only his attitude has changed. The episode with the pirates has miraculously allowed him to be back at court; he therefore thinks he has just to wait for another opportunity offered him by providence: 'There's a divinity that shapes our ends/Rough-hew them how we will' (V, ii, 10–11).[46] This was the advice given by Montaigne to princes when they have to depart from their 'ordinary duty': 'When all is done [...] must wee often, as unto our last Anker and sole refuge, resigne the protection of our vessell unto the onely conduct of heaven' (III, i: Florio vol. III, p. 18; VS 799). After killing Polonius, Hamlet already saw himself as 'the scourge and minister' of heaven (III, iv, 159). Horatio's call for flights of angels to sing the unshriven 'sweet prince' to his rest (V, ii, 313) is morally questionable but dramatically consistent, since Hamlet himself had thrice called on 'angels and ministers of grace' to defend him (I, iv, 20, 92; III, iv, 93–4).

'At the centre of Hamlet', we are told, 'there is, in short, nothing'.[47] I could agree if it only meant that introspection may be self-defeating, that pure reflectivity cannot apprehend substance and that only the 'nothing' of the kind Amiel, Valéry and Sartre diversely proposed is made evident.[48] Shakespeare's characters, however, were not intended to illustrate the workings of introspection, but to 'hold, as it were, the mirror up to nature' (III, ii, 22). Notice the cautious phrasing 'as it were'. It acknowledges that mimesis is bound to be imperfect, but maintains that the aim is nevertheless mimesis. In this context, this means the creation of a character whose 'form' (Shakespeare here uses the word like Montaigne) must seem to be true. Terry Eagleton also claims that Hamlet has no 'essence of being', which is obvious since he is a *dramatis persona*, not a person; but this does not make him 'pure deferral and diffusion, a hollow void'.[49] From a historical point of view, it would be wiser to stress the Renaissance insistence on the protean nature of man emphasized by Michel Grivelet.[50] Yet this perspective can hardly be invoked to justify post-modern claims for the 'unfixity' of some Shakespearean characters: Pico, and those who echoed him, were thinking of human nature in metaphysical and ethical terms, as ranging freely from the animal to the divine, which is quite different from plasticity in one's individual character. Also, as Thomas Greene noted, both Montaigne and Shakespeare substituted 'horizontal manoeuvrings and adaptations' for 'the vertical flexibility' which allowed Renaissance man to rise towards 'the upper limits of humanity'.[51]

In *Shakespeare's Hamlet and the Controversies of Self*, John Lee argues, not for a second Hamlet within the play in the chronological order, but for different princes in the second quarto and in the folio.[52] After the cuts practised in the folio, the prince's sense of 'that within' and of his own 'mystery' is said to be more dominant. The argument is persuasive, but too much is made, I think, of Hamlet's ironic remark about Guildenstern's attempt 'to pluck out the heart of [his] mystery' (III, ii, 353). In context, it may mean no more than 'pierce his real intentions'. In none of his soliloquies is Hamlet intent on discovering his true self, his own 'essence' or 'form'. Yes, he is concerned with 'the uses of this world' and the ends of life, with the 'ill about [his] heart', and his doubts as to what he should do, but not what he is. His preoccupations are not essentially different when he is back in Denmark. With or without the cuts, the coherence of the character is thoroughly maintained.

2. Macbeth and Lady Macbeth

Macbeth first appears to us as a fearless warrior through the description of a battle (I, ii). Soon after, in his reaction to temptation, he is depicted as a man inclined in a feudal setting to be loyal to his liege lord and desirous to keep the 'golden opinions' he has won 'from all sorts of people' (I, vii, 31–4). Yet he allows himself to be persuaded by his wife to kill his king in his sleep and, as a usurper, becomes a prey to ceaseless fears, which will dictate his conduct as a bloody tyrant. Lady Macbeth plans a regicide and, after the murder of Duncan, keeps her composure, her cool-headedness, her imperious language well articulated on all occasions. When she reappears after a long interval, she is a prey to a crisis of sleep-walking, has lost her bearings and is haunted by her remembrance of bloodshed; there is little coherence in her talk. But while it is apparent that the characters of Macbeth and his wife do evolve, should we speak, like Alan Sinfield, of a 'swaying between divergent selves'?[53]

In answering this, I can demonstrate rapidly that some fundamental traits of character persist in Macbeth through the gradual dehumanizing of the originally presented hero. I do not think he experiences a change in his nature but that his view of life is transformed at the instant of the murder: 'there's nothing serious in mortality./All is but toys. Renown and grace is dead;/The wine of life is drawn' (II, iii, 92–5). And yet the man who becomes the butcher of Scotland, out of fear of treason, is still the man who had wished to wear 'in their newest gloss' the honours and golden opinions won (I, vii, 32-5). That is why, unlike Richard III, he will ultimately regret that all that 'should accompany old age, / As honour, love, obedience, troops of friends, / [He] must not look to have' (V, iii, 24-6), a regret consistent with his original nature, warped by ambition and by the murderous deed. Macbeth is led to repeated crimes less by his aspirations than by a constant disposition to be fascinated by a possible murderous act evoked by his imagination: 'Present fears / Are less than horrible imaginings. / My thought, whose murder yet is but fantastical / Shakes so my single state of man that function / Is smothered in surmise, and nothing is / But what is not' (I, iii, 137-41). To commit this murder he must be in a state of hallucination: 'Is this a dagger which I see before me, / The handle toward my hand?' (II, i, 33-4). When writing these scenes, Shakespeare may have had in mind Montaigne's essay 'On the power of the imagination' (II, xxi). Admittedly, the crimes that follow are committed or ordered cool-headedly, but they are always dictated by a fear of the future, entertained by a man whose 'fell of hair / Would at a dismal treatise rise and stir / As life were in't' (V, v, 11-12). When fighting, however, the warrior remains dauntless and when the promise of the weird sisters proves deceptive he overcomes his fear in a final encounter (V, vii).

Macbeth is not prevailed upon by female charm. Lady Macbeth is no temptress; she incites, almost compels her husband to carry out his own 'thought' – 'whose murther yet is but fantastical' (I, iii, 138) – into act. She appeals to his 'love' for her only incidentally (I, vii, 39), and he himself chiefly admires her strength (I, vii, 73-5). Unlike her husband, Lady Macbeth has little imagination and no fear of the future. Unlike him, she is not afraid of the supernatural; she welcomes 'metaphysical aid' (I, v, 28) and invokes spirits in a tone of command (I, v, 39-49). She draws up a practical plan for action (I, vii, 61-73). She speaks as if she meant to kill Duncan herself (I, v, 52-4 and perhaps I, v, 73). In action, however, her determination is apt to flinch: 'had he not resembled / My father as he slept, I had done't' (II, ii, 12-13). Her fainting-fit after the murder may be pretended (II, iii, 118), but it may herald a disintegration of her willpower; she certainly had to steel herself for action. This would not make her resolution less savage: her violation of 'nature', of womanly and motherly instinct, is stressed (I, v, 41-52; I, vii, 54-9). In the third act she is joyless but calm (ii, 4). She retains her self-control in the banquet scene and again chastises her husband for his lack of 'manhood' (III, iv, 57-72). Illustrating their contrasting yet complementary characters, in this instance Macbeth once more is moved by his imagination, projecting a ghost, while his wife, as ever, is only dismayed when facing reality.

Different interpretations have been offered of the sleep-walking scene, either sentimentalized or presented as a case of demoniacal somnambulism, since the heroine believes herself already in hell (V, i, 33), which is in keeping with her initial call to evil spirits. But the continuity of character is best illustrated by an alternation between her resolution – only achieved, however, through a straining of the will – when she addresses her husband, and her revulsion before the sight of blood pouring out of Duncan's body or staining her own hands (V, i, 33–41, 48–9). This is, of course, an imagined sight, but she does not know it and speaks as if confronting reality.

The end of *Macbeth* thus illustrates and supports Dryden's statement on 'the constant conformity of each character' cited at the start of this chapter. Shakespearean characters have more facets than Jonsonian characters; their actions and reactions are less predictable; they may be 'compact of jars'; they are affected by their experiences and are apt to learn from experience; but their creator has endowed each of them with a noteworthy self-consistency.

3. The characters in *King Lear*

Today, we no longer expect from Shakespeare's characters the kind of verisimilitude the nineteenth-century French critic Émile Faguet regretted not finding in *King Lear* in contrast to Balzac's *Le Père Goriot*. But to reduce them to a function or to an emblematic meaning would be another mistake: they can be convincing only if their language rings true. The epoch still defined 'character' in the Theophrastan sense, as in the moral sense of Aristotle. The dramatist portrays certain character types, such as Kent, the honest servant who pathetically tries, just before his death, to make himself known to the king whom he has served in disguise (V, iii, 256–63). True to type is his spontaneous hatred of Oswald, himself the generic effeminate sycophant and one of the new breed of servants. The character can even become emblematic in a play where the influence of the moralities is generally acknowledged and where the forces of good and evil confront each other through two groups of characters. However, only Cordelia lends herself to a symbolic interpretation. Exiled from the start, she does not reappear until the denouement. On stage she speaks few words, far fewer than her sisters. In those moments that are heaviest with meaning her discourse embeds itself in the simplest forms of negation and affirmation: 'Nothing, my lord' (I, i, 87), 'And so I am, I am' (IV, vi, 63). Her words resound without her voice ever being raised on this stage where others scream. Lear remembers that 'Her voice was ever soft, / Gentle, and low' (V, iii, 247-8). Some see in her a symbol of divine grace when the king is told: 'Thou hast a daughter / Who redeems nature from the general curse' (IV, v, 201-3). Still, she is not an allegorical figure. Every human action calls forth a series of associations: it owes its underlying signification to the resonances that it awakes.

Psychological criticism, beginning with Coleridge, has at times emphasized a kind of inflexibility, of hardness even, in the attitude of the heroine towards a loving father in the first act. But Cordelia needs to have the intransigency of the one who speaks the truth – 'So young, my lord, and true' (I, i, 107) – the truth that is rejected – 'Thy truth then be thy dower' (108). She is the one who sees the lie, distinguishes reality from appearances: 'I know you what you are' (I, i, 268). When she announces 'Time shall unfold what plighted cunning hides' (I, i, 280) she speaks as if she were Time itself, as in its chorus in act IV of *The Winter's Tale*.[54] Once the passions are let loose and the masks are ripped away, the perspective is a completely different one. Cordelia is at once the one who exerts control over the passions (*History*, scene 17, ll. 17-25) and the source of compassionate love for the humiliated king, this 'child-changed father' (I, vii, 15). Oddly, while we neither hear her speak one word to the king whom she has married (I, i), nor speak of him, she becomes a mother image and a representation of life in her call to all the restorative virtues of nature (IV, iii, 16). When Lear's eyes open up to reality, and when he recognizes his daughter, she, who represents truth, resorts to lying, out of mercy for him. To this father, to this king, who reminds her that she has reasons not to love him, the one who was cursed and banished by him answers: 'No cause, no cause' (IV, vi, 68). Confronted with the shame of a public solicitation of love, her purity had been in the silence and refusal; in front of repentance and humility the inalterability of love is asserted in her ability to 'forget and forgive' (words spoken by Lear, IV, vi, 76). But, after the battle is lost, Cordelia, again an image of the truth, does not, like the king, give herself up to the illusion of happiness together in the ageless time of a blissful captivity. She holds fast to a language of Stoicism, and suggests a last confrontation with Goneril and Regan (V, iii, 7), but she knows that no victory is promised to love and truth in this world. She responds to the idyllic vision again with silence – the silence of lips forever dumb when she reappears, dead, in the arms of her father.

To humanize Goneril and Regan instead of making them monsters is today the aim of most directors. They have arguments that make sense – the impossibility of housing two bands of armed men in the same house under two leaders (II, ii, 410-17) – and some reason to fear that Lear will seek to take back his power (I, iv, 303–7). Shakespeare allows his characters to justify their actions. Nevertheless, Cordelia's words at the close of the first scene are a clear warning addressed to the spectators. This is why we cannot trust Goneril's statements when she claims that Lear's knights engage in 'rank and not-to-be-endured riots' (I, iv, 186; see also I, iv, 225–30). Lear's word may certainly be equally suspected, but the only knight whom the dramatist has placed on the stage must be representative: and his speech and conduct (I, iv, 58–77) support Lear's description, not the accusations made by Goneril. The pact between the two sisters (I, i, 283–305) and the provocation planned to unleash the king's fury (I, iii) reveal a conscious perfidy. In the interview at Gloucester's castle, the text barely justifies the effort of some actresses to appear more conciliatory than Lear: from the first, his two daughters insist (without mincing words) on his 'dotage' (II, ii, 319–25). Nevertheless, from their first false declarations of love the author seeks to differentiate them: Regan means to outdo her elder sister and already seems to disclose her sensuality when she measures all against those joys 'the most precious square of sense possesses'.[55] Goneril is a rival for Edmund's love and she expresses an obsessive jealousy when she is eager to know if he has had access to 'the forfended place' (V, i, 11). The torture of Gloucester stimulates her sadism: she wants the bonds to hurt him, pulls out the hairs in his beard, insists on gouging the second eye. It has been suggested that she sees her father in Gloucester: this does not make her less cruel. The love rivalry between the two sisters is a plot necessity to shed light on Albany and lead to the duel between the two brothers. But each falls in love in her own way. The imperious Goneril seeks a 'man' who corresponds better than her own husband to her ideal of brute force: she enlists him in her service (IV, ii, 20–4). Regan, more feminine, burns with desire to give and give herself (V, iii, 67–71). Goneril takes the initiative from the first very dialogue with her sister (I, i, 283–306) and suggests to Edmund that he murder Albany (IV, v, 261–67). Regan dies poisoned by her; Goneril kills herself with a dagger. Cordelia's sisters do not evolve in the course of the play, but their 'hard hearts' (III, vi, 37) are gradually revealed to the world.

Cornwall is also of a piece. He is not a stupid brute, but a depraved Renaissance nobleman with a haughty mien (II, v), adroit at corrupting Edmund (if that was necessary). His outraged amazement when a 'peasant' dares speak back to him is that of an aristocrat (III, vii, 73–8). Albany, however, has to change, because of the necessities of the action: he must be slow in discovering the true nature of his wife (I, iv). Once informed and indignant, he remains master of himself (IV, ii). It is understandable that Edmund portrays him as hesitant (V, i, 1–40) and that Goneril does not find in him a perfect image of virility: each character speaks from his or her own point of view. In fact, Albany adroitly manoeuvres to isolate Edmund (V, iii, 77–84) and he is ready to confront him in single combat (V, iii, 84–6). Is his decision not to govern a weakness in his character? It is an indication of a certain philosophical detachment with regard to action, but it is also a dramatic necessity if Edgar is meant to reign.

Gloucester's fate is parallel to Lear's; their personalities, however, are very different. Without doubt they both present the same lack of discernment, ironically emphasized when Gloucester boasts he does not need glasses (I, ii, 36). This credulous and superstitious father is from the start an Old Comedy *senex* who complacently recalls the good old days of yesteryear (I, i). Lear sinned in his mind, while Gloucester has sinned in the flesh, and therefore loses his sight, whereas Lear loses his reason. He reveals himself first, as opposed to Kent, anxious not to offend those in power; he remains silent during the banishment of Cordelia, gives way to Cornwall (II, ii, 143–50), all the while endeavouring to help Lear 'in secret' (III, iii, 14), for he is a good man. '[T]ied to th' stake' (III, vii, 52), he acts with courage and dignity. But while the ordeal rouses a vehement indignation in Lear, the blind Gloucester is passive in despair: he seeks death, but only lest he should 'fall to quarrel' with the 'great opposeless wills of the gods' (IV, vi, 38) and he allows himself to be persuaded that a miracle has saved him (IV, ii, 56). Always ready to relapse into hopelessness (V, ii), he submits to the will of others. The meeting at Dover with Lear becomes a symbolic confrontation when the old king, lucid in his madness, reveals the world as it is to an old man who stumbled when he saw (IV, i, 19); Gloucester, still passive, answers: 'I see it feelingly' (IV, v, 145).

Edgar and Edmund make up another pair of opposites. The bastard is more captivating than the legitimate son: nature has been very generous to him and his first monologue shows that he knows it. At the beginning of the play, when his father alludes in his presence to his illegitimate birth, calling his mother a whore, and states that he will exile this son again after having already kept him away for nine years, our sympathy is with him. When he invokes nature and stands up against the injustice of custom with reference to illegitimate children (I, ii, 1–15), some of the spectators of the period would have been as affected by his arguments as we are today: Montaigne testifies to this.[56] Yet his understandable bitterness cannot justify his scheme to destroy his brother Edgar – to expose him to banishment and death – since, according to tradition in the Elizabethan theatre (on this point quite removed from psychological verisimilitude), he proclaims his own vices and publicly recognizes the 'nobility' of the one he deceives (I, ii, 168). It was a rule written into law that the sins of the parents 'contaminated' illegitimate children:[57] Edmund is subject to this convention here in the same way as Don John in *Much Ado About Nothing*. Yet, in *King John*, as in real life, a bastard such as Faulconbridge (though, it is true, of royal blood) could play the role of the hero. In *Lear*, Shakespeare defers to convention because it serves his dramatic design, but he embellishes Edmund with certain qualities such as charm, courage and wit without making him less criminal. Cornwall spares him the sight of his father's torment (III, vii, 6–7), but he leaves in order to kill the blind man, supposedly in order 'to dispatch / His 'nighted life', but actually because his pathetic condition 'moves / All hearts' against his tormenters (IV, iv, 12–15). It is for a similar reason (V, iii, 46–51) that Edmund gives the order to assassinate Lear and Cordelia. Yet Shakespeare knows that this blackness of soul prevents neither bursts of chivalry, as in his farewell to Goneril (IV, ii, 25), nor a certain strength of spirit. If Edmund accepts the challenge of the unknown knight, it is because the despised bastard, now so close to the throne, is anxious for his own glory. It is in order to conduct himself as a real knight that he grants the victor his pardon (V, iii, 156–7). Is the will to accomplish something good before dying (218) less believable? Is he really moved by Edgar's narrative (191)? One may doubt it; but when the bodies of the two dead queens are brought to the stage, there is a haughty but nostalgic irony in his comment: 'I was contracted to them both; all three / Now marry in an instant' (V, iii, 203–4). The feeling that 'Edmond was belov'd' (215) makes plausible his decision 'some good [...] to do, / Despite of mine own nature' (V, iii, 218–19). The return of the word 'nature' is characteristic, recalling the initial invocation (I, ii, 1). All the evil he has done seems to have emerged out of his 'given' nature: will he overcome these constraints in the final moment? One can imagine it, but it is never said, nor even suggested.

Edgar is contrasted with his brother Edmund as Cordelia is with her sisters, in a manner reminiscent of the morality plays. Gloucester's legitimate son, as sententious as Albany is pious and moralizing, has everything to make him unpopular today. Some directors have sought to make the two brothers similar. Others have ascribed to Edgar in the duel a disloyalty and a ferocity that have no basis in the text.[58] Short of rewriting the play, it is necessary to admit that Edgar is indeed, as Edmund himself says, 'a brother noble, / Whose nature is so far from doing harms, / That he suspects none' (I, ii, 168–70). He becomes, as he presents himself (the Shakespearean hero has the right to define himself), a 'man, made tame to Fortune's blows, / Who, by the art of known and feeling sorrows, / Am pregnant to good pity' (IV, v, 220–2). The fact that he waits to reveal his identity to his father, whom he helps and saves from suicide

(IV, v), and without doubt from a more painful death than at the hands of his enemies (V, ii), has been attributed to spite. But neither his behaviour nor the pain that he expresses in his asides at the sight of the old blind man (IV, i, 10–53), nor his speeches, betray such a state of mind. If he recalls that the adultery of Gloucester, in resulting in the birth of a bastard, is the source of a chain of events that has led him to lose his eyes, it is only after the death of his father and in addressing the unnatural son (V, iii, 166–9). His ethics are those of his time and he takes up a biblical argument (Wisdom, xi, 16). That he has chosen to disguise himself first as a mad beggar, that he speaks in a peasant dialect when he confronts Oswald, seems to place him on an initiatory course that leads him to identify with the most destitute, then with the lowly, before re-emerging as a knight and a defender of the right. But it is true that these metamorphoses are an artifice of the dramatist and are not convincing, except for the first change into 'poor Tom'.

The importance of Edgar, then, is not in his character, but in his multiple functions. Dramatic function, since the movement of the wheel of fortune, the emblem of medieval tragedy nearly always present in Elizabethan tragedy, brings him low in elevating Edmund, until he puts an end to the rise of the bastard: 'The wheel is come full circle' (V, iii, 165). Edgar is the one who knew to wait for 'the mature time', the 'time [that] shall serve' (IV, v, 275; V, i, 38). It is a choric function, since the commentary calls attention to a constant feature of the action: the awakening of a hope or of an expectation which is immediately disappointed and the inexorable progress from worse to worst. Believing that he has nothing more to dread in his extreme destitution, Edgar learns, in seeing his father with his gouged eyes before him, that no one can say he is at the 'worst' (IV, i, 8–25). Hardly has he pulled his father out of despair than the mad king comes on stage, 'thou side-piercing sight!' (IV, v, 85). And it is after his victory over Edmund, at the moment when the officer is about to give the counter-command, that Lear appears, holding the dead Cordelia in his arms (V, iii, 232). The subtlety is in the intermingling of the main plot *commented upon* by Edgar, which leads to entropy in a scene strewn with corpses, and a secondary plot, *led* by him, which has its point of departure in emptiness when the hero chooses to be 'nothing' ('Edgar I nothing am'; II, ii, 184), but which provides an opportunity for renewal in bringing the criminal characters to their doom. Finally, Edgar fulfils a symbolic function in his appearance as the naked madman, 'poor Tom', triggering Lear's madness in presenting him as the image of a man reduced to 'the thing itself' (III, iv, 100) and acting as the Fool in order to carry on with him the dialogue of lucid madness.

His role in this context is significant. In none of the sources of *Lear* does the king lose his reason. In the story of the king of Paphlagonia, the loyal son, the model for Edgar, does not feign insanity. Thus the presence of the Fool next to Lear is also a major innovation and the meeting of the three forms of insanity in act III is a representation of a cosmic and mental chaos without precedent in an English Renaissance theatre nevertheless full of scenes of madness.

The monarch who enters the stage majestically and announces his 'darker purpose' (I, i, 36) offers no sign of mental senility or insanity. He demonstrates selfishness and naïveté in wishing to unburden himself of his responsibilities all the while preserving 'the name, and all th'addition to a king' (I, i, 136). He shows a lack of judgement with regard to his daughters, but also with regard to the consequences of dividing the kingdom. When the father, betrayed in his love, the ruler publicly humiliated, utters curses, it is the result of the impatience of his character, made worse by his age. Goneril comments on this, but Regan notes: 'he hath ever but slenderly known himself' (I, i, 292–3). To represent *Lear* as 'a tragedy of wrath' is to simplify things.[59] The 'tragic fault', *hamartia*, is above all the lack of knowledge: knowledge of oneself and knowledge of others. As in the Aristotelian tragedy, the hero must be led to 'recognition', an *anagnorisis*, through his trials.[60]

Is it necessary to explore the unconscious of these characters? When Lear says to Cordelia 'Now, our joy' (I, i, 82), it is clear that he awaits her declaration of love with a more eager desire than with his solicitations of love from his other daughters. Is it an incestuous desire that provokes the intensity of his response? Is her refusal to express herself felt as a refusal to give herself? It is true that Lear first gives his daughter a second chance to prove her love (94–5) and that his fury bursts when she declares that she must divide her love between her husband and her father. But it seems that this aged king wishes above all to find a mother in a second childhood (123–4). The staging of the division of the kingdom reveals that Lear likes playing a part.[61] He lives in a world that he thinks he makes according to his own humour and he refuses to see what is unpleasant to him. Powerful, he pushes away from his purview those who contradict him: Cordelia, then Kent (I, i, 124, 157). Powerless, he will go from Goneril to Regan, then will flee them both in the storm (II, iv, 305). The insistent reminder of impinging reality in these flights is the role of the Fool.

In *King Lear*, then, the Fool is the voice of common sense and of common wisdom. His language is indirect, embellished with images and riddles to better express the unpleasant truths without revealing the whip. But he alone sees the world upside down, as in the prophecy of

Merlin (II, ii, 95), because he sees clearly. Rather than being a professional clown he is one of the 'innocents' or simple-minded (called *naturals*) who became pupils of the king or a peer. Lear often calls him *boy*, as he has preserved from childhood an absence of inhibition and a taste for riddles. It is notable in this role that the Fool accuses Lear of that which the king has begun to accuse himself of without wishing to admit it. The Fool, whom he loves, had pined away after the departure of Cordelia; he has noticed it, but he interrupts the knight who tells him: 'No more of that' (I, iv, 73). Exasperated by Goneril, he begins to understand that the 'most small fault' (I, iv, 245) of his favourite daughter had taken his own nature 'out of joint', as Pascal would say about reason.[62] Yet, at that very moment, Lear, who had invoked Apollo until then (I, i, 159), speaks like Edmund to nature, hailed by the name of 'dear goddess' (I, iv, 254). And he intends also to make her the instrument of his desire: to punish the unthankful. But as he calls to her to make his daughter sterile, or to give her a child who would be a 'disnatur'd torment' (262), his own wish is against nature.

Until his reconciliation with Cordelia, Lear vacillates between blindness and insight, in the same way as he vacillates between bursts of anger and the effort to master himself. Confronting Goneril again in Gloucester's castle, he goes from renewing his curses to prayer – 'do not make me mad' (II, ii, 391) – and to the recognition that she is his flesh, his blood or, rather, a disease in his flesh (396–7). He claims to be patient (403), but he calls to the heavens to fill him with an exalted anger and he can barely hold back his tears (445–57). Exposing himself to the fury of the elements which he had invoked against Goneril (II, ii, 338–41), he summons heavenly fire to destroy the universe and scatter the seeds of creation, an impious prayer, similar to the wish spoken to the witches by the tyrant Macbeth (IV, i, 66–77). Lear identifies himself with the storm in order to defy it by way of the power of speech, but he continues to pity himself, a 'poor, infirm, weak, and despis'd old man' (III, ii, 20). And yet it is the ordeal of powerlessness, cold and deprivation that leads Lear to think of others: of his Fool shivering next to him (III, ii, 68–73), of the 'poor naked wretches' to whom he has given too little thought during his reign (III, iii, 28–36).

Another aspect of the 'recognition' process is the discovery of a true self through the destruction of a false self. Lear had played the role of an absolute and dreaded monarch, of a generous and loved father. As deference towards him disappears, he ceases to recognize himself, since he does not know himself as he sees himself or as he still wishes to be: 'This is not Lear [...]. Who is it that can tell me who I am?' 'Lear's shadow', answers the Fool (I, iv, 208-13). When he is left with only fifty of his hundred knights, then twenty-five, then none, it is the fragments of his identity that are being torn away from him, for the symbolic number represented the fullness of those prerogatives which constituted him in his eyes. The Fool had already told him that he was no more than an 'O without a figure' (I, iv, 174).

It is in relation to Edgar, himself reduced to 'nothing' (II, ii, 184), that Lear first finds again a 'minimal' identity, that of a naked man. But it is also the moment when he enters madness. He had a premonition of it after the first confrontation with Goneril (I, v, 46). Finding his manservant in the stocks, he had felt a pain rise to his heart, *hysterica passio* (II, ii, 294). He had shouted into the storm 'O Fool! I shall go mad' (II, ii, 459), a pregnant conjunction of related yet different words that foreshadows the cry of the perceptive Fool: 'This cold night will turn us all to fools and madmen' (II, iv, 73). In the storm, Lear realizes that his 'wits begin to turn' (III, ii, 67); the cosmic chaos will be nothing after 'the tempest in [his] mind' (III, iv, 12). He knows it: 'O, that way madness lies', but he adds, 'let me shun that' (21-2). He even shows a new clear-sightedness when, imagining all those who suffer, he prays. The actor John Gielgud got on his knees at this moment. Is it the harsh irony of the gods? The next moment, the mad naked man appears and Lear asks him, 'Didst thou give all to thy daughters?' (III, iv, 46), revealing the obsession fixed in his wandering wits. A comment by Kent confirms this: 'His wits begin t'unsettle' (152). *Begin* only, for his address to the 'poor, bare, forked animal' is still coherent (96-102). But its meaning is ambiguous. The weakness of man and the precariousness of his condition needed to be uncovered before this proud king. But was he completely wrong when, claiming for himself the 'superflux' that comes with civilization, he said to Regan: 'Allow not nature more than nature needs, / Man's life is cheap as beast's' (II, ii, 440-1)?[63] Lear's desire to undress himself (III, iv, 97-103) alludes ironically to the scene where the monarch wishes to 'divest' himself both of his power and his cares (I, i, 49); this is a necessary stage in the 'recognition' of his true condition: the truth is naked. Nevertheless, this is not an act of wisdom: undressing is also the characteristic gesture of the madman. The truth is twofold.

However, during the night of the storm, Edgar, as poor Tom, plays at being possessed, but draws his inspiration from a recent book in which Samuel Harsnett denounced false cases of possession (III, iv, 46-130). Edgar will later invoke a fake miracle on the cliff (IV, v, 55). We could make a case for Shakespeare's scepticism but Tom's feigned insanity is more unsettling than entertaining at the moment when Lear's reason begins to turn. The English public of the period, even if they had doubts about the powers of exorcists, believed in the reality of demonic possession, attested to in the Old as well as the New Testament (see, for example, 1 Kings 16; Matthew 8:28). Tom's raving is, furthermore, associated with feelings of guilt: the possessed imputes to himself all the deadly sins (III, iv, 78–93). For Edgar, as for Hamlet, feigning is an aspect of a real problem. The mention of 'nightmare' (114) and the enigmatic allusion to Nero and to the 'Lake of Darkness' (III, vi, 6–7) seem to hint at an obscure obsession, perhaps also to the 'dark and vicious place' where Edmund had been conceived (V, iii, 163). But the same disgust for sexuality expresses itself in Lear's satirical curses. One thinks of Hamlet, of Othello and of the sonnets to the dark lady: the obsessions of the playwright may be revealed through these characters.

Yet Lear succumbs to madness with dignity: Gielgud and the best actors in the role have understood this. The grotesque is there, but to emphasize it is to weaken the tragic element. The king addresses his 'philosopher' with extreme courtesy and enrols him among the hundred knights he still believes escort him (III, iv, 144–65). The questions he asks make sense, whether they refer to 'the cause of the thunder' or the search for 'a natural cause' for Regan's 'hardness of heart' (III, vi, 34–6). He observes customary forms when he creates a jury in which a beggar and a madman fill the part of the highest magistrates of the land. We note that the Fool, as opposed to Edgar, is wary of participating in Lear's hallucination and thinks that in joking he can burst the bubble of the illusion: this is his last call to reality. The king is now a prey to fantasies and to fits of rage, before falling asleep, exhausted (III, vi).

Listening to the conversation between Lear and Gloucester at Dover, Edgar cries out to himself: 'O matter and impertinency mixed, / Reason in madness!' (IV, v, 170–1). The description is apt: the mistake would be to believe that it is all reason or all madness. Lear's hallucinations persist; his talk is often subject to nothing other than mere associations of ideas and words. On the other hand, the denunciation of hypocrisy and injustice is perfectly coherent: Lear takes up, as we have seen, themes found throughout the satiric and homiletic literature of the period and the Shakespearean imagination gives them a particular power. But even here a certain excess is inherent in the genre. The one who curses, the king who wished to punish, swings to the other extreme when he states that 'none does offend' (IV, v, 164). Does the nausea towards sexuality which finds an expression in the allusion to the 'sulphurous pit', the female sex, lead to seeing all women as 'centaurs' (122–7)? What about Cordelia? It is true that denouncing the 'indistinguish'd space of woman's will' (271), as Edgar also does, enables the Baroque imagination to place into relief a heroine pure and unique against a foil of black and universal corruption.

The cure, like Lear's madness, is natural: sleep, the virtues of plants and, in the quarto, music (*History*, scene 21). Lear awakes believing he has been pulled out of the grave and thinks that Cordelia, bending towards him, is a heavenly spirit, while he himself is in a hell of torments. Like Hercules after his attack of madness in the tragedies of Euripides and Seneca, he is initially in a state of amnesia, wondering where and who he is. When finally the revelation comes, it is expressed with perfect simplicity, in a language where a painful past and the timid tenderness of the present weigh down and slow down the succession of words magically linked by their subdued sounds, the movement of the phrase, the enjambment of the line:

> Do not laugh at me,
> For, as I am a man, I think this lady
> To be my child, Cordelia.
> And so I am: I am.
> (IV, vi, 62–3)

So, a triple 'recognition' is achieved. The father recognizes his daughter – this is the first example of *anagnorisis*. He recognizes his error – the model is Oedipus – and Cordelia's forgiveness expunges it. He recognizes himself – the model is Socrates and Erasmus – as he is: 'a very foolish, fond old man' (vi, 53). As he is and as he is no longer, from the moment that he realizes it. Age also has its twofold truth. The tragedy has shown all its weakness, cruelly and publicly proclaimed by Goneril and Regan. But Cordelia does not want to let her father kneel; by kneeling herself, with respect, in order to receive the benediction of the one who had cursed her, she returns to Lear his lost fatherhood and royalty. The play could have ended with this scene and *King Lear* would have been the first of the 'tragi-comedies' of 'recognition': *Pericles*, *The Winter's Tale*, *Cymbeline*. But the inexorable movement towards the worst starts again. Captured after losing the battle, the old king strangely cherishes a dream of happiness in prison beside his beloved daughter: the illusion is of a poignant sweetness, but clearly unrealistic (V, iii, 8–19). Cordelia, still true to her nature, replies only by her silence.

To come to the tragic end is to come to the heart of the controversy concerning the interpretation of the tragedy, as I demonstrated in my general introduction to King Lear.[64] Yet my concern here is only with the continuity of character. The old king has not been deprived of his vigour and dignity by his trials. To make him enter the stage on a wheelchair, as some producers choose, is absurd. At the end of the tragedy, though his strength is declining, he is still able to tell his lifeless daughter 'I killed the slave that was a-hanging thee' (V, iii, 245–53). He is still 'this old majesty' in the eyes of Albany (275). These fundamental features have persisted throughout the play.

My insistence on continuity, far from harming the genius of Shakespeare, enhances it in my eyes. Discontinuity, which some modern critics and producers find so attractive, is more easily achieved than coherence, which has been the hallmark of all great works throughout the ages.

Notes

1   In Brian Vickers, ed., *Shakespeare: The Critical Heritage* (London: Routledge and Kegan Paul, 1978), vol. III, p. 40.
2   McGinn, *Shakespeare's Philosophy*, p. 25. The term 'fluid identity' is used in relation to characters in a comedy, but reflects his general thesis.
3   John Sterling in an essay in the *Westminster Review* quoted by Jacob Feis in *Shakespeare and Montaigne* (Genva: Slatkine, 1984).
4   Harry Levin, *The Question of Hamlet* (Oxford University Press, 1959).
5   William Cornwallis, *Essayes* (London, 1600), p. 92 (essay 46).
6   Cited by Michael Goldman, 'Acting values and Shakespearean meaning', in David Bevington and Jay L. Halio, eds, *Shakespeare: Pattern of Excelling Nature* (University of Delaware Press, 1998), p. 191. To Kenneth Muir, '*Hamlet* the play is all questions': 'The singularity of Shakespeare', in Bevington and Halio, *ibid.*, pp. 72–3, 91. Maynard Mack had elaborated this point in 'The world of Hamlet', *Yale Review*, 41 (1952), pp. 502–23.
7   Belsey, *The Subject of Tragedy*, p. 41.
8   Brian Vickers, *Appropriating Shakespeare* (Yale University Press, 1993), p. 338.
9   Harold Jenkins, Arden Shakespeare (London: Thomson Learning, 1982); Philip Edwards, New Cambridge Shakespeare (Cambridge University Press, 1985); and G. R. Hibbard New Oxford Shakespeare (Oxford University Press, 1987); John Lee, *Shakespeare's Hamlet and the Controversies of Self* (Oxford University Press, 2000); and N. N. Holland, who offers a survey in *Psychoanalysis and Shakespeare* (New York: Octagon Books, 1979.), pp. 163–206. A. Kirsch made a sensible use of Freud's views in 'Mourning and melancholia' in 'Hamlet's grief', *English Literary History*, 48:1 (1981), pp. 17–36. Janet Adelman's perceptive interpretation is so closely based on the text that it hardly requires an acceptance of the tenets of psychoanalysis; it confirms my views concerning the essential part played by sex nausea: cf. note 25 below. Janet Adelman, *Suffocating Mothers: Fantasies of Maternal Origin in Shakespeare's Plays*, Hamlet to The Tempest (London: Routledge, 1992). Most psychoanalysts after Freud 'continue to find the

idea of an organically unified psyche useful', and they have the support of neuroscientists: see N. N. Holland, S. Homan and J. Paris, eds, *Shakespeare's Personality* (University of California Press, 1989), p. 3. Lacanians, however, argue that 'identity is neither unified, autonomous, nor knowable, but the product and process of entrapment in representational and relational paradoxes alike': Barbara Freedman in *Shakespeare's Personality*, p. 259. Cf. Philip Armstrong, 'Watching *Hamlet* watching: Lacan, Shakespeare, and the mirror stage', in T. Hawkes, ed., *Alternative Shakespeares* (London: Routledge, 1996), vol. II, pp. 216–37.

10 Alastair Fowler, 'Shakespeare's Renaissance realism', *Proceedings of the British Academy*, 90 (1996), pp. 29–64.

11 See Harold Bloom, *Shakespeare: The Invention of the Human* (London: Fourth Estate, 1999).

12 In Stefan Collini, ed., *Interpretation and Over-interpretation: Umberto Eco with Richard Rorty, Jonathan Culler, Christine Brooke-Rose* (Cambridge University Press, 1992), p. 83.

13 As Bradshaw rightly insists in *Shakespeare's Scepticism*, p. 100.

14 Jenkins in the Arden Shakespeare edition of *Hamlet*, pp. 106–8. After all, Hamlet himself believed in the influence of 'some complexion': I, iv, 11 in Q2 (p. 688).

15 Robert Burton, *The Anatomy of Melancholy* (1621), pt I, sect. ii, mem. iv, subsect. 7. More general causes were 'passions and perturbations of the mind', 'the force of imagination' and 'sorrow' (pt. I, sect. ii, mem. iii, subsect. 1, 2, 4), which again fits Hamlet's case.

16 See *supra*, chapter 1, pp. 10–11.

17 *Hamlet*, II, ii, 295–301; cf. Bright, quoted by Jenkins in the Arden Shakespeare edition (p. 108) and the quotation from *The French Academie* (1594) given by Lily Campbell in *Shakespeare's Tragic Heroes* (Cambridge University Press, 1952.), p. 118: 'grief [...] causeth a man to hate & to be weary of all things, even of the light and of a mans selfe, so that he shall take pleasure in nothing but his melancholy'. Hamlet has lost the sense of wonder.

18 A note by Hibbard in his New Oxford edition of *Hamlet* calls attention to the proverb: 'A man is weal or woe as he himself thinks so' (p. 254).

19 Andrew Mousley, 'Hamlet and the politics of individualism', in M. T. Burnett and J. Manning, eds, *New Essays on Hamlet* (New York: AMS Press, 1994), p. 76.

20 Mousley recognizes his ability to 'try out and test truths'. *Ibid.*, p. 78.

21 Timothy Bright, *A Treatise of Melancholy* (1586), p. 200; quoted by Jenkins in the Arden Shakespeare edition of *Hamlet*, p. 106.

22 Cf. A. Kirsch, *The Passions of Shakespeare's Tragic Heroes* (Virginia University Press, 1990), p. 33, and the other critics cited by Fowler, 'Shakespeare's Renaissance realism', pp. 41–2. Alison Findlay argues for a 'tamed' madness; I would go no further than mental disturbance. Alison Findla, 'Hamlet: a document in madness', in Burnett and Manning, eds, *New Essays on* Hamlet, pp. 189–96.

23 Philip Maurice Davis, *Sudden Shakespeare: The Shaping of Shakespeare's Creative Thought* (London: Athlone, 1996), p. 86.
24 As Terence Cave notes, Freud 'is supplementing the text of the play, adding a recognition of his own': *Recognitions: A Study in Poetics* (Oxford: Clarendon Press, 1990), p. 175. John Rassell's argument based on identity formation in the 'pre-Oedipal' stage seems even more hazardous: *Hamlet and Narcissus* (University of Delaware Press, 1995).
25 Jacqueline Rose comments on Hamlet's 'sexual anxiety' from a different point of view in 'Sexuality in the reading of Shakespeare: *Hamlet* and *Measure for Measure*', in J. Drakakis, ed., *Alternative Shakespeares* (London: Methuen, 1985). Hamlet's sexual disgust is essential in Adelman's interpretation: *Suffocating Mothers*, pp. 17–18 and note 14. I had earlier insisted on the widespread 'sex nausea' in poetry and drama at the turn of the century in my *L'inspiration personnelle*, vol. III, pp. 52–70: its extent invites more than a purely psychological exploration centred on one character or on Shakespeare alone.
26 The term is not ambiguous in its context: why should he send her to a brothel?
27 Adelman, *Suffocating Mothers*, pp. 31–5. On Hamlet's rejection of the body, his mother's, Ophelia's and his own, see also Michel Remy, 'Hamlet: perte du corps et crise d'origine', in Gilles Mathis and Pierre Sahel, eds, *Hamlet, ou le texte en question* (Paris: Messene, 1997).
28 Particularly Stanley Cavell, *Othello: The Claims of Reason* (Oxford University Press, 1979), p. 494. Cavell himself notes that 'Shakespeare's heroes are incapable of taking their imperfections with the "gay and sociable wisdom" of Montaigne', in *Shakespeare and the Experience of Love* (Cambridge University Press, 1981), pp. 122–7, and 'Sexuality and marriage in Montaigne and *All's Well That Ends Well*', *Montaigne Studies*, 9 (1997), pp. 187–202. Arthur Kirsch offers safer parallels, but may overstate the influence of Montaigne: Kirsch, *The Passions of Shakespeare's Tragic Heroes*.
29 On the other hand, with his usual balance and clear-sightedness, Montaigne is aware of the ridiculous aspects of physical sex, the beast with two backs, and wonders, like Yeats, why love has pitched its tent in the house of excrement, lodging 'our joyes and our filthes together' (III, v: 991–2B; VS 877).
30 Cf. *Hamlet*, III, i, 124ff.; see also 'who shall scape whipping', II, ii, 533. Cf. *All's Well That Ends Well*, IV, iii, 74–7 on virtues 'whipped' by our faults and crimes 'cherished by our virtues'.
31 *Essays*, III, ii: 916 B; VS 813; *Hamlet*, II, ii, 573–80 and III, i, 123–30.
32 *Essays*, III, ii: 916 B; VS 813. Montaigne condemns the man 'that makes himselfe a horror to himselfe' (*Essays*, III, v: 994 B, my translation; III, 879) and even refuses to repent: 'My actions are squared to what I am and my condition. I cannot doe better' (III, ii: 916 B; VS 813).
33 Arthur Schopenhauer, *Die Kunst, glücklich zu sein*.
34 Bright, *Treatise*, p. 124; quoted by Jenkins in the Arden Shakespeare edition, p. 106.

35 *Essays*, II, 17: 743 A; VS 654; Petrarch, *Canzoniere*, cxxxv. Petrarch was also a forerunner of modern self-consciousness. Besides, 'conscience', a cause of Hamlet's hesitation (III, I, 85), was sometimes taken by Montaigne in a sense close to 'self-consciousness': see D. L. Schaefer, *The Political Philosophy of Montaigne* (Cornell University Press, 1990), pp. 329, 335.

36 Adelman, *Suffocating Mothers*, p. 32, ably argues that this opportunity to kill Claudius comes as 'an interruption of his fundamental purpose', which is to reclaim his mother. This interpretation does not contradict my views.

37 As Fortinbras will 'recast' Hamlet as a soldier in his stage directions (V, ii, 350); cf. Sinfeld, *Faultlines*, p. 250.

38 See Edwards' introduction in his New Cambridge edition of *Hamlet*, pp. 16–18. This balance was recognized by Graham Bradshaw in *Shakespeare's Scepticism* (Brighton: Harvester Press, 1987), pp. 6–10, but, to my mind, the text does not support the assumption that Hamlet's first response to the Captain's words really 'showed shock and moral revulsion'.

39 James Supple, *Arms Versus Letters: The Military and Literary Ideals in the Essais of Montaigne* (Oxford: Clarendon Press, 1985), p. 273.

40 Hibbard, New Oxford edition of *Hamlet*, p. 54.

41 Belsey, *The Subject of Tragedy*, p. 42. Other critics have the impression that 'Hamlet changes [...] from the undergraduate age to the near-maturity of thirty' (Fowler, 'Shakespeare's Renaissance realism', p. 34), but this would not create a 'second self'. Marjorie Garber's comparison with a 'rite of passage' is interesting: *Coming of Age in Shakespeare* (London: Routledge, 1997), p. 215.

42 *Hamlet*, I, ii, 129 and I, iii, 3; cf. V, i, 95–206.

43 Cf. V, i, 250–4 and I, ii, 76–86.

44 Here again I find myself in agreement with Janet Adelman's sensitive analysis of Hamlet's serenity acquired through the 'repossession' of the 'internal good mother' and 'the idealized father': *Suffocating Mothers*, p. 34.

45 As Harold Bloom insists in *Ruin the Sacred Truths* (Harvard University Press, 1989), ch. 3.

46 I agree with Sinfield's comment on Hamlet's 'amazing delivery from the pirates' (*Faultlines*, p. 227), but think his insistence on Calvinistic predestination and/or Stoic fatalism unjustified; Hamlet (like Graham Greene!) believes the soul's fate may be changed by a last-minute prayer or confession, which is irreconcilable with Calvinism.

47 Barker, *The Tremulous Private Body*, pp. 36–7.

48 As I suggested in chapter 1, and in *Genèse de la conscience moderne*, pp. 421–3.

49 Terry Eagleton, *William Shakespeare* (Oxford: Blackwell, 1986), p. 72.

50 Michel Grivelet, 'A portrait of the artist as Proteus', *Proceedings of the British Academy*, 61 (1975), p. 166.

51 Thomas Greene, 'The self in Renaissance literature', in P. Demetz, T. Greene and L. Nelson Jr, eds, *The Disciplines of Criticism* (Yale University Press, 1968), pp. 258–62.

52 Lee, *Shakespeare's Hamlet*, ch. 8.

53 Sinfield, *Faultlines*, pp. 64–6.
54 *The Winter's Tale*, IV, i, 1–2. Concerning the common origin *Veritas filia temporis*, see Erwin Panofsky, *Studies in Iconology* (New York: Harper and Row, 1962).
55 I, i, 74. The 'joys' procured by 'the most precious square of sense' may allude to 'the forfended place', the female genital region: Regan seems to renounce the strongest pleasures of the senses in favour of love for her father.
56 See *Essays*, II, viii, on the tyranny of fathers who 'deprive their children of their natural share of the property during their long lifetime' (445 A).
57 Sir John Fortescue, *De laudibus legum Angliae* (1546). When his daughters reveal themselves to be monstrous, Lear wishes to believe them illegitimate: see I, iv, 218; and II, ii, 302–3.
58 Particularly Peter Brook in his 1971 film, James Dunn in California (1960) and Jan Bull in Norway (1971).
59 '*King Lear*: a tragedy of wrath in old age' is the title of ch. 14 in Campbell's *Shakespeare's Tragic Heroes*.
60 See Cave, *Recognitions*, pp. 159–60.
61 He is one of the 'player kings' studied by Anne Barton Righter, *Shakespeare and the Idea of the Play* (London: Penguin, 1962).
62 Blaise Pascal, *Pensées*, II, 82.
63 This passage may have been influenced by Montaigne's description of man as 'sophisticated' in Florio's translation (vol. III, p. 305; Screech, III, xii: 1188 B).
64 Robert Ellrodt, 'Introït: *King Lear* revisited', in François Laroque, Pierre Iselin and Sophie Alatorre, eds, *'And That's True Too': New Essays on King Lear* (Cambridge: Cambridge Scholars Publishing, 2009), pp. 6–33.

Chapter 5

Subjective time in Montaigne and Shakespeare

1. From Antiquity to Montaigne

Chapter 2 traced the progress of subjectivity in the awareness of the passions and the exploration of the self from Antiquity to the Renaissance. This evolution had a consequence for the perception of time, but the change may be analysed more briefly, since its effects were not so complex and neither Montaigne nor Shakespeare initiated it.

Like the experience of self-consciousness, the conception of time was originally characterized by its objectivity. In her scholarly study *Montaigne et le problème du temps* Françoise Joukovski acknowledged this.[1] According to the ancient philosophers, time was either movement, or something moved, or something related to movement, as Plotinus himself pointed out (*Enneads*, III, vii, 7). Plato had been interested in the relations between time and the cyclical movements of the planets. Considered as a visible manifestation of the eternal, time was 'a moving image of eternity' (*Timaeus*, 37 c–d). Its mathematical nature also made it a projection of the intelligible onto the world of appearances, but this projection was described as if it were effected outside human consciousness. In this global time, divisible only after the manner of a melody, there was no privileged instant. Yet the instant will play an essential role when attention is focused on the perception of time by human consciousness.

Time was the measure of movement in Aristotelian physics. Though still related to the motions of the heavens, it was mainly considered from an earthly perspective. And since time was a measure, it could not exist without an operation of the human mind. This, however, Aristotle limited to measuring the interval between two instants (*Physics*, IV, 223a). Duration was thus reduced to a succession of instants without any extension, making it analogous to an abstract numerical series.[2] Pierre Aubenque argues:

The whole Aristotelian philosophy of time rests on the notion of the permanence of the now, for, without this permanence, time would be nothing since the past is no longer and the future has no existence yet, and what is a compound of nonbeing must be nonbeing too.[3]

Montaigne took up this argument.[4] But where Aristotle 'dissolved time in his effort to isolate the instant as an indivisible point', the author of the *Essays* recovered the 'compactness of the present' through his own subjective experience of duration.[5] The intellectual and logical definition of the structure of time in Aristotelian physics did not invite a careful observation of the succession of impressions in an individual consciousness.

Plotinus showed himself well informed about the confusion of time with 'numbers of movement or measure' when he reviewed all the theories, refuted them and set forth his own explanation of the origin of time. This denoted an evolution towards a subjective approach (*Enneads*, III, 7, 7–10). He suggested there was in the World Soul, a 'restlessly active nature', an 'unquiet power' that 'did not want the whole [of the intelligible world] to be present to it all together'. Its desire of variety and succession gave birth to the uninterrupted continuity of time: 'since the world of sense moves in Soul [...] it moves also in the time of Soul'.[6]

Time as a subjective phenomenon thus had its origin in the soul, the World Soul, one of the three Plotinian hypostases. This argumentation was not based on the workings of an individual human consciousness. As the activity of an ever existing soul, time remained independent of the human mind that apprehends it. Moreover, it is clear that Plotinus focused his attention on a conceptual object, as Greek thought had always done previously. If this soul 'turned back to the intelligible world and to eternity, and rested quietly there, what would there still be except eternity?' (III, 7, 12, p. 143). In this return to unity, 'time is abolished' (III, 7, 12, p. 145). In the *Enneads*, however, to the Greek concept of being a sense of life seems to be associated, for the eternity to which the soul aspires is defined as 'a life wholly present, together and full' (III, vii, 3).[7] The pulse of existence begins to beat in the motionless essence. Yet, at the end of this treatise, 'On eternity and time', to the question 'is time, then, also in us?' the answer is: 'It is in the universal soul and, by conformity, in all the souls; accordingly time will not be dispersed among them, no more than eternity is dispersed among beings of the same form' (III, vii, 13).[8]

More than the Platonizing philosophers, the Stoics and the Epicureans, or at least their Latin interpreters, paid attention to the personal experience of time in an individual consciousness. They stressed the importance of the instant, no longer abstractly or mathematically conceived, but as a moment of personal experience. Their discussions on time were enriched with subtle psychological observations which apparently seduced Montaigne.[9] The *Essays* alternately praise the Stoic firmness manifested as a mastery over the instant and the Epicurean invitation to the full enjoyment of a pleasurable moment.[10] Their incitements, however, were dictated by a practical wisdom which is still present in the *Essays*, but in association with an interest in the self far less evident in the writings of the Ancients.

As in the case of self-consciousness, Augustine more deeply analysed and interiorized the perception of time than his predecessors. In the *Confessions*, he defined time as an activity of the individual soul, not the World Soul. He still placed the process of becoming in the created world at its origin, but he tried to discern the nature and the effects of time on the activities of his own mind, in a manner that betrayed his anxieties over the subject. Starting from his experience of measure in poetry, he came to conceive time as a *distensio animi*: 'time is nothing else but a stretching out in length; but of what, I know not, and I marvel [wonder], if it be not of the very mind'.[11] Through the action of memory and anticipation, time is thus measured in the individual mind and allows it to govern a disorderly flood of impressions (XI, xxvii; Watts, vol. II, p. 272). Though he admitted that neither the future nor the past has 'any being', Augustine thought it more accurate to say that 'there be three times: a present time of past things; a present time of present things; and a present time of future things'. These three times are in our souls and 'otherwhere do I not see them' (XI, xx; Watts, vol. II, p. 253). Philosophical reflection, particularly the Aristotelian analysis, had reduced the present 'instant of time' to a particle which 'flies with such full speed from the future to the past, as that it is not lengthened out with the very least stay' (XI, xv; Watts, vol. II, p. 243). Yet, when we sing a well known air, 'the present attention conveys over the future into the past: by the diminution of the future, the past gaining increase; even till by the wasting away of the future, all grows into the past' (XI, xxvii; Watts, vol. II, p. 275). This is an intuition of a present perceived, not merely conceived. It may be also an anticipation of the modern phenomenological conception of a dense or 'outspread' present moment 'oriented toward an emerging perception, or momentarily preserving a vanishing experience'.[12]

When tackling the problem of time, medieval scholasticism chose to lay stress on its logical, mathematical and metaphysical aspects rather than on psychological experience. The thirteenth-century Aristotelians defined time as 'the number of movement before and after'.[13] According to Thomas Aquinas 'the intellect is above time which numbers the motions of corporal things'.[14]

The Nominalists, whom Montaigne sometimes followed, took more interest in the psychological aspects. For Occam, 'the term time designates the primary movement – continuous and uniform – of the heavens', but it 'consignifies the soul and the actions by which the soul numbers what comes before and after in movement'. In the fourteenth century, God is 'remote and rejected into an inconceivable eternity unrelated to time'.[15] This disconnection may have favoured a concentration of attention on human time.

Narrative fiction in the Middle Ages was at first 'wholly a literature of the past'.[16] Progressively, however, through the presence of the author in the opening lines of a story situated in the past, the attention of the reader of a song, a romance and especially a 'Dit' (a familiar tale), will be called to the present time.[17] The author will 'find the matter of the poem in the circumstances of life, in the present and in the presence of life'. For Rutebeuf, for example, this time may be 'the real time, the date of a particular event' such as the marriage of the poet.[18] Thus, what will be partly recovered is the dramatization of a moment of experience which had been present in the lyrical poems and the satires of Antiquity.[19] In the same way, an identification of the narrator and his *persona* at a particular moment of his life occurs in the *Divina commedia* when the poet says 'Nel mezzo del cammin di nostra vita / mi ritrovai' (*Inferno*, I, 1), and Beatrice will confirm it when she will address him as 'Dante' (*Purgatorio*, XXX, 55).

A confirmation of this tendency to privilege present subjective time will be found in the Renaissance authors. Yet they also took up again the major objective themes of Antiquity: the cycles of the seasons and labours in the fields, the blessings and ruins of time, the decline of age, poetic immortality. From a historical perspective the dominant theme was Machiavelli's blunt assertion in *The Prince* that 'time brings forth all things'. There is little originality in these considerations, apparently dictated by convention rather than by any personal exploration of the nature and the effects of time. More personal was the recollection of the moment of *innamoramento* described by Dante at the beginning of the *Convivio* and insistently invoked throughout Petrarch's *Canzoniere*. In the celebration of Laura, as in the Roman elegies, a definite moment in a definite setting is often recreated. When reproducing the ebb and flow of his inner life, Petrarch creates a sense of duration, heightened by the frequent recall of an increasing distance from his first vision of Laura. The present is thus invested with the depth and homogeneity of a life in which the past determines the future:

> Life flees before, not stopping on the way,
> and death with daylong marches follows fast,

and all things present join with all things past
and with the future to make war on me;
forethought and memory bring such dismay,
now one and now the other, that at last,
but for self-pity that still holds me fast,
I would already from these thoughts be free.[20]

Petrarch is a man encircled and besieged by time. In the French poetry of the Renaissance I have found fewer examples of this inner apprehension of fleeting impressions. Du Bellay's *Regrets* about 'three unbearably long years' were sincere but unattended by an exploration of his mind.[21] The greatest poet, Ronsard, openly cultivated 'the art of well Petrarchizing' in *Les amours de Cassandre*.[22] He also never tired of alluding to 'L'an mil cinq cens avec quarante et six' (*Cassandre*, CXXX), the year 1546, and 'the day on which an eye in the April of her age / Shot a thousand arrows into his flank' (LIX).[23] But the allusions to the passage of time, chronologically out of order,[24] rather invite us to question the reality of this passion. Ronsard himself considered that 'it is very necessary for the poet never to follow truth step by step in his art, but only care for verisimilitude'.[25] When 'time is treated in a mythical mode', as Bellenger observes, 'it can hardly be subjective'.[26] Ronsard's *Hymns* explore long mythical periods which are wholly impersonal. The poet's individuality asserts itself only through his obsession with immortality and his anxious apprehension of the flight of time.[27]

In prose, Rabelais rebelled against the regulation of time imposed by religious orders: 'Gargantua used to say that the greatest waste of time that he knew was to watch the clock'.[28] Yet he never pondered on his own perception of time and in the *Tiers livre* his consciousness, engaged in space, 'mainly seeks to apprehend itself outside itself'.[29]

By contrast, Montaigne was mainly interested in subjective time: the time of his life, the present moment. The past and Plutarch's illustrious men, no doubt, fascinated him, but not from a historical perspective: they provided examples for an interpretation of the present. His essential ambition, his self-portrait, did not call for general considerations of the universal effects of time: he enclosed himself in his life span. Mentioning his year of birth, 1533, he adds precision: 'between eleven and noon the last day of February' (II, xx: 93 A; VS 84). In several places he evokes his family origins, his father, his childhood, his education. He describes the rooms of his house in which he spends 'most days of [his] life, and most hours of each day' (III, iii: 933 C; VS 828). He paints himself ageing while writing his essays (II, xxxvii: 958 A; VS 759) and notes the effects: 'having long since passed forty […]. From now on, what I shall be is but half a being; it will no longer be me' (II, xvii: 729–30 A; VS 641–2); he has 'fallen from excessive gaiety into excessive seriousness' (III, v: 948 B; VS 841); he can only offer 'the droppings of an old mind' (III, ix: 1070 B; VS 946), a mind which 'becomes constipated and squat' (II, xii: 1198 B; VS 1057); his memory is 'growing cruelly worse every day' (III, ix: 1089 B; VS 962); he notes 'I belong entirely to the past [...]. Time is quitting me' (III, x: 1142–3 C; VS 1010–11). He, however, maintains that 'it is the privilege of the mind to escape from old age' (III, v: 951 B; VS 844). This is, indeed, his own, highly personal time, a time he feels as intensely as Shakespeare does in his *Sonnets*.

This time, which leads to death, can also prove a theme for a *leitmotif* enriched with literary and historical illustrations, with appeals to the Stoics, to the Epicureans and Lucretius. A thoughtful obsession with his own prospect of death is, however, perceptible when Montaigne asks: 'Can we ever rid ourselves of thoughts of death or stop imagining that death hath us by the scruff of the neck at every moment?' (I, xx: 95 A; VS 85). That is why 'Your life's continual task is to build your death' (I, xx: 103 C; VS 93). Nevertheless, his conclusion is that 'death is the ending of life, but not therefore its End' (III, xii: 1191 C; VS 1051). It fascinated Montaigne because this instant can be an ultimate assertion of our personal identity.[30] Yet he had also discovered that a sense of fullness could be attained in any moment of life and that the wise man should not let these opportunities slip. He had originally thought that the instant could provide 'a determination of the self through constancy'.[31] He seems, however, to have always lived 'from day to day', aware of 'the value of pleasure, plaything or pastime' (III, iii: 934 B–C; VS 829).

In the essay 'An apology for Raymond Sebond', when tackling philosophical problems, Montaigne apparently followed Aristotle when he denied any reality to time:

> Time is a thing of movement, appearing like a shadow in the eternal flux and flow of matter, never remaining stable or permanent, to Time belong the words *before* and *after*, *has been* and *shall be*, words that show at a glance that Time is evidently not a thing which is. (II, xii: 682 A; VS 603)

Yet, though past and future have no existence, Montaigne will restore reality to the present moment when apprehended *hic et nunc* by his consciousness. When he considers his own life he can declare:

> When I see my span so short, I want to give it more ballast, I want to arrest the swiftness of its passing by the swiftness of my capture, compensating for the speed with which it drains away by the intensity of my enjoyment. (III, xiii: 1263 B; VS 1111)

This resolution appears the more daring since, although a Christian, Montaigne opened no eschatological perspective. In his meditation on human life he even dared to ask: 'why do we give the dignity of *being* to that instant which amounts to no more than a flash of lightning against the infinite course of an eternal night?' (II, xii: VS 526).[32]

In the Platonic or Aristotelian tradition and in Christian thought, time was always conceived in relationship to the divine and the everlasting. With the exception of the 'Apology' and a few passages in other essays, Montaigne showed little interest in these relations. When he mentions them, it is always in order to introduce an irremediable separation between the temporal and the eternal, between becoming and being. Yet, while describing the passage of time and laying stress on the evanescence of the present, he came to confer its proper fullness to the instant, though unconnected with the eternal.

2. Shakespearean time in the *Sonnets*

The usual commonplaces on the universal aspects of time are often evoked objectively in the plays of Shakespeare as well as in the *Sonnets*. There is no clear assertion of his originality in this field, and from a thematic point of view there is probably little to add to previous studies. As in my study of John Donne and the Metaphysical poets, my aim is to discover constant subjective structures.[33] My search is not based on a philosophical and literary structuralism averse to the recognition of personality: I am concerned with permanent individual modes of perception and thought, imagination and sensibility which are not altered by the evolutions, larger changes and even conversions that may occur in the life, the inspiration and the style of a writer.

Concerning the Metaphysical poets, it appeared that the present was dominant, with the exception of Henry Vaughan. However, the dense, dynamic present of Donne and George Herbert, concentrating on an instant loaded with life and substance, is not the timeless present of Lord Herbert, a discontinuous succession of empty moments. It is different, too, from the static and boundless present of Thomas Traherne. And both Andrew Marvell and Richard Crashaw seem to struggle in order to impose the rhythms of human aspirations on a continuously gliding or ever fluid present.

In a historical comparison with other periods, this very diversity reveals an evolution and is in keeping with a stronger assertion of individual subjectivity. An attempt to discern the constant and distinctive features of Shakespeare's apprehension of time will therefore require a confrontation with his predecessors and his contemporaries. Just as I discovered various ways of perceiving time in the poetry of Donne and his successors, Ricardo Quinones has later called attention to the emergence of an increasing variety of attitudes to time in Renaissance authors.[34] This diversity was placed by Quinones, and shortly after by Gary Waller,[35] within the frame of a general evolution which, after Dante and Petrarch, would have led to a 'laicisation of time' different from the earlier progression from 'Church's Time' to 'Merchant's Time' described by Jacques Le Goff.[36] From another perspective, Gisèle Venet has also traced the evolution of concepts from Augustine to the Reformation and studied various aspects of the 'conflict of temporalities' in the tragedies of Christopher Marlowe and John Marston, Shakespeare and John Webster.[37] To this unavoidable conjunction of the collective and the individual, the historical and the personal, critics should always be heedful.

The search for constant structures or individual traits, however, might be in vain if totally different approaches to time were discernible in the plays of Shakespeare at different moments, as Quinones and, to a lesser extent, Waller, argue.[38] An evolution in Shakespeare's 'conception' of time and its dramatic handling would be perceptible from the first to the second historical tetralogy, then in the tragedies, with a further change in the romances.[39] There is a large part of truth in these observations; yet, in my study of the Metaphysical poets, I have noticed the persistence of some structures despite obvious thematic or stylistic variations. With 'myriad-minded' Shakespeare, the demonstration of constancy proves more difficult. On the stage, one has to take dramatic requirements into consideration. Each character, when clearly individualized, may have a particular mode of expression. In an attempt to discover an idiosyncratic perception of time in Shakespeare's writings one has to start from his lyrical poems, for, with due reservations, they are more likely to reveal individual characteristics. I shall add only brief remarks on some plays when they apparently confirm the dominant features discerned in the *Sonnets*, and pass over the narrative poems, which obey their own conventions. The *Sonnets*, too, were influenced by conventions, but I have shown elsewhere how their author either departed from them or renovated them.[40]

A comparative study is required to bring out the personal characteristics of the perception of time in Shakespeare's *Sonnets*. I have examined the sonnet cycles composed by Sidney, Spenser and Daniel that Shakespeare may have read before writing his own sonnets (or a majority of them).[41]

A comparison with Petrarch's *Canzoniere* also proves necessary even in the probable absence of direct influence. Besides, in drawing constant parallels with Roman and Renaissance authors, J. B. Leishman has clearly brought out the similarities and the differences between Shakespeare and his predecessors or contemporaries in their approach to such themes as the reign of mutability, their defiance of time the destroyer, their search for a compensation, and their desire to confer immortality on the beloved. Yet his accurate analysis has not led him to ascribe personal and constant features to the Shakespearean imagination.[42]

One may first note a quantitative difference, though I am aware of its limited interest. Obviously attention is more often called to time and its effects in Shakespeare's sonnets than in the other cycles, even when including the *Canzoniere*. Petrarch's *Familiar Letters* do disclose an obsession with time, but chiefly with the right use of time in the perspective of a life beyond death.[43] In the *Canzoniere* attention is focused on the moment of *innamoramento* and its rememoration.[44] In a comparison with other Elizabethan sonneteers, one may notice the insistent recurrence of the conjunction *when* in the 126 sonnets written by Shakespeare for the young man, a sequence which may be isolated from the less coherent series of sonnets for or about the dark lady.[45]

Anne Ferry has called attention to the logical and almost syllogistic value of the construction 'when [...] then' in Shakespeare's sonnets 12, 15, 30 and 64: 'When I do count the clock that tells the time [...]. Then of thy beauty do I question make'. In a vast majority of cases, however, *when* has only a temporal value.[46] I can agree that Shakespeare imposes a verbal order on the temporal succession to create the timeless world of his art, yet reject the assumption that he turns it into a 'continuous present'.[47] In his sonnets, the present is at times haunted by the past, but more often projected towards the future, in suspense or expectation.

My reading of the *Sonnets* leads me to think that Shakespeare's intuition of time has two essential characteristics: a personal experience of time as a continuous and irreversible progression towards an end; and a simultaneous attention to phenomena of growth and decline. Time can be personified, and actually is, in a dozen sonnets,[48] but it is always a personal experience, not an allegorical figure.

Of course, time's flight is a universal theme. Augustine reminded us that the time of our life is nothing more than a race towards death in which no one is allowed to stop or slow down.[49] That Shakespeare should speak of time's 'continual haste' (sonnet 123), of 'never-resting Time' (sonnet 5), 'swift-footed Time' (sonnet 19) is not distinctive; it is a commonplace theme revivified only by the freshness of the phrasing, as in the abrupt metaphor 'what strong hand can hold his swift foot back?' (sonnet 65). What I find personal is the way in which the poet in the opening lines of many sonnets places himself in time and adopts its movement.

In his *Songs and Sonnets* Donne pitched himself in a present moment which, though definite and localized, opened – or seemed to open – access to the timeless.[50] In *Astrophel and Stella*, Sidney often chose to speak in the present moment – 'now' appears twenty-seven times – but seldom in a definite setting, and the episode or his emotion seldom opened on the future or any transcendence.[51] Spenser frequently isolated his emotion in an indefinite, motionless or iterative present in his *Amoretti*, delaying the expression of a wish or an expectation reserved to the final couplet.[52] In a few poems the narrative is wholly enclosed in the past.[53]

In his *Sonnets*, Shakespeare's imagination most often takes two directions regarding time: either in succession or simultaneously, starting from the past, or even from the future, to enter the present; or projecting from the present into the future. Accordingly, the present cannot have the same quality as in Montaigne's *Essays*; it is rarely self-sufficient.[54] The only privileged instants are moments of close intimacy with the friend, 'some special instant special blest', but these rare moments are 'in the long year set,/Like stones of worth [...] thinly placed' (sonnet 52). Neither punctual like Donne's, nor indefinite or immobile like Spenser's, the Shakespearean present tends to spread over a space of time: moments of anxious waiting (sonnets 57, 58) or a slow trip on horseback (sonnet 50). The poet will not call, like Sidney, 'Come, Sleep, O Sleep, the certain knot of peace';[55] he will make us aware of the unending length of a sleepless night (sonnets 27, 28, 61).

The present can also be a recurrent moment, several times repeated, or ever present, as a moment of meditation: 'When I consider every thing that grows'.[56] This moment, however, is often linked to a past which is still alive in the memory and may surge up again: 'When I have seen by Time's fell hand defaced/The rich proud cost of outworn buried age [...] This thought is as a death'.[57] Time passes, yet a whole space of time may be present in the poet's mind: 'For term of life thou art assurèd mine'.[58] Nevertheless, the anticipation of a future moment is also characteristic: 'When thou shalt be disposed to set me light' (sonnet 88). Donne also practises this kind of anticipation, but projects himself into it as if it were already realized;[59] Shakespeare keeps aware of the distance before reaching an expected moment and makes himself ready for it: 'Against that time (if ever that time come)', 'Against my love shall be as I am now' (sonnets 49, 63).[60] Many of the sonnets end on an expectation; they are never enclosed in a moment, though the final couplet creates a sense of closure. What is asserted is conclusive, yet still projected into the future: 'And all in war with Time for love of you / As he takes from you, I ingraft you new' (sonnet 15).

Sonnet 60 is a poem in which Shakespeare's distinctive perception of time may be traced:

> Like as the waves make towards the pebbled shore,
> So do our minutes hasten to their end,
> Each changing place with that which goes before,
> In sequent toil all forward do contend.
> Nativity, once in the main of light,
> Crawls to maturity, wherewith being crowned,
> Crooked eclipses 'gainst his glory fight,
> And Time that gave doth now his gift confound.

Apparently this sonnet expresses only a universal conception of time, traceable to Antiquity, since it echoes a speech ascribed to Pythagoras by Ovid which had often been echoed or paraphrased. Shakespeare's universality rests, I think, on his reliance on the most obvious impressions and the most natural emotions. Nothing here is apparently distinctive apart from the stylistic expressiveness, the forceful play on polysemous abstractions and abrupt metaphors. At first sight the opening lines only condense Golding's translation of the Ovidian text:

> Things ebb and flow, and every shape is made to passe away.
> The tyme itself continually is fleeting like a brooke.
> For neyther brooke nor lightsomme Tyme can tarry still. But looke,
> As every wave dryves other foorth, and that that commes behynd
> Both thrusteth and is thrust itself: Even so the tymes by kynd
> Do flye and follow bothe at once, and evermore renew.
> For that that was before is left, and streyght there dooth ensue
> Anoother that was never erst.

Yet slight differences become significant when attentively examined. To evoke universal transience, Pythagoras said that time flows like a continuous stream, and light hours (*levis hora*) no more than a stream can stay: a wave pushes another wave and that which is ahead is pressed by that which comes behind while pressing that which runs before.[61] In Shakespeare's sonnet the waves must be sea waves, since they break on a 'pebbled shore'. That Pythagoras in the preceding lines described himself as carried away on a vast sea may have influenced the imagination of the English poet, but could not dictate this transposition of the Ovidian image, a transposition which makes the comparison inaccurate, since the ebb and flow of the tide does not create the impression of a continuous stream.[62] Shakespeare's imagination here is focused only on the way in which the waves come after each other, to break and die isolated on the shore. When his attention turns to their 'end', he designedly hides the fact that, like the waves, the times 'evermore renew' as Ovid said.

This, I think, is Shakespeare's own way of conceiving and experiencing a universal mutability. In the *Sonnets*, and also in his plays, he is chiefly alive to the disappearance of an individual being. Like the young man he loved, any flower, any thing of beauty, and any human being, is unique, precious and mortal. In sonnet 15 his imagination embraces the whole universe, but a universe still perceived as a single object of contemplation, a theatrical stage, 'this huge stage' described by Prospero when he sees 'the great globe itself' dissolve and leave not 'a rack behind' (*The Tempest*, IV, i, 146–56); or again a single cloud, like the single cloud described by Hamlet (III, ii, 364–70); or by Antony when 'even with a thought / The rack dislims' (IV, xv, 2–11). We are far from a cosmic sense of life and even from the Neo-Platonic vision of a universe animated by a World Soul.

The irreversibility of time is not deterministic. The word 'fate', frequent in the tragedies, appears once only in the *Sonnets*.[63] As in Montaigne's *Essays*, an unpredictable fortune creates 'millioned accidents' (sonnet 115).[64] Summing up the tragedy of Hamlet, Horatio spoke of 'accidental judgments, casual slaughters' (V, ii, 56) and the freely chosen death of Cleopatra is 'that thing that ends all other deeds, / Which shackles accidents and bolts up change' (V, ii, 6–7). Shakespeare's conception of time is not dominated by an 'impersonal determinism' as Waller claimed.[65]

One thing is inevitable for all living beings: ageing, a prelude to death. Petrarch had felt this anxiety, awakened by the change on his face reflected in a looking-glass.[66] The theme is more widely used in Shakespeare's *Sonnets*. The consequences of ageing are seen in the whole world (sonnets 19, 60, 65), obvious in the young man though he seems for a while preserved from them (sonnets 7, 100 [l. 10], 108 [ll. 10–11], 126) and felt by the poet himself (sonnets 22, 62, 73, 138). His harping on the difference in age between himself and both the young man and the dark lady is a distinctive feature.[67] It is possible that he may be obeying a convention, yet the intensity of personal feeling seems genuine.[68]

Though swift-footed time carries all things to their end, different meanings can be attached to this progression. It may first give access to maturity, followed by a decline and extinction: 'men as plants increase, [...] / Vaunt in their youthful sap, at height decrease' (sonnet 15). The speech of Jaques on the seven ages in *As You Like It* (II, vii) and the monologue of Time in *The Winter's Tale* (IV, i) only revive various commonplaces. Shakespearean time, however, has more complex functions when it leads to what Hamlet calls 'readiness' and Edgar names 'ripeness' in the tragedies – an achievement of maturity before the extinction of life – whereas the romances seek a conjunction of death and birth: 'thou met with things dying, I with things new-born' (*The Winter's Tale*, III, iii, 110–11). This conjunction is anticipated in the *Sonnets* in which growth and decline are simultaneously envisaged. Yet the imagination can move along this cycle in one way or another and the tone changes. The first sonnets invite the young man to choose the ways of generation, for thus 'As fast as thou shalt wane, thou grow'st / In one of thine' (sonnet 11). He would thus, like Spenser's Adonis, 'by succession [be] made perpetual' (*Faerie Queene*, III, vi, 47, 6), with this difference: Spenser accepted change and death as a way to a cosmic regeneration,[69] whereas Shakespeare, too much concerned with the individual to consent to his disappearance, will drop this theme in the *Sonnets*. It is by the celebration of the young man in the poems that his perfection will survive, though time alters it: 'As he takes from you, I ingraft you new' (sonnet 15). This hope, however, never alters his perception of 'the wastes of time' (sonnet 12), nor his consciousness that 'every thing that grows / Holds in perfection but a little moment' (sonnet 15). Sonnet 126 is a melancholy adieu to the 'lovely boy' who has 'by waning grown', whereas his lovers were 'withering'. But it is also a reminder that nature, after heaping favours on him, will ultimately forsake him: 'Her audit (though delayed) answered must be / And her quietus is to render thee'.

The permanence of a personal and particular intuition of time in the writings of Shakespeare is disclosed in this simultaneous consciousness of two movements, growth and decline. The solar cycle is also an image of this double reality: 'the sun is daily new and old'.[70] And when he chooses to direct his gaze towards one object, his gaze remains horizontal. It does not rise, like Spenser's (at the end of the Mutability Cantos), to a world resting on the pillars of eternity.[71] And this brings Shakespeare closer to Montaigne.

The author of the *Essays* seeks to take hold of the present instant and give it more intensity (III, xiii: 1263 B; VS 1111), as in the 'special instant special blest' of Shakespeare's sonnet 52. In his first two books Montaigne relies on constancy to preserve these discontinuous moments of life, but in the third he chiefly insists on the enjoyment that can be found in each moment: 'when good, I do not want to "pass time", I savour and hold on to it' (III, xiii: 1262 B–C; VS 1111). This epicurean moment may be tasted even when imagining the approach of death, which will overwhelm him (III, ix: 1099 B; VS 971), a death which can be made 'luxurious', like Antony's and Cleopatra's, 'those fellows in death' (III, ix: 1113 B; VS 984), an evocation which may have caught the attention of Shakespeare.

Montaigne ascribed to man no 'permanent existence', since 'we have no communication with being' (III, xii: 680 A; VS 601), which is the attribute of a transcendent God. Combining scepticism and fideism, he recommended a *docta ignorantia* concerning impenetrable mysteries. That is why, protected by his faith (probably more sincere than some critics admit), he took no interest in eternity, while enjoying the ordinary moments of life so intensely. Shakespeare, who feels himself always carried along by the stream of time, cannot seek refuge in the present moment: he needs to forge for himself a special eternity in love and in poetry, for the world of his *Sonnets*, unlike Petrarch's in the *Canzoniere*, is wholly enclosed in time – in the totality of time, since the horizon is the end of time, and 'love bears it out to the edge of doom' (sonnet 116). 'So long as men can breathe or eyes can see', this love will live in the poem (sonnet 18). Yet the word 'eternal', whether used for brass or the poem, is an echo of the *perenius* of Horace and has no metaphysical implication.[72] In sonnet 122, 'lasting memory' is wanted to extend 'Beyond all date, even to eternity', but this ambition is corrected: 'Or, at the least, so long as brain and heart / Have faculty by nature to subsist'. In sonnet 77, a single line conjures up 'Time's thievish progress to eternity', but the poet never projects himself into this eternity as Petrarch had done, and he does not even indulge in the evocation of Cydnus or an Elysian field in which the loved one could be met (cf. *Antony and Cleopatra*, V, ii, 224–5, 282–3).[73] Love by itself and by its poetic expression creates a sense of eternity in the *Sonnets*. Hence the ambiguity of the words 'my love', which may designate either the beloved or the love felt for him, or combine both meanings. The beloved is mortal, the lover may be unfaithful, but in the solemn statement 'Let me not to the marriage of true minds / Admit impediment' (sonnet 116), the love which alters not 'when it alteration finds' is not a reciprocal love, always tainted with imperfection, but the poet's love, capable of realizing this miracle: 'That in black ink my love may still shine bright' (sonnet 65). This is not merely the classical proclamation of an immortality conferred on the beloved (who, paradoxically and deliberately, remains anonymous), nor even a poet's pretension to a literary immortality: it is the inner conviction that this love awakes by itself a sense of eternity enshrined in the poem. Not the fragile and melancholy hope – as in Keats's 'Ode to a nightingale' – that this voice, heard in ancient times, will be heard by all the generations to come, but, as Virginia Woolf experienced it through her heroine

Mrs Ramsay, reciting in solitude the sonnet 'from you have I been absent in the spring', the calm certainty of having, through the perfection of form, created an immutable essence, 'the essence sucked out of life and held rounded there – the sonnet'.[74]

Notes

1. F. Joukovski, *Montaigne et le problème du temps* (Paris: Nizet, 1972).
2. J. S. Callahan, *Four Views of Time in Ancient Philosophy* (Harvard University Press, 1948), pp. 194–5.
3. Pierre Aubenque on *Physics*, IV, 10, 217 b 32 – 218 a 6, in *Le problème de l'être chez Aristote* (Presses Universitaires de France, 1962), p. 436.
4. *Essays*, II, xii: 682 A: 'Time is evidently not a thing which is […]'.
5. Joukovski, *Montaigne et le problème du temps*, p. 121.
6. I use the translation by A. H. Armstrong, *Plotinus: In Seven Volumes* (Harvard University Press, 1995), III, vii, 11; p. 142.
7. I follow here the translation of E. Bréhier in *Plotin, Ennéades* (Paris: Belles Lettres, 1925), vol. III, p. 130.
8. Closer to Bréhier's translation, p. 148. In a footnote, however, Bréhier points out that this unity of all the souls 'does not absorb and contradict their individuality and might therefore leave a proper individual character to the duration of each soul': cf. *Enneads*, IV, 3, 2–7.
9. Joukovsky, *Montaigne et le problème du temps*, p. 41.
10. *Ibid*., pp. 38–45, 56.
11. *Saint Augustine's Confessions*, with an English translation by William Watts (1631) (Harvard University Press, 1960), XI, xxvi, vol. II, p. 269. Watts kept closer to the Latin text than most translators.
12. Gaston Berger, *Phénoménologie du temps* (Presses Universitaires de France, 1964), pp. 122, 128. Cf. the role of the instant in the poetry of Donne analysed in Ellrodt, *Seven Metaphysical Poets*, vol. II, p. 6.
13. See Miha Pintaric, *Le sentiment du temps dans la littérature française (XIIIe s. – fin du XVIe s.)* (Paris: Champion, 2002), p. 40.
14. Thomas Aquinas, II, *Sent.*, d. 15, q 1, a 3; quoted by Joukowsky, *Montaigne et le problème du temps*, p. 138, n. 57.
15. Pintaric, *Le sentiment du temps*, p. 45.
16. Zink, *La subjectivité littéraire*, p. 83.
17. *Ibid.*, p. 90.
18. *Ibid.*, pp. 111, 115.
19. See Ellrodt, *L'inspiration personnelle*, vol. III, pp. vi, 4.
20. Petrarch, *Canzoniere*, trans. A. Mortimer (London: Penguin, 2002), p. 272.
21. See Yvonne Bellenger, *Le temps et les jours dans quelques recueils poétiques du XVIe siècle* (Paris: Champion, 2002), p. 190. Nakam notes that Du Bellay and Ronsard are mainly concerned with perishable forms in the sphere of

history rather than in the time of matter, whereas Montaigne will be more deeply concerned with universal instability – and first of all, one may add, with the instability he discovered in himself, that time had become subjective. Nakam, *Le dernier Montaigne*, p. 69.

22 'Elégie à Cassandre', in *Ronsard: oeuvres complètes* (Paris: Pléiade, 1958), vol. I, p. 99, included in *Premier livre des Amours de Ronsard*.
23 Cf. *Cassandre*, XLVII, LXI, LXIV, LXXI, XCII, XCIII, CI, CX, CXI, CXII, CXLIV, CCXIV.
24 CII, 'depuis sept ans'; CXXII, 'six ans'; Madrigal, p. 70, 'trois ans'; CCXIX, 'l'an s'est tourné sept fois'.
25 In H. Lemonnier, ed., *Ronsard* (Paris: Société Des Textes Français Modernes, 1914–75), vol. XVI, p. 336.
26 Bellenger, *Le temps et les jours*, pp. 64–5.
27 *Ibid.*, pp. 162, 166.
28 Rabelais, *Gargantua*, ch. 50, in *Gargantua and Pantagruel*, trans. M. A. Screech (London: Penguin, 2006), p. 360.
29 Pintaric, *Le sentiment du temps*, p. 201.
30 See Ellrodt, *Seven Metaphysical Poets*, ch. 6.
31 Joukovski, *Montaigne et le problème du temps*, p. 41.
32 My translation, based on the texts of Thibaudet and Villey. Screech's substitution of 'light' for 'night' (p. 589) seems unsupported by any text I know.
33 See Ellrodt, *L'inspiration personnelle*; Ellrodt, 'Unchanging forms of identity'; Ellrodt, *Seven Metaphysical Poets*.
34 Ricardo Quinones, *The Renaissance Discovery of Time* (Harvard University Press, 1972), p. xiii: 'from every work one can deduce a time sense. But *time as a concept* [my italics] is essentially different in the *Purgatorio*, in Petrarch's *Rime*, his Letters, or his *Trionfi*, in Spenser's *Complaint* volumes and the much grander interludes, the *Bower of Bliss*, the *Garden of Adonis*, and the *Cantos of Mutabilitie*; in Shakespeare's sonnets and, in fact, almost all his plays'.
35 Quinones, *ibid.*, pp. 16ff.; Gary F. Waller, *The Strong Necessity of Time: The Philosophy of Time in Shakespeare and Elizabethan Literature* (La Haye: Mouton, 1976), ch. 3.
36 Jacques Le Goff, *Time, Work, and Culture in the Middle Ages*, trans. A. Goldhammer (University of Chicago Press, 1982).
37 Gisèle Venet, *Temps et vision tragique chez Shakespeare et ses contemporains* (Paris: Publications de la Sorbonne Nouvelle, 1985, 2002).
38 Quinones, *The Renaissance Discovery of Time*; Waller, *The Strong Necessity of Time*. Frederic Turner had offered a purely thematic approach in *Shakespeare and the Nature of Time* (Oxford: Clarendon Press, 1977).
39 Quinones, *The Renaissance Discovery of Time*, chs 8, 9, 10.
40 See Ellrodt, 'The inversion of cultural traditions in Shakespeare's sonnets'.
41 Daniel, however, proved so heavily indebted to Italian and French sonneteers that no definite personal tendency emerged, as A. C. Sprague noted in his edition of *Poems and a Defence of Rhyme* (London: Routledge and Kegan, 1950), p. xvi.

42 J. B. Leishman, *Themes and Variations in Shakespeare's Sonnets* (London: Hutchinson, 1961).
43 Quinones, *The Renaissance Discovery of Time*, pp. 106ff.
44 *Canzoniere*, poem 211; cf. poems 30 (l. 28), 50 (l. 55), 62 (l. 9), 79, 101 (l. 13), 107 (l. 7), 118, 122, 145 (l. 14), 212 (l. 12), 221 (l. 8), 271, 364. See *supra*, chapter 2, p. 45.
45 From 0.33 in Sidney's *Astrophel and Stella* and 0.45 in Spenser's *Amoretti*, the frequency of *when* rises to 0.65 in these sonnets.
46 See sonnets 2, 22, 30, 32, 43, 51, etc.
47 Anne Ferry, *All in War with Time: Love Poetry of Shakespeare, Donne, Jonson, Marvell* (Harvard University Press, 1975), pp. 13–15, 21.
48 Sonnets 12, 15, 16, 19, 55, 60, 64, 65, 115, 116, 123, 126.
49 Augustine, *City of God*, XIII, x. Quinones, in *The Renaissance Discovery of Time*, quotes a letter in which Petrarch paraphrases this text in almost Shakespearean terms, and cites *Familiares rerum libri*, ed. V. Rossi, 4 vols (Florence: Sansoni, 1935), XXI.12.
50 See Ellrodt, *L'inspiration personnelle*, vol. I, pp. 82–94, or Ellrodt, *Seven Metaphysical Poets*, ch. 6.
51 For Sidney, in the first instance, see sonnets 4, 9, 16, 21, 30, 35, 46, 48, 49, 50, 54, 55, 56, 58, 60, 61, 72, 73, 76, 79, 80, 84, 88, 89, 91, 94, 106. In the second, see sonnets 3, 14, 18, 19, 27, 28, 31, 32, 34, 37, 40, 41, 44, 67, 68, 69, 70, 81, 85, 86, 101, 107.
52 For Spenser, in the first instance, this is true of forty-seven sonnets out of eighty-nine. Some sonnets, besides, are devoted to a special day recurrently mentioned after the manner of Petrarch, though in a much shorter period (see sonnets 4, 22, 60, 68, 70, 80). In the second instance, see *Amoretti*, 6, 7, 10, 14, 24, 25, 26, 32, 36, 43, 49, 51, 52, 57, 66, 71, 73, 82, 85.
53 *Amoretti*,16, 39, 50, 64, 67, 76, 77, 87.
54 With Montaigne, however, the instant, too, may be correlated with the past and the future for its fulfilment: see Joukovski, *Montaigne et le problème du temps*, p. 122.
55 Sidney, *Astrophel and Stella*, sonnet 39.
56 Sonnet 15; cf. sonnets 12, 22, 29, 30, 33, 43, 47, 75, 78, 80, etc.
57 Sonnet 64; cf. sonnets 31, 113, 115, 119, 120.
58 Sonnet 92; cf. sonnets 102, 104, 105, 108, 123, 124.
59 See Ellrodt, *L'inspiration personnelle*, vol. I, p. 83; Ellrodt, *Seven Metaphysical Poets*, p. 112.
60 He may wish, however, for a conjunction of the future moment with the present moment: 'Then hate me when thou wilt, if ever, now' (sonnet 90).
61 Ovid, *Metamorphoses*, XV, 198–205: 'Cuncta fluunt omnisque vagans formatur imago, / Ipsa quoque assiduo labuntur tempora motu, / Non secus ac flumen; neque enim consistere flumen / Nec levis hora potest; sed ut unda impellitur unda / Urgeturque eadem veniens urgetque priorem, / Tempora sic fugiunt pariter pariterqur sequuntur / Et nova sunt semper; nam quod fuit ante relictum est / Fitque quod haud fuerat momentaque cuncta novantur.'

62 Briefly paraphrasing the Ovidian image on two occasions, Chaucer retained the image of a running stream: 'the tyme wasteth night and day [...] / As soth the streaem, that turneth never agayn, / Descending fro the montaigne to playn' (*Canterbury Tales*, group B, 3, 'The wordes of the Hoost to the companye', ll. 19–24); and 'As water that doun renneth ay' (*The Romaunt of the Rose*, ll. 369–85).
63 Sonnet 29, l. 4. There are 114 occurrences of the word 'fate' in the plays.
64 Montaigne mentions 'fortune' 349 times in the *Essays*. 'Fortune' is mentioned nine times in the sonnets (14, l. 5; 25, l. 3; 29, l. 1; 32, l. 3; 37, l. 3; 90, ll. 3, 12; 111, l.1; 124, l. 2) and 513 times in the plays.
65 Waller, *The Strong Necessity of Time*, p. 88. Yet Waller himself admits that in Shakespearean tragedy 'events continue in their unpredictable way' (p. 397).
66 'Dicemi spesso'; *Canzoniere*, poem 361.
67 In sonnets 22, 37, 62, 63, 73, 110 (l. 7), 138 (ll. 10–12); see John Klause, 'Shakespeare's *Sonnets*: age in love and the goring of thoughts', *Studies in Philology*, 80 (1993), pp. 300–23.
68 Petrarch, too, felt old when looking at himself in a mirror (*Canzoniere*, poem 361), but only when approaching the end of his life; Shakespeare's particular and rather premature insistence may be due to his aesthetic sensibility rather than a literary convention.
69 See Quinones, *The Renaissance Discovery of Time*, pp. 259–60; or Robert Ellrodt, *Neoplatonism in the Poetry of Spenser* (Geneva: Droz, 1960), pp. 66–81.
70 Sonnet 76; cf. sonnets 7, 33, 59.
71 See Edmund Spenser, 'Two Cantos of Mutabilitie: Which, both for Forme and Matter, appeare to be parcell of some following Booke of the Faerie Queene, under the legend of Constancie' (published with the folio edition of *The Faerie Queene*, 1609).
72 Horace, *Odes*, III, 30: 'Exegi monumentum aere perennius'.
73 Petrarch, *Canzoniere*, poems 126, 191, 355, etc.; cf. the 'Triumph of Eternity' in Petrarch's *Il Trionfi*.
74 Sonnet 98; Virginia Woolf, *To the Lighthouse* (London: Hogarth Press, 1927), part I, ch. 19.

Chapter 6
Scepticism and stable humanistic values

Obviously discernible in the *Essays* of Montaigne, the influence of the sceptical currents of thought which ran through the Renaissance has also been traced in the works of Shakespeare by many commentators. It is possible that this may have been overestimated. Therefore, just as I have called attention in the preceding chapters to the persistence of some features in the personality of Montaigne and the stage characters of Shakespeare despite their flexibility and their evolutions, I intend to demonstrate that these authors, though playing with sceptical notions, constantly adhered to values that may be called at once humanistic and modern, in both senses of these terms.

Milton praised Shakespeare's 'native woodnotes wild' in *L'Allegro*. Nevertheless, though not so extensive as Montaigne's, Shakespeare's debt to classical authors can no longer be called into question. It has been fully explored, notably in the critical work of T. M. Baldwin, Jonathan Bate and Robert Miola.[1] I therefore call attention only to an illuminating detail. In *As You Like It* (III, iii, 6) the fool, Touchstone, finding himself among goats in the Forest of Arden, plays upon homophones to compare himself to Ovid, exiled among the Goths. Acquired in the excellent grammar school of Stratford, Shakespeare's spontaneous familiarity with the authors and celebrated figures of Antiquity allowed him to make them vividly present as a dramatist. The literary culture of Renaissance readers often rested on allusions to the best-known texts of Antiquity and the Holy Writ. Moreover, the great humanist Erasmus, mentioned in the *Essays* (III, ii: 913 C; VS 310), compiled *Adagia* and *Apophthegms*.[2] Shakespeare's wisdom, often proverbial, was also in temper with his times.[3] This familiarity is why the profusion of classical quotations did not deter him from reading the *Essays* of Montaigne.

Although his reading in the classics was not as extensive as Montaigne's, it is interesting to notice that both took a keen interest in Ovid, whose

Metamorphoses the author of the *Essays* had read with delight in his youth (I, xxvi: 197 A; VS 175).[4] There appears also a keen interest in the historians Titus Livius and Plutarch, in whose works they both sought rather 'a true account of [Brutus'] chat with his private friends in his tent on the eve of a battle than the oration which he delivered next morning to his army' (II, x: 465 A; VS 415).[5] Both the essayist and the dramatist must have found Plutarch's usual manner of 'sustained doubt and indecision' congenial (II, xii: 626 A; VS 556). Besides, they seem to have responded in the same way to the Stoic aspiration to constancy despite the differences subtly analysed by Geoffrey Miles.[6]

These contiguities are generally known and agreed upon. Nor is it new to consider Montaigne and Shakespeare as humanists in a philosophical sense. But recent studies have laid stress on a scepticism, or pragmatism, which would exclude all fixed structure of truth or knowledge and acknowledge only 'relatively stable' values – notably in the analyses of Graham Bradshaw, Stanley Cavell, Lars Engle, Hugh Grady and John Lee.[7] Now, although the essayist and the dramatist have undisputed affinities in their emphasis on diversity and mutability, they also agree in their defence and illustration of constant values which I consider 'humanistic' and which prove particularly 'modern'.

To propose a modern conception of 'humanism' I take as a starting point the definition advanced by Tzvetan Todorov, whose *Jardin imparfait* offers a panorama of humanistic thought from Montaigne and René Descartes to the present age. Dismissing any reduction of the concept to mere 'humaneness', he put forward three characteristics described as 'the universality of the they, the finality of the you, and the autonomy of the I'.[8] The autonomy of the 'I' requires an agreement on its existence and its permanence, a problem which called for the debate in my first chapter. The finality of the 'you' is a notion of little help in the present study since Montaigne focuses his attention on himself. Instead, I shall substitute for it 'comprehension of the other', a disposition which, with Montaigne and Shakespeare, tends towards an identification rather than a recognition of otherness and of one's 'responsibility for the other' as in the *Humanism of the Other* advocated by Emmanuel Lévinas.[9] Now, 'comprehension of the other' may lead to compassion for the other, as well as the 'finality of the you'. One recovers thus the moral meaning of humanism, and even the humanitarian meaning discarded by Todorov, though it perfectly suits Montaigne's bent when he uses the term 'inhumanité' (I, xiv: VS 53)[10] to denounce 'the worst species of vice' (III, ix: 1083 B; VS 956), anticipating the condemnation of 'man's inhumanity to man' by Robert Burns. Shakespeare, as we shall see, was in harmony with this view. To acknowledge the 'universality of the they' means you admit that an individual experience can be universalized, which will require coping with the problem of 'essence'. It also implies the existence of universal values and the possibility of applying rules to all people and all communities at any moment of history.

At first glance, Montaigne's interest in Pyrrhonism, a philosophy which denies any possibility of certainty, seems to exclude this universality. As Claude Lévi-Strauss argues, 'that Montaigne is a thorough sceptic is beyond question'.[11] Yet his interest in Pyrrhonism was chiefly manifested within the frame of an 'Apology of Raymond Sebond', which mainly aimed at contesting all dogmatic positions. Montaigne was aware of the difference between those sceptics who disbelieved in the very existence of truth and the Pyrrhonists, who advocated a suspension of judgement called 'epoché'. He states that according to the 'Academicians', from Arcesilas and Carneades to Cicero, 'truth is swallowed up in deep abysses where Man's vision cannot penetrate' (II, xii: 633 A; VS 561). But the author of the *Essays* does not only proclaim his preference for Pyrrhonism; he goes beyond it when he acknowledges the existence of a truth whose 'essence [...] is to be constant and uniform' and admits 'fortune arranges for a little of it to come into our possession', though corrupted by our weakness (II, xii: 622 A; VS 553). He assumes nevertheless that this world is but a school of enquiry (III, viii: 1051 C; VS 928), and 'no desire is more natural than the desire of knowledge', adding that 'truth is so great a matter that we must not disdain any method which leads us to it' (III, xiii 1207 B; VS 1065). He is conscious that the notions he himself is 'propounding have no form and reach no conclusion' and declares he is 'seeking the truth not laying it down' (I, lvi: 355 A; VS 317). His aim, however, is not to reach the Pyrrhonian ataraxy, or tranquillity, freeing man from worry. It is only in some pages of the 'Apology' that he leaves us under the impression that no kind of certain knowledge is attainable. We should note, though, that the celebrated question 'what's the truth limited by these mountains if it is a lie for the world beyond?' (II, xii: 653 C; VS 579; my translation) bears on the diversity of laws and customs, not on the distinction between the real and the false.[12]

The systematic survey of the shortcomings of reason and the errors of the senses in the 'Apology', like the demonstration of the superiority of animals over man, has some analogy with those paradoxes in prose cultivated by Renaissance writers from Francesco Berni to Donne.[13] Moreover, Terence Cave has resorted to a comparison with a rhetorical figure, antiperistasis, cultivated by poets contemporary with Montaigne. He showed that in the 'Apology' there is not simply a *coincidentia oppositorum* but 'a movement of transvaluation which allows the mind to adopt successively – if not simultaneously – two, or even several attitudes though radically different'. This would account for the unexpected final rejection of the epistemological pessimism displayed in the 'Apology'. The obvious contradiction between the elaborate sceptical argument and the sudden return to orthodoxy at the end should, according to Cave, preserve us from the temptation of 'ascribing a radical and anachronistic Pyrrhonisn to the writers of this period'.[14]

Another fundamental contradiction may be discovered in the progress of a speculation which starts from a proclamation of the necessity of faith to embrace 'the high mysteries of our religion' (II, xii: 492A; VS 441). Observation, however, reveals that Christians who profess to be believers do not hesitate to commit sinful acts to such an extent that their conduct is worse than that of Moslems or pagans. Furthermore, they are often led to hatred, cruelty and ambition by a pretended religious zeal. Hence this lapidary conclusion, which Lucretius might have inspired:[15] 'Our religion was made to root out vices: now it cloaks them, nurses them, stimulates them' (II, xii: 495 C; VS 444).[16] Since a faith which comes to 'dwell within us as something infused, beyond the natural order' (492 A; VS 441) should keep us off these vices, one is compelled to assume that a great majority of Christians do not possess this faith. Montaigne does not say it explicitly, but their behaviour implies that they are not in good faith when they pretend their actions are guided by this faith. The detection of a human propensity to self-deceit about one's own motives or the origin of one's passions breeds a scepticism unrelated to the scepticism of pagan philosophers; it proceeds from an attention to the inner life akin to Christian self-scrutiny.

There are other reasons not to exaggerate the influence of Pyrrhonism on the thought of Montaigne. Pyrrho and the Sceptics are mentioned only some twenty times in the *Essays*, and almost exclusively in the 'Apology'.[17] There are more than 200 mentions of Plato and Platonism, often, I admit from a critical point of view, especially concerning the doctrine of Ideas, but the author of the *Republic* and the *Laws* is declared a 'master-theoretician of all political government' (III, ix: 1078 C; VS 925). Géralde Nakam points out that Pyrrho, after playing a prominent part in the original, 1580 edition of the *Essays*, is in the second book only a prefiguration of Socrates.[18] Besides, when advocating doubt, Montaigne invokes St Augustine: 'I am of Saint Augustine's opinion, that in matters difficult to verify and perilous to believe, it is better to incline toward doubt than certainty' (III, xi: 1168 B; VS 1032). Only fools have made up their minds and are certain, and he will even quote Dante to justify this view: 'Che non men che saper dubbiar m'aggrado'.[19] Since Augustine and Dante can hardly be considered sceptics, it may have been a way of assigning limits to doubt. The search for a kind of balance is obvious when the author of the *Essays* writes: 'The arrogance of those who attributed to man's mind a capacity for everything produced in others (through irritation and emulation) the opinion that it has a capacity for nothing' (III, xi: 1172 B; VS 1035).

In this study of Montaigne's thought, it did not appear to me necessary to take into account an evolution which would have led him from Stoicism to Pyrrhonism before achieving a well balanced outlook.[20] The fundamental features I have brought forth in chapter 1 were present all through the composition of the *Essays*. With Marcel Tetel I think that 'the progress of Montaigne has not the characteristics of an evolution, but rather marks a greater depth' – a position supported by Eva Kushner in the conclusion of a wide-ranging debate.[21]

Lars Engle concedes that Shakespeare 'treated scepticism in a rather sceptic way'.[22] Montaigne himself indulges in mockery when he writes that 'Pyrrho, the man who built up ignorance into so pleasing a science' behaved foolishly on some occasions (II, xxix: 800 A; VS 705).[23] The suspension of belief does not imply renouncing all certainty nor giving up all action, as Bacon insisted in his preface to the *Novum Organum*.[24] Terence Cave has called attention to a surprising passage in the 'Apology' in which Montaigne presents a 'plausible opinion', ascribed to 'conciliatory men', which gives pre-eminence to the present and the future over the past, implying a possibility of progress in the search for truth:

> The assays of experience have taught me that where one man fails another succeeds; that what is unknown to one century is clarified by the next; that the sciences and the arts are not just cast in a mould all at once, but have to be gradually shaped by repeated handling and polishing [...]; I may not be strong enough to uncover anything, but I can still take soundings and make assays; by kneading and working the dough of this new subject-matter, by blending it and warming it through, I make it easier for my successor to enjoy it at leisure; [...] A second man will do the same for the third; that is why no difficulty should drive me to despair – nor should my own powerlessness. Man is capable of understanding everything as well as something. (*Essays*, II, xii: 631–2 A; VS 560–1)

Throughout the *Essays*, however, we are constantly reminded that the human mind cannot penetrate the 'essences'.[25] Montaigne would not have been in sympathy with intransigent rationalists but rather with the scientists of our own age who acknowledge the presence of a mystery at the core of reality.[26] Heisenberg's 'uncertainty principle' would have delighted him since he ascribed a great influence to chance (*hasard*, often called *fortune*) over the course of events.[27] Yet he might also have acknowledged that the scientific probabilism of our present age does not preclude a degree of determinism.[28]

The recent and precise researches of William Hamlin reveal a fairly widespread knowledge of Pyrrhonist views in Renaissance England, denoted by the presence of many copies of the translation of Sextus in English libraries from 1562 to 1635, and by the debates held in the universities, as well as by the first refutations of his theses. Allusions can be spotted in the works of Spenser and Marlowe, Donne and Cornwallis.[29] Yet nothing allows us to assume that Shakespeare had direct access to texts representative of academic or Pyrrhonian scepticism, apart from his reading of Montaigne. Besides, the expression of doubt in proverbial wisdom had anticipated its philosophical expression and the two were often combined in Renaissance writings.[30]

Hamlin has also shown how fragile and anachronistic is Stanley Cavell's assumption that 'the advent of scepticism as manifested in Descartes' *Meditations* is already in full existence in Shakespearean tragedy'. Descartes starts from a 'radical' scepticism, more intransigent than the Pyrrhonism of Montaigne, but his aim is to pass beyond it and he succeeds. Besides, Cavell associates scepticism with the creation of 'a world deprived of the assurance of God's existence and providential supervision', which is never the case with Montaigne and is only suggested at times by some Shakespearean characters.[31] Hamlin notices that the reception of the philosophy of the Sceptics in Renaissance England was an 'appropriation rather than a faithful reflection'. He makes useful distinctions between 'genuine epistemological scepticism' and a more widespread form of 'common sense doubt': a 'sense of human weakness and mental frailty', or of 'humanity's limited comprehension', an 'awareness of conflicting judgments and appearances'.[32] When scepticism is reduced to a state of mind it is not surprising that this type of doubt should arise in any dramatic work pervaded by a spirit of interrogation, from *Doctor Faustus* to *King Lear*. Montaigne himself admitted his contradictions, but he ascribed them to 'varied and changing occurrences', adding: 'I may happen to contradict myself but, as Demades said, I never contradict truth' (III, ii: 908 B; VS 805). Just as he saw himself different at different moments, yet retained a sense of identity, Montaigne can examine the same object, the same problem, the same situation from different angles and each time perceive a different facet of a complex truth. This capacity also conduced to an attitude of impartiality.

Impartiality is also present in Shakespeare's histories and tragedies when he allows different characters to hold divergent views and leaves us free to adopt any of the different points of view, for instance when Mowbray and Bolingbroke charge each other with high treason in *Richard II* (I, i) or when Caesar's greatness is acknowledged despite some ridiculous traits in *The Tragedy of Julius Caesar*, or when Antony and Cleopatra, after a revelation of all their failings, are raised to the sublime at the end of the play. He shows us two aspects of a complex reality when Shylock is presented as a man pitilessly thirsting for revenge because he is a victim of Christian prejudices. Shakespeare, indeed, like Montaigne, never contradicts truth, for each man has his personal vision, each character his own contradictions. For Falstaff, lying is 'part of a life-style'.[33] When he is charged with lying, yet brazenly asks 'Is not truth the truth?' (*Henry IV, Part I*, II, v, 233–4), he speaks in accordance with his nature and yet proclaims what the extremely numerous occurrences of the words 'true' and 'truth' in Shakespeare's works suggests: the poet's attachment to truth and reality.[34]

To consider different views with an open mind does not mean that truth cannot be approached. Yet some critics consider that the multiple perspectives of Shakespeare's drama and poems are best understood as illustrations of a methodological 'pragmatism' in which 'the competing values and ideologies of a transitional period are put into circulation in a market-like free play of intellectual contestation'.[35] I rather incline to think that Shakespeare, like Montaigne, would prefer to say: 'I welcome truth, I fondle it in whatsoever hand I find it' (III, viii: 1047 B; VS 924). Neither of them to my mind has anticipated the pragmatism of Richard Rorty and considered truth as 'a mutable human commodity rather than a natural or God-given certainty'.[36]

I will not, therefore, compare the positions of Montaigne and Shakespeare's manifestations of doubt as the expression of a cultural and moral relativism supposed to be constant in the *Essays*. Montaigne does insist on the diversity of customs (notably in I, xxiii; II, xii; and III, xiii), but to notice a diversity does not mean you countenance it. In the tragic circumstances of contemporary wars of religion, he was led to consider conservatism preferable to innovation. This, however, does not mean that he rejected the possibility of more justice in laws and institutions. Reading Florio's translation of the *Essays*, Samuel Daniel praised the denunciation of custom, tyrant of the universe, whom 'wee may plainly see [...] upon every occasion to force the rules of Nature'.[37] Montaigne knew that 'laws remain respected not because they are just but because they are laws. That is the mystical basis of their authority' (III, xiii: 1216 B;

VS 1072). But the cause of all cases of injustice is 'the Imbecility of Man' (III, xiii: 1214 C; VS 1070).

The *Essays* proclaim that there are 'desirable laws'. They are:

> Those which are fewest, simplest and more general. [...] Nature always gives us happier laws than those we give ourselves. Witness that Golden Age portrayed by the poets and the circumstances in which we see those peoples live who have no other laws. (III, xiii: 1208–9 B; VS 1066)[38]

This assertion must be qualified, as we shall see, but it is an implicit admission that there is an ideal model from which our laws diverge 'by their chaotic deformity' (III, xiii: 1216 B; VS 1072). Would Montaigne 'to some extent' justify 'our disobeying them' (1217 B) and, in cases 'producing a hard and dubious choice', give his preference 'for hiding and escaping', that is, for abstention (III, ix: 1124 B; VS 994), if he was not convinced that better laws might have been elaborated? On this question I cannot offer any precise parallel with Shakespeare. Yet mercy, which both ancient humanism and Christian humanism advocated, stretches the law and both Montaigne and Shakespeare celebrated it. The dramatist even borrowed arguments from the essayist in *Measure for Measure* and *The Tempest*.[39]

I am conscious that there is a serious obstacle to my tempering of Montaigne's and Shakespeare's relativism: in two essays and in *Hamlet* and *Troilus and Cressida* the relativity of values seems to be proclaimed. Yet when the essayist asserts 'that the taste of good and evil things depends in large part on the opinion we have of them' (I, xiv), he considers only man's fear of death, pain and poverty, starting from a saying of an 'old Greek', Epictetus. And when he writes in the essay 'We can savour nothing pure' that 'the best of the goodness in me has some vicious stain' (II, xx: 766 B; VS 674), he only confesses what many moralists, Christian or not, have observed. What is indisputable is that Montaigne in his acute self-examination discerned that 'it is our opinion which confers value' on things and 'value consists not in what they give to us but in what we bring to them' (I, xiv: 66 C; VS 62; my translation); which need not imply that our subjective valuing is unjustified.

When Hamlet says 'there is nothing good or bad, but thinking makes it so' (II, ii, 251–2), he may echo a proverb, as Hibbard points out in his Oxford edition of the play: 'A man is weal or woe as he himself thinks so'.[40] Besides, Hamlet here is explaining why Denmark now is to him a prison rather than pursuing Montaigne's trend of thought in the essay 'That the taste of good and evil things depend in large part on the opinion we have of them'. In *Troilus and Cressida* moral relativism seems to prevail when

Hector's claim that Helen 'is not worth what she doth cost the keeping' sparks Troilus's question: 'What's ought but as 'tis valued?' Again, the idea may be found in Dent's list of proverbs, but the question here, I admit, is debated.[41] Hector's retort does not wholly wipe out the subjectivity of judgement, but balances it against an objective reality: 'value dwells not in particular will. / It holds his estimate and dignity / As well wherein 'tis precious of itself / As in the prizer' (II, ii, 52–5). One may think that Ulysses' earlier plea for order was politically minded and dictated by circumstances, but the sincerity of Hector cannot be doubted.[42] In his plea for honour, Troilus, however, is no less sincere, for honour and beauty are constant values in the plays and poems of Shakespeare. Therefore I cannot agree with Hugh Grady when he sees in this dialogue 'a diagnosis of the process of value creation in the commodification which is so relentlessly enacted [...] at so many levels of this play', for Hector, when accepting war, 'gives over a world of values now revealed as baseless and arbitrary'.[43] Yet Hector sees clearly that the reasons 'superficially' alleged by Troilus and Paris cannot 'make up a free determination' (II, ii, 162–9); his decision to 'keep Helen still' (190) and wage war is obviously wrong because it is based on the consideration only of 'our and several dignities' (192), mere outward honour. The absurdity of this war is obvious. Hector should have remembered the statement of Montaigne: 'Any honourable person prefers to sully his honour than to sully his conscience' (II, xvi: 717 C; VS 630). The play makes it clear that Troilus is no less deluded in extolling the worth of Helen than in trusting Cressida. Both women are successively described by him as an inestimable 'pearl' (I, i, 100; II, ii, 80); but Cressida turns out to be a spurious pearl, and so is Helen, as presented in the play. Conversely, Othello will discover that, in his suspicion of Desdemona, he 'threw a pearl away' that was true (V, ii, 356). I think the dramatist does not leave us in doubt about 'baseless and arbitrary values' in *Troilus and Cressida*. His aim may be, as Lars Engle suggests, to 'demystify codes of value', but not to subvert them.[44] The play illustrates the defeat of those who believed in the true values, a fairly common occurrence in the practical realm.

Montaigne incessantly mentions moral values. He has been considered a 'moralist who mainly resorts to his own experience in order to highlight the contradictions of any moral judgement'.[45] I agree that he usually abstains from prescribing definite ways of behaving, but he does not refrain from approving or disapproving of some of them. Even when he starts from his personal experience, he openly or implicitly offers a general judgement of value. When he declares himself 'nice to the point of superstition in keeping [his] promises', it is clear that he highly values loyalty and honouring one's pledges. He prizes truthfulness in public as in private life, which implies the possibility of discerning truth. He calls on Pindarus and Plato to remind us that 'the first sign of corrupt morals is the banishing of truth. [...] Our understanding is conducted solely by means of the word: anyone who falsifies it betrays public society.'[46] Robert Bennett has called attention to the Erasmian spirit of this requirement and shown that truthfulness is also a means of forming a community in the 'humanistic comedies' of Shakespeare.[47] When Montaigne writes that 'truth and falsehood are both alike in form and faith', it is not to muddle them, but to invite us not to be 'slack about guarding ourselves from dupery' (III, xi: 1162 B; VS 1027). He confesses he may happen to lie in a conversation 'because of the excitement of the actual telling' but he is always ready to return to 'native truth' (III, xi: 1163 B; VS 1028), thus disclosing his clear-sightedness in self-scrutiny. Shakespeare shows himself equally clear-sighted when he discerns how he and his mistress lie to each other.[48] He may seem deluded when he calls the young man 'kind, and true' (sonnet 105), but other sonnets reveal he is conscious of trying to deceive himself. In his plays the fool is the spokesman of truth, which is in keeping with a tradition, but Inga-Stina Ewbank noticed that to be called a liar is the worst insult for both Shakespeare and Montaigne.[49]

In a long exposition on man's ignorance the 'Apology' declares that certainty is unattainable in the realm of the senses and the intellect, but it preserves the humanistic values of the Ancient world and Christian ethics. Montaigne has his personal perspective and preferences, but, without rejecting all influence of Machiavelli's realism, one may maintain that the author of the *Essays*, like the author of *The Prince*, never rejects what Victoria Kahn calls 'the Ciceronian and humanist equation between *honestas* and *utilitas*'.[50] Yet he always gives prominence to *honestas* and to what he calls *bonté*, *débonnaireté*, *humanité*, noting that Cyrus and Scipio the Elder rated 'generosity and benefactions', 'affability and humanity' above 'valour and conquests in war' (III, ix: 1098 C; VS 970). It does not prevent him from showing respect for arms as well as letters, as a man of the Renaissance would.[51] He has, however, little sympathy for *virtus* when it is displayed only in warlike or Stoic ways and proves inhuman towards others and even towards oneself.[52]

The humanistic values privileged by Montaigne and by Shakespeare require 'an understanding of the other' which may manifest itself in a relation of personal friendship, a favourite theme with Renaissance humanists. Montaigne thought it could ensure a 'perfect and absolute communication' (II, viii: 445 A; VS 396). His friendship with La Boétie, 'having captured my will, brought it to plunge into his and lose itself and [...] having captured his will, brought it to lose itself in mine' (I, xxviii: 212 A–C; VS 189). The same aspiration to lose oneself in the other was expressed by Shakespeare in his *Sonnets*, though he found it only momentarily or deceitfully in the young man loved. Both writers raise a memorial to the friend, from whom Montaigne was separated by death and Shakespeare by life. And by so doing, each of them raises a memorial to himself: 'My life hath in this line some interest; / Which for memorial still with thee shall stay' (sonnet 74).

Beyond relations of friendship, they both extend their sympathy to men of a lower condition. They, no doubt, retained the reverence due to rank, even in the humanist ideal, though it could celebrate *il cor gentile* in the low-born. Montaigne was a magistrate but he claimed to belong to the old nobility, the *noblesse d'épée*. Shakespeare took advantage of his growing prestige to apply for a coat of arms in his father's name. Like the author of the *Essays*, who described the mob as 'that mother of ignorance, of injustice and inconstancy' (II, xvi: 709 B; VS 624), the dramatist obviously abhorred the volatility and cruelty of crowds, repeatedly illustrated in the English histories and in *Julius Caesar*. On the other hand, when an individual is concerned, he generally stages or speaks of low-born people with sympathy, and shows compassion for the destitute, such as the naked beggar in *King Lear*. The 'seigneur de Montaigne' declared: 'I have seen in my time hundreds of craftsmen and ploughmen wiser and happier than University Rectors – and whom I would rather be like' (II, xii: 542 A; VS 487). He acknowledged that 'examples of virtue rarely make their home among the "rich and noble"' (II, xxxv: 844 A; VS 745). Yet, like Shakespeare, he knew that a mob is a monster from whom nothing is less to be hoped than 'mildness or humanity' (I, xxiv: 147 B; VS 130; cf. *Julius Caesar*, III, iii), and he was aware of the 'indiscriminate and prodigious facility which peoples have for letting their beliefs be led and their hopes be manipulated towards what has pleased and served their leaders' (III, x: 1146 C; VS 1013).

This understanding of the other is extended to foreigners. Montaigne proclaims: 'I reckon all men my fellow-citizens, embracing a Pole as I a Frenchman' (III, ix: 1100 B; VS 973). He reminds us that Socrates, when asked where he came from, 'did not say from "Athens", but from the world' (I, xxvi: 176 A; VS 157). Shakespeare can mock the French, the Spaniards and the Welsh for a comic purpose, but without the hostility of the satirists and pamphleteers of his age. He probably wrote the scene in the collaborative *Sir Thomas More* in which More urges the rioters to spare 'wretched strangers', immigrants in London, inviting them to imagine themselves subjected to such 'mountainous inhumanity'.[53]

This sympathy is extended to those whom their race and religion might have made most distant. It can embrace a Moor, Othello, who, despite his lack of judgement, is the noblest character in the play. The author of *The Merchant of Venice* can allow a despised Jewish usurer to speak his most comprehensive assertion of the universality of human nature. I need not quote Shylock's well known speech (III, i, 54–66): his urgent interrogations could be taken up at any time by the representative of any other oppressed community or religion in any part of the world. If Shylock is eventually condemned, it is largely because he has ignored Portia's plea for mercy (IV, i, 181–99); whereas Prospero, exiled, then threatened with assassination on his island, timely remembers that 'The rarer action is / In vertue [here = mercy] than in vengeance' (V, i, 27–8), probably echoing the opening of Montaigne's essay 'On crueltie', as Eleanor Prosser discovered, a parallel later expanded by David Quint.[54]

This mercy Prospero will extend to Caliban, who is at once a victim of oppression and a would-be rapist and murderer. Caliban was born 'a freckled whelp', 'not honour'd with a human shape' (I, ii, 283–4); he is spoken of as a 'monster', but for Shakespeare such monsters were not outside humanity as the American Indians were for a time in the eyes of certain theologians. Prospero finally says: 'This thing of darkness I / Acknowledge mine' (V, i, 278–9). Montaigne reminded us in his essay 'Of a monstrous child' that 'what we call monsters are not so for God' and that 'whatever happens against custom we say is against Nature' (II, xxx: 808 C; VS 713). Yet Caliban as a savage is not idealized in the way in which Montaigne apparently vindicated the way of life of the cannibals in an essay which Shakespeare did read and which he may seem to be parodying when the utopian dream of Gonzalo is punctured by the ironic comment of the realists (*The Tempest*, II, i, 153–73). Yet the dramatist and the essayist are not so far apart as one might think and to claim that Shakespeare has 'reversed Montaigne' may be an overstatement.[55]

The Golden Age cannot be revived. Montaigne only *seems* to admit it survived in these nations of the New World that:

> have no trade of any kind, no acquaintance with writing, no knowledge of numbers, no terms for governor or political superior, no practice of subordination or of riches or poverty, no contracts, no inheritances, no divided estates, no occupation but leisure, no concern for kinship [...], no clothing, no agriculture, no metals, no use of wine or corn. Among them you hear no words for treachery, lying, cheating, avarice, envy, backbiting or forgiveness. How remote from such perfection would Plato find that Republic which he thought up! (I, xxxi: 233 A; VS 206)

The mention of Plato reminds us that humanists liked to dream up utopias. Montaigne asserts nothing, since in the same essay he writes:

> it *seems* [my italics] to me that what experience has taught us about these people surpasses not only all the descriptions with which poetry has beautifully painted the Age of Gold [...], but also the very conceptions and yearnings of philosophy. (I, xxxi: 232 A; VS 206)

The opening ('il me semble') is a deliberately subjective and cautious judgement. Besides, as Todorov pointed out, Montaigne himself would not have enjoyed a primitive way of life. He uses the image of the cannibals and later of the Mexican Indians in the essay 'Of coaches' mainly to criticize the society of his time, and his preference as a humanist comes out when he regrets they were not conquered by the Greeks and the Romans, who would have polished their native qualities (III, vi, 1031; VS 910).[56] Genuine humanism, whether Christian or not, knows that man is always subject to violent impulses, whether proceeding from a mythical Fall or from the Freudian id.

Montaigne and Shakespeare are also at one in relying on compassion to mitigate 'man's inhumanity to man'. Under the influence of Antonin Artaud and Ian Kott, and of recent or present horrors, theatre directors nowadays often turn Shakespearean tragedy into a theatre of cruelty. Cruelty, of course, is present on stage; but it always evokes compassion for its victims. For Shakespeare, as for Aristotle, pity is an essential component of tragedy. This is perceptible even in his first and most Senecan tragedy, *Titus Andronicus*. Tamora's exclamation at the murder of her son, 'O cruel irreligious piety' (I, i, 130), is no less genuine for coming from a character who will prove no less cruel. But some modern representations or reshapings of *King Lear* best illustrate this misinterpretation of Shakespeare. In the folio text, the compassionate dialogue between the servants after the blinding of Gloucester, the moralizing of Albany (IV, ii) and the scene in which Cordelia is described as an emblematic figure of pity (IV, iii, 11–32) are cut out, but the cuts need not be interpreted as an attempt to eliminate pathos in an authorial revision: I have suggested other reasons in the recent Pléiade edition of the tragedies. Furthermore, despite these cuts, the play is still studded with recurrent expressions of pity.[57] *King Lear* has been said to end in nihilism. Yet, at the very end, around the lifeless bodies of Cordelia, an innocent victim, and Lear, a redeemed offender, those who survive, Kent, Edgar and Albany, exemplify the same moral values they have throughout: loyalty, respect for natural and social bonds, human kindness.

In *Macbeth*, the contemplated murder creates a hallucinated vision of 'pity, like a naked new-born babe / Striding the blast' (I, vii, 21–5), and shortly before his reduction of life to 'a tale / Told by an idiot, full of sound and fury, / Signifying nothing' (V, v, 25–7), the tyrant, in a wiser moment, comes to deplore that he 'must not look to have that which should accompany old age', 'honour, love, obedience, troops of friends' (V, iii, 24–8) – true and enduring values. Macduff's lament over his murdered children (V, iii, 217–20) had been anticipated by all the scenes of indignation and mourning for the killing of children in the histories, and it is characteristic that the author of *King John* should have chosen to make the murder of young Arthur the essential reason (though unhistorical) for the revolt of the barons. Was 'the gentle Shakespeare' only intent on pathos, making dramatic use of pity? Partly perhaps, but I think his personal and genuine interest in the value of compassion might be vindicated in a comparison with Marlowe's or Middleton's handling of scenes of cruelty.

Montaigne had in France a direct experience of 'that horrifying moral corruption which [...] civil wars and political upheavals bring in their wake' (I, xxiii: 135 B; VS 120), exclaiming 'What a monstrosity this war is! Other wars are external: this one also gnaws at itself and destroys itself with its own poison' (I, xii: 1178 B; VS 1041). He has, like Shakespeare, a spontaneous aversion to cruelty, writes a whole essay (II, xi) to denounce it, and often reverts to this theme, not only about the tortures inflicted on the American Indians, but also about the inhuman treatment of the Jews in Portugal (I, xiv: 55–6 C; VS 53).[58] Géralde Nakam speaks of the 'wide-ranging indictment of cruelty in the *Essays*'.[59]

This arraignment of cruelty is constant also in the works of Shakespeare and he extends it to the pains inflicted on animals: the hunted hare in *Venus and Adonis* (ll. 679–708), the dying stag in *As You Like It* (II, i, 26–43). Montaigne also could not 'witness without displeasure an innocent defenceless beast which has done us no harm being hunted to the kill' (II, xi: 484 A; VS 432) and he criticized mothers who think 'their boys are playing when they see them wring the neck of a chicken or find sport in wounding a dog' (I, xxiii: 124 B; VS 110). When Valeria thinks her grandson 'a noble child' because he tears a butterfly – 'how he mammocked it!' – and Volumnia comments 'one son's father's mood' (I, iii, 59–70), Shakespeare may be hinting at the presence of furious rage in the heroism of Coriolanus. In the Middle Ages John of Salisbury had already demonstrated that the slaughter of animals revealed man's own bestiality and both Erasmus and Sir Thomas More had disapproved of hunting.[60]

On what basis did this condemnation of cruelty, and more generally all humanistic values, rest for Montaigne and Shakespeare? They did not assume that man is naturally inclined to kindness. Indeed, Montaigne feared 'that Nature herself has attached to Man something which goads him on to inhumanity' (II, xi: 485 B; VS 433). Quoting the *Suave mari magno* of Lucretius, he even admitted that 'we feel deep down some bitter-sweet pricking of malicious pleasure at seeing others suffer' (II, i: 892 B; VS 791). He himself, however, ascribed his own 'hatred of cruelty' to a soft disposition – *mollesse* – yet hated it 'both by nature and judgement' as 'the ultimate vice' (II, xi: 480–1 A; VS 429). What was Montaigne's conception of 'judgement'? He does not invoke the teachings of Christianity, ignored or distorted in a period of religious wars. Instead, he places his trust in 'a well-governed conscience' (II, xv: 708 A; VS 623). But how can it be governed? Not by nature alone, since it can incline man at times to inhumanity; nor by religion alone, since 'Men's practices reveal an inordinate distinction between devotion and conscience' (III, xii: 1201C; VS 1059; my translation).

All moral values in the age of Montaigne and Shakespeare rested on a religious basis which they rarely invoke. Yet it cannot be denied that they considered themselves Christian, though the author of the *Essays* acknowledges 'we are Christians by the same title that we are Perigordians or Germans' (II, xii: 497 B; VS 445), that is, by an accident of birth. The nature of Montaigne's faith is not a problem essential to my purpose in this book. Some orientations, however, must be discerned. He seems sincere when he thanks the Christian God for establishing his belief 'on the changeless foundation of his holy Word' (II, xii: 653 C; VS 579). Yet he acknowledges that our religion, made to root out vices, now 'cloaks them, nurses them, stimulates them' (II, xii: 495 C; VS 444). It is not improbable that some of his declarations of allegiance to the Catholic Church were meant to help him escape censure for his occasional unorthodox 'fantasies'. That the 'unpremeditated philosopher' should find the rational arguments in favour of the immortality of the soul definitely weak is not surprising and is in keeping with his unquestioning acceptance of the mysteries of faith: 'God alone tells us this, and faith' (II, xii: 623 A–C; VS 554). One should note, however, that in his incessant meditations on death he never speaks of the life beyond. It has been noticed that although he alludes to the dogma of the resurrection of the body, he asserts with more conviction that 'we are built of two separate parts, which together form our being: to separate them is death and the collapse of our being' (II, xii: 580–1 A; VS 519) – an assertion which, however, would be compatible with the 'mortalist' interpretation of the dogma of the resurrection, a heresy which may have been entertained for a while by John Donne, no less convinced of the essential character of the union of body and soul.[61]

Yet the frequent mention of God in the *Essays*, obvious in the *Concordance*, seems spontaneous rather than called for by a pretence of conformity. Montaigne's sincerity cannot be doubted when he says he recites the Paternoster regularly, adding 'it is the only prayer I can ever remember' (I, lvi: 356 A–C; VS 318), which might awake suspicion: as a Catholic he would be expected to recite also the Ave Maria.[62] The mention of this prayer, uncalled for in the *Essays*, seems to me testimony to a genuine attachment to the message of Christ. Like Shakespeare, however, he seems to select in Scripture what is in harmony with his own inclinations. He emphasizes 'the most holy mildness and justice of God's word' (III, xii: 1181; my translation) and never speaks of God's wrath. He alludes only once to original sin (II, xii: 555 A; VS 498) and might seem to call it into doubt when he writes: 'Man commands himself to be necessarily at fault' (III, ix: 1120 C; VS 990). He is 'fully armed' against superstition (III, vii: 1039 C; VS 917), but makes it clear that 'because I loathe superstition I do not go straightway mocking religion' (III, v: 962 B; VS 853). He apparently believed that 'God in his goodness' had protected him on certain occasions (III, xii: 1205 B; VS 1062) and, like Hamlet in the fifth act of the tragedy (ii, 165–70), he thinks 'we are often obliged to commit our ship to the sole guidance of Heaven' (III, i: 902 C; VS 799). Yet he mentions 'fortune' 349 times in the *Essays*. He sometimes spontaneously speaks as if he believed in a life after death[63] but, unlike Hamlet or Claudio in *Measure for Measure* (III, i, 118–28), he does not hazard speculations about it and does not seem to feel 'the dread of something after death' (*Hamlet*, III, i, 80).

Montaigne seems also to be hostile to any use of 'the express words of the Bible' (III, xiii: 1208 B; VS 1065) in order to dictate laws, hence to fundamentalism; but he acknowledges the 'true' foundation of the simple laws given by Moses (II, xvi: 71 C, VS 630). One might therefore expect a theological justification of love for one's neighbour, yet Montaigne finds it unnecessary to offer it, perhaps because he has a spontaneous and 'marvellous weakness towards mercy and clemency' (I, i: 4 B; VS 8).

The plays of Shakespeare are studded with allusions to the Old and New Testaments.[64] The fate of man after death is anxiously evoked by Hamlet and Claudio. Portia and Isabella, pleading for clemency, base their appeal on the reminder that mercy 'droppeth as the gentle rain from heaven' (*Merchant of Venice*, IV, i, 182) and 'He which is the top of judgment' exercised it (*Measure for Measure*, II, ii, 75–9). Providence is mentioned in several plays.[65] Shakespeare, however, like Montaigne, takes liberties with orthodoxy. As Maurice Hunt observes, one finds in his theatre a surprising medley of motives and ideas of Protestant and

Catholic origin assembled in the same images, the same concepts and the same characters. The plots did not always call for this blending and as the personal convictions of the dramatist remain hazy it is difficult to discern an origin for it. Hunt legitimately speaks of a tolerant attitude.[66] Shakespeare would be close to Montaigne in this respect, since he always showed a moderation which made him appear 'Guelph to the Ghibelline, Ghibelline to the Guelph' (III, xii: 1182 B; VS 1044).

Nothing can be proved, but I think it is acceptable to posit that a personal inclination rather religious faith originated these appeals to compassion and tolerance in the case of Shakespeare as in Montaigne's. Would a philosophical justification be possible? Some thinkers have tried to offer one. Schopenhauer based his ethics on compassion, considered as the only non-selfish motive for our actions. In *The World as Will and Idea* (1818) he presented life as the manifestation of a single will operating in nature, but each man was invited not to consider himself as a distinct individual and was urged to identify himself with any suffering man. In our own time, Lévinas asked himself in *Humanism of the Other* whether 'the most humble experience of the one who puts himself in the other's place, that is, accuses himself of the other's illness or pain, is not already animated by the most eminent sense in which "I is another"?'[67] We have seen that Montaigne thought himself capable of putting himself in another's place as well as any dramatist, and he also declared: 'the sight of another man's suffering produces physical suffering in me'.[68]

The mention of two thinkers with a different approach, Schopenhauer and Lévinas, only aims to reveal the modernity of Montaigne and Shakespeare when they base ethical conduct on compassion and care for the other without resorting to a theological argument. As such feelings had emerged in the earliest times of human history, they provide an argument in favour of a universal human nature.[69]

This established, I may therefore now come to the first characteristic of humanism according to Todorov. These moral values must be acknowledged and assumed by an 'I' capable of constantly exercising judgement with a certain freedom. The existence of this 'I' is supported by my argument in favour of 'an unchanging self' in my *Seven Metaphysical Poets*. In Montaigne's particular case, the first chapter of the present volume has offered further arguments. I may add that the autonomy of the 'I' justifies Montaigne's reliance on free will, in full conformity with the doctrine of Sebond.[70] He had always felt free to govern his impulses in accordance with his 'maistresse forme'.

Shakespeare proclaims 'I am that I am' (sonnet 121). Having set forth the presence and the workings of this 'I' in several soliloquies I must tackle another problem.⁷¹ The action of this 'I' is guided by the exercise of an individual judgement, which must rely on human reason. There's the rub: human reason is fallible, as Montaigne insistently reminds us. Yet, as even Lévi-Strauss admits, the essayist constantly appeals to this deficient reason, for it is 'the seed of that universal reason which is stamped upon every man who is not disnatured' (III, xii: 1201 C; VS 1059).⁷² Is there no inconsequence here? Montaigne at times appeals to nature against a ratiocinating reason; at other times he relies on reason to correct the bad instincts given us by nature. The paradox is that reason alone allows man 'not to be slavishly subject to the laws of Nature as the beasts are, but [...] conform to them by our free-will and judgement' (II, viii: 434 A; VS 387). That is why 'philosophy believes she has not made a bad use of her resources when she has bestowed on Reason sovereign majesty over our soul' (II, xxxiii: 825 A; VS 728).

Reason, then, must guide us in our difficult search for truth. Montaigne repeats Cicero's warning that 'the false and the true are in such close proximity that the wise man should not trust himself to so steep a slope'.⁷³ He himself agrees that 'all *grosso modo* judgments are lax and defective' (III, viii: 1069 C; VS 943). He dislikes idle or biased discussions when their fruit is only 'the destruction and annihilation of truth' (III, viii: 1048 C; VS 926) and yet he says 'I welcome truth, I fondle it, in whosoever hand I find it' (III, viii: 1047 B; VS 924). It implies that truth is attainable, at least in certain cases. Hamlin observes that it is in this way that Montaigne 'can maintain a hostile stance towards rational theorizing while exhibiting sympathy towards reasoning on local, practical contexts'.⁷⁴

Donald Frame had proposed a distinction between the 'ratiocinating reason' of philosophers and theologians, whose speculations Montaigne thought hazardous, and a 'reasonable reason', whose operations in the realm of human conduct were safer.⁷⁵ In my eyes this reasonableness is akin to the 'common sense' later invoked by Reid and the Scottish School of Common Sense, who rejected both the idealism of Berkeley and the scepticism of Hume in favour of immediate perception and common-sense truths. It may include the kind of reasoning which proceeds from an objective assessment of facts, after the manner of experimental science or a judicial inquiry. Montaigne was a magistrate and this influenced his attitude to history. He knew 'what a delicate thing our quest for truth is' when writing 'good histories', yet, unlike Agrippa in his *De incertudine et vanitate scientiarum et artium* (1531), he did not consider all recording of history as uncertain. He did not either assimilate historical narratives to fictions, as Hayden White does in our own time, or look upon facts as interpretations or signifiers after the manner of Roland Barthes or Michel de Certeau.[76] He thought truth accessible when the historian could, 'as in a judicial inquiry, confront witnesses and accept objections to alleged proofs on the finer points of every occurrence' (II, x: 469 A; VS 418). Truth is attainable, but, as Donne later warned us, 'On a huge hill, / Cragged, and steep, truth stands, and he that will / Reach her, about must, and about will go' (satire III). In this regard, Montaigne expressly condemned Sextus Empiricus, for whom no impartial judgement was possible.[77]

In the essay devoted to the demonstration of 'the uncertainty of our judgement' (I, xlvii) it appears that 'fortune' or 'chance' (*hazard*) is responsible for the course of events and the failure of foresight (I, xlvii: 320 A–C; VS 286). This is different from entertaining a false opinion. Personally, Montaigne seems inclined to trust his own judgement.[78] He ascribed to his soul 'sure and open judgements about subjects which she knew' (I, xxvi: 198 C; VS 176). He even proclaimed: 'With me judgement holds the rector's chair, or at least it anxiously strives to do so' (III, xiii: 1219 B; VS 1074).[79] He does not believe in the possibility of 'universal assent' (II, xii: 64A; VS 562), but he believes he owes to himself a capacity 'for sifting the truth' (II, xvii: 747 A; VS 658) when examining the available facts 'without penetrating their origin and essences', for 'to know causes' belongs only to God (III, xi: 1161 C; VS 1026).

In the restricted field of experience this 'sceptic' will sometimes hammer home his convictions. While he does call attention to his love of 'terms which soften and tone down the rashness of what we put forward, terms such as "perhaps", "somewhat", "some", "they say", "I think", and so on' (III, xi: 116 5B; VS 1030), this circumspection does not lead to a systematic rejection of judgement, nor a refusal to take sides. Under his pen such phrases as *en vérité, de vrai, il est vrai, il est bien vrai* and *bien est vrai que* constantly recur.[80] He acknowledges that one may be in a 'state of indecision and perplexity' and yet concludes: '*There is no doubt* that it was fairer and nobler [...] not to act otherwise but to forgive' (I, xxiv: 144 A; VS 128; my italics). Truth may be evident, at least for moral choice.

Furthermore, there is a natural link between 'truth' and 'essence': 'belief endows itself with essence and truth' (I, xiv: 71 C; VS 67; my translation); 'the essence and truth' of a sickness appear jointly (II, vi: 418 A; VS 372). Essence and reality are also associated; man 'enjoys his goods only in fantasy, but knows ills in their essence' (II, xii: 544 B; VS 489; my translation); 'those who have the face of virtue do not have her essence' (I, xxxvii: 258 A; VS 230); rhetoricians pride themselves on 'corrupting things in their very essence' (I, li: 341 A; VS 305). Montaigne had no opposition to essentialism, but his conception of essence calls for a distinction Locke will later formulate: 'essence' is used in the primary sense of *essentia*, the real existence of a particular thing, '*the very being of anything*', its nature and constitution.[81]

A thing always has an essence for the author of the *Essays*, who follows Aristotle on this point, as Michael Screech demonstrates; but it is not the 'nominal essence' which is of man's making and determines a genus or species: such an essence has no existence outside language.[82] Montaigne, like the jurists and the nominalists, thought more attention should be paid to things than to words, as the opening of his essay 'On glory' proclaimed (II, xvi).[83] Nor had he in mind an ideal essence representative of a transcendent reality.

The present tendency among literary critics is to reject any presence of essentialism in the thought of Montaigne and Shakespeare.[84] It is only justified if one has in mind a Platonic type of essentialism. Whereas Pyrrho ascribed no essence to things, Montaigne admits the reality of particular essences, but he considers, like Locke, that we cannot penetrate 'their origins and essences' (III, xi: 1161 C; VS 1026) for an essence is 'hidden and secret' (III, ii: 916 B; VS 813: 'abstruse et occulte'). He also acknowledges the imperfection of man's essence, but in an Augustinian perspective: man is nothing because he is a creature and, as such, radically separated from God, the only Being.[85] From this point of view Montaigne's self is nothing, but he is no more deprived of an essence than are other creatures. One may think that Montaigne, as a 'chance philosopher, not a premeditated one' (II, xii: 614 C; VS 546), makes loose use of such terms as 'essence' or 'form'. What seems to me significant is that he could at once acknowledge the difficulty of penetrating essences and yet proclaim: 'It is not what I do that I write of, but of me, of what I *am*' (II, vi: 426 C; VS 379: 'c'est mon essence'). This means not only that the 'self' has an essence but that it may be discovered and set down on paper. Some will say that this self is only a trace on paper, which is obviously true for the reader, but this trace would not have appeared if this 'self' had not existed.

In his celebrated statement that 'every man bears the whole form of the human condition' (III, ii: 908 B; VS 805), Montaigne does not only mean that one may find in any man the universal form which distinguishes man from an animal or an angel. In the context, he asserts that the private life of an individual can bear testimony to all the possibilities offered to any man by 'the human condition'. The particular and the universal are closely associated, but the essence, the reality of existence, is almost always linked with the individual, thus giving pre-eminence to diversity.[86] The nature of men, Todorov observes, is precisely 'their capacity for having an individual culture, history and identity'.[87] In his translation of Sebond, Montaigne had already written: 'there is nothing more familiar, more interior and proper to each man than he himself is to himself' ('que soy-mesme à soy').[88] This is what his *Essays* proclaim throughout, but it is also an extension of the Augustinian tradition.

Shakespeare resorts metaphorically to the word 'essence' when Valentine, speaking of Sylvia, says 'She is my essence' (*Two Gentlemen of Verona*, III, i, 182). In *Measure for Measure* (II, ii, 123), when 'glassy essence' emphasizes the frailty of man, 'essence' may have its primary philosophical meaning. But when Iago ironically claims that Desdemona's honour 'is an essence that's not seen' (IV, i, 16), he is suggesting that this essence of her personal honour, usually invisible, is in reality absent. In the poem 'The phoenix and turtle', the essence of a love defined in metaphysical terms is still the real essence of an individual being: 'So they loved as love in twain / Had the essence but in one'. In Shakespeare's sonnet 53, all the graces that tend on the beloved are not a Platonic incarnation of an ideal beauty, as they are in Petrarch or Sidney, but 'millions of strange shadows' embodied in his individual 'substance'. Lévinas nowadays writes that 'the other is not initially characterized as freedom, from which alterity would then be deduced: the other bears alterity as an essence'.[89] La Boétie and the young man of the *Sonnets* have an essence perceived as an individual essence, which implies at once a sense of otherness and an intuition of identity.

The fact that Montaigne and Shakespeare had not the conception of essence predominant in Platonic idealism does not mean that they could not have a certain intuition of transcendence. Transcendence may be conceived in different ways. The Stoics and the Renaissance humanists, Seneca and Samuel Daniel, had the same message: 'unlesse above himselfe he can / Erect himselfe, how poore a thing is man!'[90] Yet Montaigne rejects it: 'A pithy saying, a most useful aspiration, but absurd withal' (III, xii: 683 A–C; VS 604). He does not think like Sebond that one can 'in one stride stalk from man to God'.[91] His 'conscience is happy with itself – not as the conscience of an angel is nor of a horse, but as behoves the conscience of a man' (III, ii: 909 C; VS 806). He 'can desire to be entirely different', but he makes no effort to change: 'I cannot do better' (III, ii: 916 B; VS 813). In sonnet 121 Shakespeare also consents to be what he is: 'I am that I am'.

Nevertheless, Montaigne, through his 'perfect friendship' with La Boétie, and Shakespeare, in his conception of a love which alters not 'when it alteration finds' (sonnet 116), have 'transcended themselves' in a way.[92] This is not a merely 'horizontal transcendence', for the 'other', the friend, in both cases, is identified with an absolute beyond words: Montaigne speaks of 'some inexplicable quintessence' (I, xxvii: 212 A; VS 188). This 'force of destiny' (*ibid*.) is divine, since this 'loving-friendship' lasted 'as long as it pleased God' (207 A; VS 184). Shakespeare, too, imparted a transcendental value to the feeling which united him with the young man of the *Sonnets*, by conferring on him the attributes of a vaguely Neo-Platonic trinity (sonnet 195) or by resorting to a liturgical language.[93]

A fascination with the notion of absolute transcendence cannot be denied to Montaigne when he celebrates a God who is 'but ONE existing in reality' and 'fills Eternity with a single Now' (II, xii: 683 A; VS 603). This evocation, however, was borrowed from Plutarch and, as in the eyes of Pythagoras, who 'closely adumbrated truth' when he judged that our conception of the First Cause must be 'free of limits, restrictions or definitions', this transcendence might be only 'the utmost striving of our intellect towards perfection, each of us enlarging the concept according to his capacity' (II, xii: 573 C; VS 513).[94]

Now, this absolute perfection, contemplated by Montaigne from outside, seems something foreign to his nature and desire: 'Those humours soaring to transcendency terrify me as do great unapproachable heights' (III, xiii: 1268 C; VS 1115). Therefore the existence of God, in his mind, appears to me in a way 'purely transcendental', unlinked to any living intuition or inner experience of His presence. One may wonder whether his insistence on 'the nihility of the human condition' (II, vi: 426 B; VS 380; my translation), asserted in a general way but contradicted by the moderation and diversity of his judgements on individuals and his admiration for some exemplary figures, may not have been mainly inspired by a desire to magnify a divine transcendence he was unable to conceive and of which he could not perceive any confirmation.

An intuition of the transcendence of being seems to me to be absent in Shakespeare, but I cannot commit myself on this point. I shall put forward only an impression: what seems to have haunted his imagination was the idea that the whole world of sense, the spectacle offered by the universe, was bound to fade away, 'leave not a rack behind', and that 'we are such stuff / As dreams are made on' (*The Tempest*, IV, I, 155–7).[95] The idea that life might be a dream was widespread long before Pedro Calderon's *La vida es sueño*, a play of 1635. It appears in the *Essays* of Montaigne, but without any insistence or emotion: 'Those who have compared our lives to a dream are right – perhaps more right than they realized' (II, xii: 674 B; VS 596). With Shakespeare, the prospect of an inevitable annihilation of the visible universe may be interpreted as a genuine intuition of what might be called a hollow transcendence.

Both Montaigne and Shakespeare, however, had an intuition of a full transcendence through the poetic function of language, which by itself can induce the aesthetic ecstasy through which, as Schopenhauer will claim, 'subject and object escape from time's whirlwind'.[96] It is on a joint exaltation of poetry that I wish to bring the parallel to a close. Montaigne confessed a literary ambition when he wrote: 'I am not at all sure whether I would not much rather have given birth to one perfectly formed son by commerce with the Muses than by commerce with my wife' (II, viii: 451 B; VS 401). According to Lévinas, the subject transcends himself in paternity and may claim: I am my son.[97] In the same way, Montaigne thought 'I am my book', and the Shakespeare of the *Sonnets* seems to have shared this feeling.

One might think Montaigne regretted not being able to write in verse, since he declared 'From my earliest childhood poetry has had the power to transpierce and transport me' (I, xxxvii: 260 C; VS 232).[98] Yet prose in his eyes could shine with the 'vigour and boldness' of poetry and he voiced the quintessence of the humanistic ideal of the Renaissance when he placed 'good, enrapturing divine poetry above reason and rules' (I, xxxvii: 260 C; VS 231), considering it 'the ancient theology', as well as 'the first philosophy' and 'the original language of the gods' (II, ix: 1126 C; VS 995).

Notes

1. See T. M. Baldwin, *William Shakespeare's Small Latine and Lesse Greek* (University of Illinois Press, 1944); Jonathan Bate, *Shakespeare and Ovid* (Oxford University Press, 1993) and *The Genius of Shakespeare* (Oxford University Press, 1997), as well as 'Montaigne and Shakespeare', a radio essay available on the BBC iPlayer; Miola, *Shakespeare's Reading*. On Montaigne's original use of the classics see R. Aulotte, 'Montaigne et l'humanisme', in C. Blum, ed., *Montaigne, apologie de Raymond Sebond. De la theologia a la théologie* (Paris: Champion, 1990).
2. Translations were published in England in 1539, 1542, etc.
3. F. P. Wilson, *The Proverbial Wisdom of Shakespeare* (London: Modern Humanities Research Association, 1961).
4. See Nakam, *Le dernier Montaigne*, p. 3.
5. See also *Essays*, II, xxxii, 'In defence of Seneca and Plutarch'; III, v: 987 B, VS 875; III, vi: 1018 B, VS 899.
6. Miles, *Shakespeare and the Constant Romans*, pp. 89–91, 105–9.
7. Bradshaw, *Shakespeare's Scepticism*; Graham Bradshaw, *Shakespeare and the Materialists* (Cornell University Press, 1993); Graham Bradshaw, T. Bishop and P. Holbrook, eds, *Shakespeare and Montaigne Revisited*, Shakespearian International Yearbook No. 6 (Aldershot: Ashgate, 2006); Stanley Cavell,

8   *Disowning Knowledge in Six Plays of Shakespeare* (Cambridge University Press, 1987); Lars Engle, *Shakespearean Pragmatism: Market of His Time* (University of Chicago Press, 1993); Hugh Grady, *Shakespeare's Universal Wolf* (Oxford University Press, 1996); Hugh Grady, ed., *Shakespeare and Modernity* (London: Routledge, 2000); Hugh Grady, 'Shakespeare's links to Machiavelli and Montaigne', *Comparative Literature*, 52 (2000), pp. 119–42; Lee, *Shakespeare's Hamlet*.
8   Todorov, *Le jardin imparfait*, p. 48.
9   See Emmanuel Lévinas, *Humanism of the Other*, trans. Nidra Poller (University of Illinois Press, 2003), pp. 87–8. Cf. Emmanuel Lévinas, *Of God Who Comes to Mind*, trans. Bettina Bergo (Stanford University Press, 1998), pp. 137–71.
10 Rendered as 'inhuman treatment' in Screech, p. 55.
11 Claude Lévi-Strauss, 'En relisant Montaigne', in *Histoire de Lynx* (Paris: Plon, 1991), p. 286.
12 Donald Frame and Geoffrey Miles also consider the 'Apology' not as an affirmation of Pyrrhonism but a rejection of Stoicism and of the conviction that an ethic can be based on reason. Donald M. Frame, *Montaigne's Discovery of Man: The Humanization of a Humanist* (Columbia University Press, 1955), pp. 175–80; Miles, *Shakespeare and the Constant Romans*, p. 86.
13 See Ellrodt, *L'inspiration personnelle*, vol. III, ch. 7, sec. 2.
14 Terence Cave, *Préhistoires: textes troublés au seuil de la modernité* (Geneva: Droz, 1999), pp. 34–49.
15 M. A. Screech has published *Montaigne's Annotated Copy of Lucretius* (Geneva: Droz, 1998).
16 Cf. 'tantum religio potuit suadere malorum', in Lucretius, *De rerum natura*, I, 101.
17 Outside the 'Apology', Pyrrho reappears only twice in the *Essays*, and only in relation to virtue, in II, xx.
18 Géralde Nakam, *Montaigne: la manière et la matière* (Paris: Klincksieck, 1991; Paris: Champion, 2006), p. 123.
19 *Essays*, I, xxvi, 170 C-A; VS 151: 'For doubting pleases me as much as knowing'.
20 This evolution, set forth by Villey, was agreed upon by many critics, notably Joukovsy, *Montaigne et le problème du temps*, and Miles, *Shakespeare and the Constant Romans*.
21 See *Bulletin de la Société des Amis de Montaigne*, 7ème série, 13–16 (1988–9), pp. 12 and 249–531. See also the observations of George Hoffman on the origin of the successive 'additions' to the *Essays*, in *Montaigne's Career* (Oxford: Clarendon Press, 1998), ch. 5.
22 Lars Engle, '*Measure for Measure* and modernity: the problem of the sceptic's authority', in Hugh Grady, ed., *Shakespeare and Modernity* (London: Routledge, 2000), p. 86.
23 Thomas Harriot mocked the Sceptics, who 'make there knowledge certayne to doubt assuredly'. Quoted by William M. Hamlin, *Scepticism in Shakespeare's*

England, Shakespeare International Yearbook No. 2 (Aldershot: Ashgate, 2002), p. 298.
24 Bacon rejected two extremes: 'the presumption of pronouncing on everything, and the despair of comprehending anything'. See John M. Robertson, ed., *The Philosophical Works of Francis Bacon* (London: Routledge, 1903), p. 256.
25 See *infra*, pp. 162–3.
26 Notably Bernard d'Espagnat in *A la recherche du reel: le regard d'un physicien* (Paris: Gauthier-Villars, 1979).
27 See III, viii (1058 B; VS 934) and the words 'fortune' and 'hasard' in Roy E. Leake, *Concordance des Essais de Montaigne* (Geneva: Droz, 1981).
28 As d'Espagnat argued in *A la recherche du réel*.
29 William Hamlin, *Tragedy and Scepticism in Shakespeare's England* (Houndmills: Macmillan, 2005), pp. 29–72.
30 *Ibid.*, pp. 29ff. The proverbial expression of these doubts 'lends support to the idea that a lay scepticism pre-dated any manifestation of philosophical scepticism in early modern Britain'.
31 *Ibid.*, pp. 145–7. See Cavell, *Discerning Knowledge*, pp. 3–4.
32 Hamlin, *Tragedy and Scepticism*, pp. 124–8.
33 Inga-Stina Ewbank, 'Shakespeare's liars', *Proceedings of the British Academy*, 69 (1983), pp. 137–68, p. 140.
34 See Leake, *Concordance*.
35 This is Hugh Grady's convenient summary of Lars Engle's position. Grady, *Shakespeare's Universal Wolf*, p. 36.
36 See Engle, '*Measure for Measure* and modernity', p. 88.
37 In Florio's translation of the opening paragraph of I, xxii (= xxiii in modern editions), vol. I, p. 105.
38 This assertion seem to be contradicted by the acknowledgement that there is not one law 'universally accepted by the agreement of all peoples' (II, xii: 654 A; VS 580). But Montaigne is speaking here of existing laws, not of those that might be 'desirable'. Besides, his opposition to dogmatism is more extreme in the 'Apology' than in other essays.
39 See David Quint, *Montaigne and the Quality of Mercy* (Princeton University Press, 1998), ch. 2; Eleanor Prosser, 'Shakespeare, Montaigne, and the rarer action', *Shakespeare Studies*, 1 (1965), pp. 261–4.
40 G. R. Hibbard, *Hamlet*, New Oxford Shakespeare (Oxford University Press, 1987).
41 See Robert William Dent, *Shakespeare's Proverbial Language* (University of California Press, 1981).
42 Jonathan Dollimore claims that this appeal to the respect of an order inscribed in natural law is contradicted by the evidence of the disorder reigning in society. But this contrast was universally acknowledged and invoked in order to remind man of his straying from the law of nature and from God's will. Jonathan Dollimore, *Radical Tragedy* (Brighton: Harvester Wheatsheaf, 2nd edn, 1984), p. 43.
43 Grady, *Shakespeare's Universal Wolf*, pp. 91–4.

44 Engle, *Shakespearean Pragmatism*, p. 49.
45 Philippe Desan, *Montaigne: les formes du monde et de l'esprit* (Paris: PUPS/ DL, 2008), pp. 19, 168.
46 II, xviii: 756–7 A; VS 666–7. Cf. I, ix: 'On liars', and II, xvii (735 A; VS 647): 'that novel virtue of deceit and dissimulation that is now much honoured I hate it unto death'.
47 Robert Bennett, 'Shakespeare and Montaigne via Erasmus', *Romance and Reformation: The Erasmian Spirit of Shakespeare's* Measure for Measure (University of Delaware Press, 2000).
48 See *supra* chapter 3, p. 67.
49 Ewbank, 'Shakespeare's liars', p. 141, n. 2. Ewbank also states that 'Lying [...] dominates the political world of *Hamlet*, the plot of *Othello*, and so much of the first act of *King Lear* that the Fool, pointedly, asks to "learn to lie"' (p. 143).
50 Victoria Kahn in A. R. Ascoli and Victoria Kahn, *Machiavelli and the Discourse of Literature* (Cornell University Press, 1993), p. 198. Cf. Grady, 'Shakespeare's links to Machiavelli and Montaigne', p. 122.
51 See II, xxi: 769–70; VS 677–8. Cf. Supple, *Arms Versus Letters*, particularly p. 273.
52 Cf. Schaeffer, *The Political Philosophy of Montaigne*, pp. 232ff.
53 *Sir Thomas More*, II, i, 82–155.
54 Prosser, 'Shakespeare, Montaigne, and the rarer action'; Quint, *Montaigne and the Quality of Mercy*, ch. 1.
55 Bate, *Shakespeare and Ovid*, p. 256.
56 Cf. Hamlin, *The Image of America*, p. 63. As Todorov observes in *Nous et les autres* (Paris: Seuil, 1989), pp. 298, 302–3. Frank Lestringant also notes that the qualities Montaigne ascribes to the Indians make them heirs of the great men of Antiquity: *Le cannibale* (Paris: Perrin, 1994), p. 188. According to Claude Lévi-Strauss in *Histoire de Lynx*, p. 281, 'Montaigne sails between two reefs: utopia, which gives a rational foundation to society, and cultural relativism, which implies a rejection of any absolute criterion'. To my mind he rejects utopia but does not advocate relativism.
57 Lear's compassion for his 'poor Fool and knave' (III, ii, 72–73; iv, 26), his address to the 'Poor naked wretches' (III, iv, 28ff.); Gloucester's pity for naked Edgar and the old man's pity for both the blind man and the beggar (IV, i, 32–51); Gloucester's giving of his purse (IV, i, 64); Edgar's compassion for Gloucester's bleeding eyes (IV, i, 54); the Gentleman's remark on 'A sight most pitiful in the meanest wretch, / Past speaking of in a king' (IV, vi, 204); Edgar's description of himself as a man 'Who, by the art of known and feeling sorrows [is] pregnant to good pity' (IV, vi, 221–3) and his moving account of his meeting with his father (V, iii, 190–9); Albany's dissolving with woe at hearing this tale (V, iii, 203) and his design to apply what comfort may come to 'this great decay'; Lear (V, iii, 298) and Kent's final urging 'O, let him pass' (314–16).
58 See I, xxx: 227 B, VS 201; III, vi: 1032–3; VS 910–15. On other instances of cruelty: II, xxvii: 795 C–A; VS 699–701.

59 Nakam, *Le dernier Montaigne* p. 65; cf. pp. 71–8, 153–4.
60 See Claus Uhlig, 'The sobbing deer: *As You Like It*, II, i, 21–66 and the historical context', *Renaissance Drama*, n.s. 3 (1970), pp. 79–109.
61 See entry for 'moi' in F. Charpentier, ed., *Le dictionnaire de Montaigne*, p. 673.
62 *Le dictionnaire de Montaigne* calls attention to his 'devotion to the Virgin Mary at Loretto' (entry for 'Catholicisme', p. 141). Yet the Virgin is mentioned only once in the *Essays* (I, xlvi: 309 A; VS 277).
63 For instance when he says 'I would willingly come back from the next world' (III, ix: 1112 B; VS 983).
64 See Steven Marx, *Shakespeare and the Bible* (Oxford University Press, 2000).
65 Notably *Richard II*, *Romeo and Juliet*, *Hamlet* and *Macbeth*, but also in the Roman plays, *Titus Andronicus* and *Antony and Cleopatra*.
66 See M. Hunt, *Shakespeare's Religious Allusiveness: Its Play and Tolerance* (Aldershot: Ashgate, 2004), p. ix.
67 Lévinas, *Humanism of the Other*, p. 62.
68 *Essays*, I, xxvi: 198 B; VS 176; see *supra*, p. 157.
69 On this issue, see Robin Headlam Wells, *Shakespeare's Humanism* (Cambridge University Press, 2005) and his *Human Nature: Fact and Fiction* (London: Continuum, 2006).
70 See E. Colomer, 'Raymond Sebond, un humaniste avant la lettre', in C. Blum, ed., *Montaigne, Apologie de Raymond Sebond, De la* Theologia *à la* Théologie (Paris: Champion, 1990), pp. 60–1.
71 See *supra*, chapter 3, section 4.
72 See Lévi-Strauss, *Histoire de Lynx*, p. 280. Cf. Montaigne, *Essays*, I, xxiii: 116 C, VS 116, 'we think that it is reason which is unhinged whenever custom is'; II, xvii: 718 A, VS 632, 'Reason forbids us to do things which are bad'; III, viii: 1059 B; VS 935, 'My reason was not made for bending and bowing'.
73 *Essays*, II, xii: 1162 B; VS 1027: Montaigne quotes Cicero's *Academica*, II (Lucullus), xxi, 68.
74 Hamlin, *Tragedy and Scepticism*, p. 135.
75 Donald Frame, 'Montaigne's dialogue with his faculties', *French Forum*, 1 (1976), p. 203.
76 See Ellrodt, 'Literary history and the search for certainty', p. 531.
77 See Sextus Empiricus, *Esquisses pyrrhoniennes*, ed. P. Pellegrin (Paris: Seuil, 1997), I, 14 [135–40], pp. 129–31.
78 This is acknowledged by Guerrier, *Quand 'les poètes feignent'*, p. 335, and by R. C. La Charité in *The Concept of Judgment in Montaigne* (La Haye: Martinus Nijhoff, 1968).
79 He distrusts mere 'testimonies', even in print (III, xiii: 1227 B; VS 1081) and knows, like Plutarch, that the same truth can be presented in 'two opposite and contrasting manners' (III, xii: 1206 B; VS 1063).
80 See 'vérité' and 'vrai' in Leake's *Concordance*.
81 John Locke, *Essay Concerning Human Understanding*, ed. A. C. Fraser (Oxford: Clarendon, 1894), III, iii, 15ff. Montaigne also uses the term 'essence réelle' (III, x, 1144 B; VS 1011).

82 Screech, *Montaigne and Melancholy*, passim (see index).
83 Cf. Maclean, *Montaigne philosophe*, p. 46. See also 'There are names and there are things' (II, xvi: 702 A). On Montaigne and nominalism, see Antoine Compagnon, *Nous, Michel de Montaigne*.
84 See Bradshaw, *Shakespeare's Scepticism*, Cavell, *Disowning Knowledge in Six Plays of Shakespeare*, Engle, *Shakespearean Pragmatism*, Lee, *Shakespeare's Hamlet*. Grady, however, admits that occasionally 'their thought appears much less assimilable to Postmodernist claims for a consistent early modern anti-essentialism'. Grady, 'Shakespeare's links to Macchiavelli and Montaigne', pp. 131–2.
85 See Claude Blum, 'L'être et le néant. *Les Essais*, voyage au bout de la métaphysique', in *Montaigne. Penseur et philosophe (1588–1988)* (Paris: Champion; Geneva: Slatkine, 1990), p. 130.
86 He may happen to write 'nostre existence estant imparfaicte' (VS II, xvi, 618 A; Screech, p. 702), which implies all men have an essence in common, but in opposition here to the divine essence.
87 Todorov, *Le jardin imparfait*, p. 82.
88 *La Théologie naturelle de Raymond Sebond*, Traduicte par messire Michel, Seigneur de Montaigne (Paris, 1581), ch. 1, fol. 5r.
89 Lévinas, *Time and the Other*, pp. 87–8.
90 In essay II, xii (end), Montaigne translates Seneca, *Quaestiones naturales* (I, preface): 'Oh, what a vile and abject thing is Man if he does not rise above humanity'. See also Samuel Daniel's poem 'To the Lady Margaret, Countesse of Cumberland', ll. 98–9.
91 Montaigne, *La Théologie naturelle*, fol. 5v.
92 According to Lévinas, 'the distance between the same and the other is the abyss of transcendence and the subject transcends himself when he goes towards the Other'. See Fabio Cimarelli, *Transcendance et éthique: essai sur Lévinas* (Brussels: OUSIA, 1989), pp. 59, 207.
93 In sonnet 106, 'prefiguring'; in sonnet 108, 'hallowed'; in sonnet 125, 'oblation'.
94 Borrowed from chs 18 and 19 of Putarch's *On the 'E' at Delphi*. Montaigne, however, may also have had in mind a passage of Sebond: 'God is a deep abyss of essence, without any bottom, edge or measure' (Montaigne, *La Théologie naturelle*, ch. 12, fol. 18r). Moreover, in *Journal de voyage en Italie* Montaigne reveals that he had a copy of the works of Cusanus, which denotes an interest in negative theology, often associated with scepticism in the early seventeenth century. See Montaigne, *Journal de voyage en Italie*, ed. François Rigolot (Presses Universitaires de France, 1992), p. 71. See also Henri Busson, *La pensée religieuse française de Charron à Pascal* (Paris: Vrin, 1933).
95 One may think I make too much of this single instance of an imaginative evocation of the world's end, but the persistent allusions to the general doom in the poems and plays may proceed from the same sense of the fundamental unreality of the world of appearances. See: sonnet 55, l. 12, 'That wear this world out to the ending doom'; and sonnet 116, l. 12, 'to the edge of doom'; *Lucrece*, l. 724, 'From the creation to the general doom'; *Henry IV, Part 1*,

IV, i, 135, 'Doomsday is near'; *Romeo and Juliet*, III, ii, 67, 'sound the general doom'; *Hamlet*, Q2, I, i, 120, 'sick almost to doomsday with eclipse' and V, i, 59, 'lasts till doomsday'; *Macbeth*, II, iii, 78, 'the great doom's image'; *Antony and Cleopatra*, V, ii, 228, 'To play till doomsday'.

96   Arthur Schopenhauer, *Le monde comme volonté et comme représentation*, trans. Auguste Burdeau (Presses Universitaires de France, 1966), pp. 253–4. The ecstasy awakened in Florimel by each action of Perdita has some kinship with it: *Winter's Tale*, IV, iv, 136–46.

97   Cimarelli, *Transcendance et éthique*, p. 195.

98   He also speaks of 'creative ecstasies which transport a poet' (I, xxiv: 143 A; VS 127) and of how poets can throw the reader into 'an ecstasy of wonder' (II, xvii: 724 A; VS 637).

Epilogue

The wisdom of Montaigne and Shakespeare

As each chapter has been presented as a self-enclosed entity, this book's wide-ranging review of the progress of self-consciousness and its consequences in the works of Montaigne and Shakespeare need not be followed by an exhaustive summary or extended series of conclusions. I wish, therefore, to offer my conclusion in one word: wisdom. In different ways, both Montaigne and Shakespeare followed the example set by Socrates, who 'brought human wisdom back from the heavens where she was wasting her time and returned her to mankind, in whom lies her most proper and most demanding task as well as her most useful one' (*Essays*, III, xii: 1174 B; VS 1038). Wisdom characterized their practice of introspection, and the balance achieved between their attention to the inner self and their observation of the outer world. Wisdom directed their vision of human nature, their discovery of the instability of the self and their acknowledgement of the permanence of some individual features, and their awareness of change and their discovery of continuity. Wisdom inspired their conception of and their use of time, which they considered at once destructive and creative. Wisdom tempered their reliance on reason, apt to unmask imposture provided it entertains no delusion about its own capacities and takes into account the requirements of sensibility and the permanence of humanistic values. Thus the superb assertion of Matthew Arnold about Sophocles cited in my preface can apply to Montaigne as well as Shakespeare: 'Who saw life steadily, and saw it whole'.

When I offered an outline of the development of subjectivity in the second chapter of this book, I attempted to prove what has been often asserted but never fully demonstrated. I believe that I have shown that Montaigne and Shakespeare were indeed the first writers to open the way to clear manifestations of a new kind of self-consciousness in the early modern age. I have also brought to light some special traits which bring them close to some writers of our own period, though they were wise enough not to fall into the excesses of the present post-modernism.

Select bibliography

The place of publication is not mentioned for university presses.

The Bibliography does not include the ancient authors, Greek, Roman, medieval, Italian, French and English, mentioned in the text. The edition used is indicated in the note giving the first reference to the author mentioned and listed in the Index.

For MONTAIGNE, references are generally given to:

Michel de Montaigne. *The Complete Essays*. Translated and edited with an introduction and notes by M. A. Screech. Harmondsworth: Penguin Books, 1991; reprinted with corrections, 2003.

Michel de Montaigne. *Les Essais*, Édition Villey-Saulnier, augmentée en 2004 d'une préface et d'un supplément de Marcel Conche. Paris: Quadrige/Presses Universitaires de France, 2004.

Other editions are occasionally mentioned:

Montaigne's Essays. Trans. John Florio. Everyman's Library. London: Dent, 1965.

Montaigne. Œuvres complètes. Texte établi par Albert Thibaudet et Maurice Rat. Paris: NRF, Gallimard, 1962.

La Theologie naturelle de Raymond Sebond. Traduicte par messire Michel, Seigneur de Montaigne. Paris, 1581.

For SHAKESPEARE references are generally given to:

William Shakespeare: The Complete Works. Compact edition: General editors Stanley Wells and Gary Taylor. Oxford: Clarendon Press, 1988.

For *King Lear*, almost all references are to *The Tragedy of King Lear*, not to *The History*; the few exceptions in chapter 4 are noted in the text.

Some critical remarks are borrowed from French bilingual editions:

William Shakespeare. Œuvres complètes. Under the direction of Michel Grivelet and Gilles Monsarrat, 8 volumes. Paris: Éditions Robert Laffont, 1995–2002.

Shakespeare. Œuvres complètes. Under the direction of Jean-Michel Déprats and Gisèle Venet. *Tragédies,* vols I and II; *Histoires,* vols III and IV. Paris: Gallimard, 2002 and 2008.
William Shakespeare: Sonnets. Ed. Robert Ellrodt. Paris: Actes Sud (Babel), 2007.

In translation only:
Théâtre élisabéthain. Under the direction of Line Cottegnies, François Laroque and Jean-Marie Maguin, 2 vols. Paris: Gallimard (Pléiade), 2009.

Critical studies on Montaigne

BAKEWELL, Sarah. *How to Live: A Life of Montaigne in One Question and Twenty Attempts at an Answer.* London: Vintage Books, 2010.
BENCIVENGA, Ermano. *The Discipline of Subjectivity: An Essay on Montaigne.* Princeton University Press, 1990.
BLUM, Claude, ed. *Montaigne, Apologie de Raymond Sebond. De la Theologia a la Théologie.* Paris: Champion, 1990.
—— *Montaigne, penseur et philosophe (1588–1988).* Paris: Champion; Geneva: Slatkine, 1990.
——, M.-L. DEMONET and A. TOURNON, eds. *Montaigne et le nouveau monde: actes du colloque de Paris* (organized by la Société des amis de Montaigne, 18–20 May 1992). Mont-de-Marsan: Inter-Universitaires, 1994.
BRAHAMI, Frédéric. *Le scepticisme de Montaigne.* Presses Universitaires de France, 1997.
BRODY, Jules. *Lectures de Montaigne.* Lexington, KY: French Forum, 1982.
—— *Nouvelles lectures de Montaigne.* Paris: Champion, 1994.
BRUSH, C. *From the Perspective of the Self: Montaigne's Self-portrait.* New York: Fordham University Press, 1994.
BULLETIN de la Société des Amis de Montaigne, 2007: *Montaigne parmi les philosophes* (with articles by B. Roger-Vasselin, P. Desan, J.-F. Mattéi, P. Magnard).
BUTOR, Michel. *Essai sur les Essais.* Paris: Gallimard, 1968.
CARRAUD, V. and J.-L. MARION, eds. *Montaigne: scepticisme, métaphysique, théologie.* Presses Universitaires de France, 2004.
CAVE, Terence. *The Cornucopian Text: Problems of Writing in the French Renaissance.* Oxford University Press, 1979.
—— *Cornucopia. Figures de l'abondance au XVIe siècle: Érasme, Rabelais, Ronsard, Montaigne.* Paris: Macula, 1997.
—— *Préhistoires: textes troublés au seuil de la modernité.* Geneva: Droz, 1999.
—— *How to Read Montaigne.* London: Granta Books, 2007.
CÉARD, Jean. 'Montaigne et l'intériorité', in M. T. Jones-Davies, ed., *L'intériorité au temps de la Renaissance.* Paris: Champion, 2005.

COMPAGNON, Antoine. *Nous, Michel de Montaigne*. Paris: Seuil, 1980.
—— *La seconde main, ou Le travail de la citation*. Paris: Seuil, 1979.
—— *Nous, Michel de Montaigne*. Paris: Seuil, 1980.
—— *Chat en poche: Montaigne et l'allégorie*. Paris: Seuil, 1993.
—— *L'été avec Montaigne*. France Inter-éditions des Équateurs, 2013.
CONCHE, Marcel. *Montaigne et la philosophie*. Presses Universitaires de France, 1996.
—— *Montaigne ou la conscience heureuse*. Presses Universitaires de France, 2007.
DEFAUX, Gérard. 'Rhétorique et représentation dans les *Essais*: de la peinture de l'autre à la peinture du moi', in F. Lestringant, ed., *Rhétorique de Montaigne*, Paris: Champion, 1985.
—— *Marot, Rabelais, Montaigne: l'écriture comme présence*. Paris: Champion; Geneva: Slatkine, 1987.
DE LAJARTE, Philippe. 'Les *Essais* de Montaigne et la naissance de l'auteur moderne', in J. R. Fanlo, ed. *'D'une fantastique bigarrure'. Le texte composite à la Renaissance. Études offertes à André Tournon* (Paris: Champion, 2000).
DELÈGUE, Yves. *Montaigne et la mauvaise foi. L'ecriture de la vérité*. Paris: Champion, 1998.
DEMONET, Marie-Luce. *Montaigne et la question de l'homme*. Presses Universitaires de France, 1999.
DESAN, Philippe, *Les commerces de Montaigne: le discours économique des 'Essais'*. Paris: Nizet, 1992.
——, ed. *Dictionnaire de Michel de Montaigne*. Paris: Champion, 2004.
—— 'Montaigne paysagiste', in Dominique de Courcelles, ed., *Nature et paysages: l'émergence d'une nouvelle subjectivité à la Renaissance*. Paris: École des Chartes, 2006.
—— *Montaigne: les formes du monde et de l'esprit*. Paris: PUPS/DL, 2008.
DONELLAN, Brendan. 'Nietzsche and Montaigne'. *Colloquia Germanica*, 19 (1986), 1–20.
DOTOLI, Giovanni. *Montaigne et les libertins*. Paris: Champion, 2007.
ELLRODT, Robert. 'Montaigne et les ordres de vérité', in Francis Jacques, ed., *La vérité une et plurielle*. Paris: Éditions Parole et Silence, 2009.
FANLO, J. R., ed. *'D'une fantastique bigarrure'. Le texte composite à la Renaissance. Études offertes à André Tournon*. Paris: Champion, 2000.
FRAME, Donald M. *Montaigne's Discovery of Man: The Humanization of a Humanist*. Columbia University Press, 1955.
—— 'Montaigne's dialogue with his faculties'. *French Forum*, 1 (1976), 195–208.
FRIEDRICH, Hugo. *Montaigne* (trans. R. Rovini). Paris: Gallimard, 1968.
FUMAROLI, Marc. *La diplomatie de l'esprit. De Montaigne à La Fontaine*. Paris: Hermann, 1994.
GARAVINI, Fausta. *Monstres et chimères: Montaigne, le texte et le fantasme*. Paris: Champion, 1993.
—— 'Quel malheur de douter qu'on croit'. *Bulletin de la Société des Amis de Montaigne*, 33–4 (1993), 109–29.

GREEN, Felicity. *Montaigne and the Life of Freedom*. Cambridge University Press, 2012.
GUERRIER, Olivier. *Quand 'les poètes feignent': 'fantasies' et fiction dans les Essais de Montaigne*. Paris: Champion, 2002.
HALL, Joan, L. 'Role playing in Montaigne and Jacobean drama'. *Comparative Literary Studies*, 22 (1985), 173–86.
HARTLE, Ann. *Michel de Montaigne: Accidental Philosopher*. Cambridge University Press, 1999.
HOFFMAN, George. *Montaigne's Career*. Oxford: Clarendon Press, 1998.
HULSE, Anne. 'Montaigne's scepticism'. *Montaigne Studies*, 12 (2000), 75–90.
JOUKOVSKY, Françoise. *Montaigne et le problème du temps*. Paris: Nizet, 1972.
KUSHNER, Eva, ed. *La problématique du sujet chez Montaigne*. Paris: Champion, 1995.
LA CHARITÉ, R. C. *The Concept of Judgment in Montaigne*. La Haye: Martinus Nijhoff, 1968.
LANGER, Ulrich, ed. *The Cambridge Companion to Montaigne*. Cambridge University Press, 2005.
LEAKE, Roy E. *Concordance des Essais de Montaigne*. Geneva: Droz, 1981.
LEMAIRE, Jacques, ed. *Montaigne et la révolution philosophique du XVIe siècle*. Brussels: J. Lemaire, 1992.
LESCHEMELLE, Pierre. *Montaigne ou la mort paradoxe*. Paris: Imago, 1993.
LESTRINGANT, Frank. *Le cannibale*. Paris: Perrin, 1994.
LÉVI-STRAUSS, Claude. 'En relisant Montaigne', in *Histoire de Lynx*. Paris: Plon, 1991.
MACLEAN, Ian. *Montaigne philosophe*. Presses Universitaires de France, 1996.
MAN, Paul de. 'Montaigne et la transcendance'. *Critique*, 9:79 (1953), 1011–22.
MATHIEU-CASTELLANI, Gisèle. 'Lire "entre ce que l'autre y a mis"'. *Montaigne Studies*, 9 (1997), 5–16.
—— *Montaigne ou la vérité du mensonge*. Geneva: Droz, 2000.
—— 'Les *Confessions* de saint Augustin dans les *Essais* de Montaigne', in N. Peacock and J. J. Supple, *Lire les* Essais *de Montaigne* (pp. 211–28). Paris: Champion, 2001.
MCFARLANE, I. D. and Ian MACLEAN, eds. *Essays in Memory of Richard Sayce*. Oxford: Clarendon Press, 1982.
MERLEAU-PONTY, Maurice. 'Lecture de Montaigne', in *Signes*. Paris: Gallimard, 1960.
MERMIER, Guy. 'Inconstance et relativité: pièces maîtresses de la modernité de Montaigne'. *Bulletin de la Société des Amis de Montaigne*, 25–6 (1978), 151–6.
MICHA, Alexandre. *Le singulier Montaigne*. Paris: Nizet, 1964.
MIERNOWSKI, Jan. *L'ontologie de la contradiction sceptique*. Paris: Champion, 1998.
NAKAM, Géralde. 'Montaigne maire de Bordeaux: à la mairie et dans les *Essais*', *Bulletin de la Société des Amis de Montaigne*, 8e série, 13–14 (1983), 7–28.
—— *Montaigne: la manière et la matière*. Paris: Klincksieck, 1991; Paris: Champion, 2006.

—— *Les Essais de Montaigne: miroir et procès de leur temps*. Paris: Champion, 2001.
—— *Le dernier Montaigne*. Paris: Champion, 2002.
NORTON, Glynn. *Montaigne and the Introspective Mind*. La Haye: Mouton, 1975.
PANICHI, Nicola. *Montaigne et Nietzsche*. Paris: Champion, 2008.
PINCHARD, Bruno. 'Montaigne: essai de lecture dialectique'. *Montaigne Studies*, 12 (2000), 63–73.
POUILLOUX, Jean-Yves. *Lire les 'Essais' de Montaigne*. Paris: Maspéro, 1969.
—— *Montaigne. L'éveil de la pensée*. Paris: Champion, 1995.
—— 'Ne sachant pas pénétrer ce que c'est que croire'. *Bulletin de la Société des Amis de Montaigne*, 50, 2ème semestre (2009), 109–18.
—— *Montaigne, une vérité singulière*. Paris: Gallimard, 2012.
QUINT, David. *Montaigne and the Quality of Mercy*. Princeton University Press, 1998.
REGOSIN, Richard L. *The Matter of My Book: Montaigne's 'Essais' as the Book of the Self*. University of California Press, 1977.
—— 'Recent trends in Montaigne scholarship: a post-structuralist perspective'. *Renaissance Quarterly*, 38 (1984), 34–54.
RENDALL, Steve. *Distinguo: Reading Montaigne Differently*. Oxford: Clarendon Press, 1992.
RIDER, Frederick. *The Dialectic of Selfhood in Montaigne*. Stanford University Press, 1973.
RIGOLOT, François. *Les métamorphoses de Montaigne*. Presses Universitaires de France, 1988.
ROGER-VASSELIN, Bruno. *Montaigne et l'art du sourire à la Renaissance*. Paris: Nizet, 2003.
SAYCE, Richard. *The Essays of Montaigne: A Critical Exploration*. Northwestern University Press, 1972.
SCHAEFFER, D. L. *The Political Philosophy of Montaigne*. Cornell University Press, 1990.
SCOLAR, Richard. *Montaigne and the Art of Free-Thinking*. New York: Peter Lang, 2011.
SCREECH, M. A. *Montaigne and Melancholy*. London: Duckworth, 1983.
SELLEWOLD, Kirsti. *L'expression linguistique du doute dans les Essais de Montaigne: une approche polyphonique*. Paris: Champion, 2004.
SMALL, Andrew. *Essays in Self-portraiture: A Comparison of Technique in the Self-portraits of Montaigne and Rembrandt*. New York: Peter Lang, 1996.
STAROBINSKI, Jean. 'Montaigne et la dénonciation du mensonge', in Odo Marquard and Karlheinz Stierle, eds, *Identität*. Munich: Wilhelm Fink, 1979.
—— *Montaigne en mouvement*. Paris: Gallimard, 1982.
—— *Montaigne in Motion* (trans. A. Goldhammer). Chicago University Press, 1985.
SUPPLE, James J. *Arms Versus Letters: The Military and Literary Ideals in the Essais of Montaigne*. Oxford: Clarendon Press, 1985.
—— *Les Essais de Montaigne: méthode(s) et méthodologie*. Paris: Champion, 2000.

—— and Noël PEACOCK, eds. *Lire les* Essais *de Montaigne: perspectives critiques*. Paris: Champion, 2001.
TETEL, Marcel, ed. *Actes du colloque international Montaigne 1980*. Paris: Nizet, 1983.
—— and G. Mallary MASTERS, eds. *Le parcours des Essais — Montaigne 1588–1598*. Paris: Aux Amateurs de Livres, 1986.
TODOROV, Tzetan. *Montaigne ou la découverte de l'individu*. Tournai: La Renaissance du Livre, 2001.
TOURNON, André. *Montaigne en toutes lettres*. Paris: Bordas, 1989.
—— *Montaigne: la glose et l'essai*. Paris: Champion, 2000.
—— *Route par ailleurs: le 'nouveau langage' des Essais*. Paris: Champion, 2006.
ZALLOUA, Zahi. *Montaigne and the Ethics of Skepticism*. Charlottesville, VA: Rockwood Press, 2005.
—— ed. *Montaigne After Theory: Theory After Montaigne*. University of Washington Press, 2009.

Critical studies on Shakespeare
(including studies on Shakespeare and Montaigne)

ADELMAN, Janet. *Suffocating Mothers: Fantasies of Maternal Origin in Shakespeare's Plays,* Hamlet *to* The Tempest. London: Routledge, 1992.
AERS, David. *Hamlet: Culture and History 1350–1600*. London: Harvester Wheatsheaf, 1992.
BALDWIN, T. M. *William Shakespeare's Small Latine and Lesse Greek*, 2 vols. University of Illinois Press, 1944.
BARKER, Francis. *The Tremulous Private Body*. London: Methuen, 1984.
BARTON (RIGHTER), Anne. *Shakespeare and the Idea of the Play*. London: Penguin, 1962.
BATE, Jonathan. *Shakespeare and Ovid*. Oxford University Press, 1993.
—— *The Genius of Shakespeare*. Oxford University Press, 1997.
—— 'Montaigne and Shakespeare'. Radio essay available on the BBC iPlayer.
BELSEY, Catherine. *The Subject of Tragedy*. London: Methuen, 1984.
BENNETT, Robert. 'Shakespeare and Montaigne via Erasmus', in *Romance and Reformation: The Erasmian Spirit of Shakespeare's* Measure for Measure. University of Delaware Press, 2000.
BLOOM, Harold. *Shakespeare: The Invention of the Human*. London: Fourth Estate, 1999.
BRADSHAW, Graham. *Shakespeare's Scepticism*. Brighton: Harvester Press, 1987.
—— *Shakespeare and the Materialists*. Cornell University Press, 1993.
——, T. BISHOP and P. HOLBROOK, eds. *Shakespeare and Montaigne Revisited*. Shakespearian International Yearbook No. 6. Aldershot: Ashgate, 2006.
BURNETT, M. T. and J. MANNING, eds. *New Essays on* Hamlet. New York: AMS Press, 1994.

Burns, Edward. *Character, Acting and Being on the Pre-modern Stage*. New York: St Martin's Press, 1990.
Campbell, Lily. *Shakespeare's Tragic Heroes*. Cambridge University Press, 1952.
Cavell, Stanley. *Disowning Knowledge in Six Plays of Shakespeare*. Cambridge University Press, 1987.
Cazamian, Louis. *The Development of English Humor*. Duke University Press, 1952.
Charnes, Linda. *Notorious Identity: Materializing the Subject in Shakespeare*. Harvard University Press, 1993.
Charney, Maurice. *Wrinkled Deep in Time: Aging in Shakespeare*. Columbia University Press, 2009.
Chauduri, Sukanta. *Infirm Glory: Shakespeare and the Renaissance Image of Man*. Oxford University Press, 1981.
Cixous, Hélène. 'The character of "character"'. *New Literary History*, 5 (1974), 383–402.
Coghill, Nevil. 'Soliloquy', in *Shakespeare's Professional Skills*. Cambridge University Press, 1964.
Colie, Rosalie and F. T. Flahiff, eds. *Some Facets of King Lear*. University of Toronto Press, 1974.
Coussement-Boillot, Laetitia. *Copia et cornucopia: la poétique shakespearienne de l'abondance*. Berne: Publications Universitaires Européennes, 2008.
Cox, John C. D. and David Scott Kastan. *A New History of Early English Drama*. Columbia University Press, 1997.
Dahl, Liisa. *Nominal Style in the Shakespearean Soliloquy with Reference to the Early English Drama, Shakespeare's Immediate Predecessors and His Contemporaries*, Torsten: University of Turku, 1969.
Davies, Michael. *Hamlet: Character Studies*. London: Continuum, 2008.
Davis, Philip Maurice. *Sudden Shakespeare: The Shaping of Shakespeare's Creative Thought*. London: Athlone, 1996.
De Grazia, Margreta. *Hamlet Without Hamlet*. Cambridge University Press, 2007.
Dent, Robert William. *Shakespeare's Proverbial Language*. University of California Press, 1981.
Dollimore, Jonathan. *Radical Tragedy*. Brighton: Harvester Wheatsheaf, 2nd edn, 1984.
Driscoll, James P. *Identity in Shakespearean Drama*. London: Associated University Press, 1983.
Dubrow, Heather. 'Shakespeare's undramatic monologues: towards a reading of the Sonnets'. *Shakespeare Quarterly*, 32:1 (1981), 55–68.
Eagleton, Terry. *William Shakespeare*. Oxford: Blackwell, 1986.
Edmonson, Paul and Stanley W. Wells. *Shakespeare's Sonnets*. Oxford University Press, 2004.
Ellrodt, Robert. 'An anatomy of "The phoenix and the turtle"'. *Shakespeare Survey*, 15 (1962), 99–110.

—— 'Self-consciousness in Montaigne and Shakespeare'. *Shakespeare Survey*, 28 (1975), 37–50.
—— 'Shakespeare the non-dramatic poet', in Stanley Wells, ed., *The Cambridge Companion to Shakespeare Studies*. Cambridge University Press, 1986.
—— 'The inversion of cultural traditions in Shakespeare's sonnets', in T. Kishi, R. Pringle and S. Wells, eds. *Shakespeare and Cultural Traditions*. University of Delaware Press, 1994.
—— 'La perception du temps dans les *Sonnets* de Shakespeare', in Louis Roux, ed., *Le Char ailé du temps*. Publications de l'Université de Saint-Etienne, 2003.
—— 'Constance des valeurs humanistes chez Montaigne et chez Shakespeare', in P. Kapitaniak and J.-M. Maguin, eds, *Shakespeare et Montaigne: vers un nouvel humanisme*. Montpellier: Société Française Shakespeare, Actes du Congrès, 2003.
—— 'Self-consistency in Montaigne and Shakespeare', in Tom Clayton, Susan Brock and Vicente Forés, eds, *Shakespeare and the Mediterranean*. University of Delaware Press, 2004.
—— 'Shakespeare's progress from the narrative poems to the Sonnets', in P. Kapitaniak and Y. Peyré, eds, *Shakespeare poète*. Montpellier: Société Française Shakespeare, Actes du Congrès, 2006.
ENGLE, Lars. *Shakespearean Pragmatism: Market of His Time*. University of Chicago Press, 1993.
FERRY, Anne. *All in War with Time: Love Poetry of Shakespeare, Donne, Jonson, Marvell*. Harvard University Press, 1975.
FOWLER, Alastair. 'Shakespeare's Renaissance realism'. *Proceedings of the British Academy*, 90 (1996), 29–64.
GARBER, Marjorie. *Coming of Age in Shakespeare*. London: Routledge, 1997.
GRADY, Hugh. *Shakespeare's Universal Wolf*. Oxford University Press, 1996.
—— ed. *Shakespeare and Modernity*. London: Routledge, 2000.
—— 'Shakespeare's links to Machiavelli and Montaigne'. *Comparative Literature*, 52 (2000), 119–42.
HALL, Joan Lord. 'Role-playing in Montaigne and Jacobean drama'. *Comparative Literary Studies*, 22 (1985), 73–86.
HAMLIN, William M. *The Image of America in Montaigne, Spenser, and Shakespeare*. New York: St Martin's Press, 1995.
—— *Scepticism in Shakespeare's England*. Shakespeare International Yearbook No. 2. Aldershot: Ashgate, 2002.
—— *Tragedy and Scepticism in Shakespeare's England*. Houndmills: Macmillan, 2005.
HILLMAN, Richard. *Self-speaking in Medieval and Early Modern English Drama: Subjectivity, Discourse and the Stage*. London: Macmillan, 1993.
HILMAN, David. *Shakespeare's Entrails*. London: Macmillan, 2007.
HIRSH, James E. *Shakespeare and the History of Soliloquies*. Farleigh Dickinson University Press, 2003.
HOENSELAARS, Tom and Clara CALVO, eds. *European Shakespeares*. Shakespeare International Yearbook No. 8. Aldershot: Ashgate, 2002.

HOLBROOK, Peter. *Shakespeare's Individualism*. Cambridge University Press, 2010.
HOLLAND, N. N. *Psychoanalysis and Shakespeare*. New York: Octagon Books, 1979.
——, S. HOMAN and B. J. PARIS, eds. *Shakespeare's Personality*. University of California Press, 1989.
HONAN, Park. *Shakespeare: A Life*. Oxford University Press, 1998.
HUNT, Maurice. *Shakespeare's Religious Allusiveness: Its Play and Tolerance*. Aldershot: Ashgate, 2004.
KERRIGAN, John. *On Shakespeare and Early Modern Literature*. Oxford University Press, 2001.
KIRSH, Arthur. 'Hamlet's grief'. *English Literary History*, 48:1 (1981), 17–36.
—— *Shakespeare and the Experience of Love*. Cambridge University Press, 1981.
—— *The Passions of Shakespeare's Heroes*. Virginia University Press, 1990.
—— 'Virtue, vice and compassion in Montaigne and *The Tempest*'. *Studies in English Literature 1500–1900*, 37 (1997), 337–52.
KLAUSE, John. 'Shakespeare's *Sonnets*: age in love and the goring of thoughts', *Studies in Philology*, 80 (1993), 300–23.
LACAN, Jacques. 'Desire and the interpretation of desire in *Hamlet*'. *Yale French Studies*, 55/6 (1977), 11–52.
LANGLEY, Eric. *Narcissism and Suicide in Shakespeare and His Contemporaries*. Oxford University Press, 2009.
LAROQUE, François, Pierre ISELIN and José NUYTS-GIORNAL. *King Lear, l'œuvre au noir*. Presses Universitaires de France, 2008.
LAROQUE, François, P. ISELIN and S. ALATORRE, eds. *'And That's True Too': New Essays on King Lear*. Cambridge: Cambridge Scholars Publishing, 2009.
LEE, John. *Shakespeare's Hamlet and the Controversies of Self*. Oxford University Press, 2000.
LEISHMAN, J. B. *Themes and Variations in Shakespeare's Sonnets*. London: Hutchinson, 1961.
Low, Anthony. *Aspects of Subjectivity: From the Middle Ages to Shakespeare and Milton*. Duquesne University Press, 2003.
MAGUIN, Jean-Marie. '*The Tempest* and cultural exchange'. *Shakespeare Survey*, 48 (1995), 147–54.
MARIENSTRAS, Richard. *Shakespeare au xxi siècle: une petite introduction aux tragédies*. Paris: Les Éditions de Minuit, 2000.
—— *Shakespeare et le désordre du monde*. Ed. Dominique Goy-Blanquet. Paris: Gallimard, NRF, 2012.
MARTINDALE, Charles and Michelle MARTINDALE. *Shakespeare and the Uses of Antiquity*. London: Routledge, 1990.
MARX, Steven. *Shakespeare and the Bible*. Oxford University Press, 2000.
MATHIS, Gilles and Pierre SAHEL. *Hamlet, ou le texte en question*. Paris: Messene, 1997.
MAUS, Katharine Eiseiman. *Inwardness and Theater in the English Renaissance*. University of Chicago Press, 1995.

MAYER, Jean-Christophe. *Shakespeare et la postmodernité: essais sur l'auteur, le religieux, l'histoire et le lecteur.* New York: Peter Lang, 2012.
MCALINDON, Thomas. *Shakespeare's Tragic Cosmos.* Cambridge University Press, 1991.
MCGINN, Colin. *Shakespeare's Philosophy.* New York: Harper/Collins, 2006.
MILES, Geoffrey. *Shakespeare and the Constant Romans.* Oxford: Clarendon Press, 1996.
MIOLA, Robert. *Shakespeare's Reading.* Oxford University Press, 2000.
MURRAY, Peter B. *Shakespeare's Imagined Person: The Psychology of Role-Playing and Acting.* London: Barnes and Noble, 1996.
NEVO, Ruth. *Tragic Form in Shakespeare.* Princeton University Press, 1972.
NEWELL, Alex. *The Soliloquies in Hamlet: The Structural Design.* London: Associated University Presses, 1991.
NUTTALL, A. D. *A New Mimesis: Shakespeare and the Representation of Reality.* Yale University Press, 2nd edn, 2007.
—— *Shakespeare the Thinker.* Yale University Press, 2007.
PROSSER, Eleanor. 'Shakespeare, Montaigne, and the rarer action'. *Shakespeare Studies*, 1 (1965), 261–4.
ROBERTSON, John M. *Montaigne and Shakespeare.* London University Press, 1897.
ROSENBERG, Marvin. *The Masks of Hamlet.* University of Delaware Press/Associated University Presses, 1992.
SALINGAR, Leo. *Dramatic Form in Shakespeare and the Jacobeans.* Harvard University Press, 1986.
SCHWARTZ, Robert B. *Shakespeare's Parted Eye: Perception, Knowledge and Meaning in the Sonnets and Plays.* New York: Peter Lang, 1990.
SKIFFINGTON, Lloyd A. *The History of English Soliloquy: Aeschylus to Shakespeare.* University Press of America, 1985.
SOELLNER, Rolf. *Shakespeare's Patterns of Self-knowledge.* Ohio State University Press, 1972.
STATES, Bert O. *Hamlet and the Concept of Character.* Johns Hopkins University Press, 1992.
TAYLOR, G. C. *Shakespeare's Debt to Montaigne.* Harvard University Press, 1925.
TURNER, Frederick. *Shakespeare and the Nature of Time.* Oxford: Clarendon Press, 1977.
VAN LAAN, Thomas. *Role-Playing in Shakespeare.* Toronto University Press, 1978.
VENET, Gisèle. *Temps et vision tragique chez Shakespeare et ses contemporains.* Paris: Publications de la Sorbonne Nouvelle, 1985, 2002.
WEIMANN, Robert. 'Society and the individual in Shakespeare's conception of character'. *Shakespeare Survey*, 24 (1981), 23–31.
WELLS, Stanley and Margreta DE GRAZIA, eds. *The Cambridge Companion to Shakespeare Studies.* Cambridge University Press, 2001.

General studies (literary, historical, philosophical)

AERS, David. *Community, Gender, and Individual Identity*. London: Routledge, 1988.
ASCOLI, A. R. and Victoria KAHN. *Machiavelli and the Discourse of Literature*. Cornell University Press, 1993.
BALIBAR, Etienne, ed. *John Locke: identité et différence, l'invention de la conscience*. Paris: Seuil, 1998.
BARBU, Zevedei. 'The emergence of personality in the Greek world', in *Problems of Historical Psychology*. New York: Grove Press, 1960. pp. 69–144.
BELLENGER, Yvonne. *Le temps et les jours dans quelques recueils poétiques du XVIe siècle*. Paris: Champion, 2002.
BLEVINS, Jacob. *Catullan Consciousness and the Early Modern Lyric in England: From Wyatt to Donne*. Aldershot: Ashgate, 2004.
BRADEN, Gordon. *Renaissance Tragedy and the Senecan Tradition: Anger's Privilege*. Yale University Press, 1985.
BREMMER, Jan. *The Early Greek Concept of the Soul*. Princeton University Press, 1983.
BRÈS, Yvon. *La psychologie de Platon*. Presses Universitaires de France, 1968.
—— 'La connaissance de soi chez Platon', in René Angelergues, ed., *Psychologie de la connaissance de soi: 15e symposium de l'Association de psychologie scientifique de langue française, Paris, 1973*. Presses Universitaires de France, 1975.
BRUGIÈRE, Bernard. 'Aspects de la conscience de soi dans le romantisme', in Robert Ellrodt, ed., *Genèse de la conscience moderne*. Presses Universitaires de France, 1983.
BRUNSCHVICG, Léon. *Le progrès de la conscience dans la philosophie occidentale*. Paris: Presses Universitaires de France, 1953.
CALLAHAN, J. S. *Four Views of Time in Ancient Philosophy*. Harvard University Press, 1948.
CARRAUD, Vincent. *L'invention du moi*. Presses Universitaires de France, 2010.
CASSIRER, Ernst. *L'individu et le cosmos dans la philosophie de la Renaissance*. Paris: Éditions de Minuit, 1983.
CASTORIADIS, Cornelius. 'L'état du sujet aujourd'hui'. *Topique. Revue Freudienne*, 38 (1986), 7–39.
CAVE, Terence. *Recognitions: A Study in Poetics*. Oxford: Clarendon Press, 1990.
CAVELL, Stanley. *Othello: The Claims of Reason*. Oxford University Press, 1979.
CERTEAU, Michel de. *Hétérologies*. Minnesota University Press, 1986.
CHEVALIER, Jacques. *Histoire de la pensée antique, vol. II: D'Aristote à Plotin*. Paris: Éditions Universitaires, 1991.
CIMARELLI, Fabio. *Transcendance et éthique: essai sur Lévinas*. Brussels: OUSIA, 1989.
COURCELLE, Pierre. *Connais,-toi toi-même: de Socrate à saint Bernard*. Paris: Études augustiniennes, 1974.
COURCELLES, Dominique, ed. *Nature et paysages: l'émergence d'une nouvelle subjectivité à la Renaissance*. Paris: École des Chartes, 2006.

DAUVOIS, Nathalie. *Le sujet lyrique à la Renaissance*. Presses Universitaires de France, 2000.
DE GRAZIA, Margreta. 'World pictures, modern periods, and the early stage', in John C. D. Cox and David Scott Kastan, eds, *A New History of Early English Drama*. Columbia University Press, 1997, pp. 7–21.
——, M. QUILLIGAN and P. STALLYBRASS, eds. *Subject and Object in Renaissance Culture*. Cambridge University Press, 1996.
DESAN, Philippe. *Naissance de la méthode: Machiavel, La Ramée, Bodin, Montaigne, Descartes*. Paris: Nizet, 1987.
DINSHAW, Carolyn. *How Soon Is Now? Medieval Texts, Amateur Readers, and the Queerness of Time*. Duke University Press, 2012.
DRAGSTRA, Henk, Sheila OTTWAY and Helen WILCOX, eds. *Betraying Ourselves: Forms of self-Representation in Early Modern English Texts*. New York: Palgrave/St Martin's Press, 2000.
ELLRODT, Robert. 'Genèse et dilemme de la conscience moderne'. *Revue de la Méditerranée*, XII, 1952–3.
—— *L'inspiration personnelle et l'esprit du temps chez les poètes Métaphysiques anglais*. 3 vols. Paris: Corti, 1960; vols I and II in a new edition, 1973.
—— 'La conscience moderne de saint Augustin à Jean-Paul Sartre', in *Actes du groupe de recherche sur la conscience de soi*. Publications de la Faculté des Lettres et Sciences Humaines de Nice, first series, vol. XVIII, 1980.
—— ed. *Genèse de la conscience moderne*. Presses Universitaires de France, 1983.
—— 'The search for identity from Montaigne to Donne', in Armand Himy, ed., *John Donne and Modernity*. Confluences XI. Université Paris X – Nanterre, 1995.
—— 'Literary theory and the search for certainty'. *New Literary History*, 17 (1996), 529–43.
—— 'Unchanging forms of identity in literary expression'. *European Review: Interdisciplinary Journal of the Academia Europaea*, 7:1 (1999), 113–26.
—— *Seven Metaphysical Poets: A Structural Study of the Unchanging Self*. Oxford University Press, 2000.
—— 'Genèse de la conscience de soi', in Francis Jacques, ed., *Anthropologie et humanisme*. Paris: Éditions Parole et Silence, 2006.
FERRY, Anne. *The Inward Language: Sonnets of Wyatt, Sidney, Shakespeare, Donne*. Chicago University Press, 1983.
FERRY, Luc and Alain RENAUD. *Heidegger et les modernes*. Paris: Grasset, 1988.
FIGURELLI, Fernando. *Il dolce stil novo*. Naples: Riccardo Riccciardi, 1933.
FOUCAULT, Michel. *Dits et écrits*. Paris: Gallimard, 2000.
—— *L'herméneutique du sujet*. Paris: Gallimard, Seuil, 2008.
FUDGE, Erica. *Brutal Reasoning: Animals, Rationality, and Humanity in Early Modern England*. Cornell University Press, 2006.
GAUNT, Simon and Sarah KAY. *The Troubadours*. Cambridge University Press, 1999.
GIDDENS, Anthony. *Modernity and Self-identity: Self and Society in the Late Modern Age*. Stanford University Press, 1996.

GREENBLATT, Stephen. *Renaissance Self-fashioning from More to Shakespeare.* University of Chicago Press, 1980, reprinted 2006.
GREENE, Thomas. 'The flexibility of the self in Renaissance literature', in P. Demetz, T. Greene and L. Nelson Jr, eds, *The Disciplines of Criticism.* Yale University Press, 1968.
GRIMAL, Pierre. *Le lyrisme à Rome.* Presses Universitaires de France, 1978.
GROETHUYSEN, Bernard. *Anthropologie philosophique.* Paris: Gallimard, 1953.
GUSDORF, Georges. *La découverte de soi.* Presses Universitaires de France, 1948.
HADOT, Pierre. *Plotin, porphyre: études néoplatoniciennes.* Paris: Belles Lettres, 1999.
HANNING, Robert W. *The Individual in Twelfth Century Romance.* Yale University Press, 1977.
HIMY, Armand and Margaret LLASERA, eds. *John Donne and Modernity.* Confluences XI. Universite Paris X, 1995.
HOLMES, Olivia. *Assembling the Lyric Self: Authorship from Troubadour Song to Italian Poetry Books.* University of Minnesota Press, 2000.
HUOT, Sylvia. *From Song to Book: The Poetry of Writing in Old French Lyric and Lyrical Narrative Poetry.* Cornell University Press, 1987.
JACQUES, Francis. *Difference and Subjectivity: Dialogue and Personal Identity.* Yale University Press, 1991.
KAY, Sarah. *Subjectivity in Troubadour Poetry.* Cambridge University Press, 1990.
KIMMELMAN, Burt. *The Poetics of Authorship in the Later Middle Ages: The Emergence of the Literary Persona.* New York: Peter Lang, 1996.
KRISTELLER, Paul O. *Studies in Renaissance Thought and Letters.* Rome: Edizione di Storia e Letteratura, 1956.
JONES-DAVIES, M. T., ed. *L'intériorité au temps de la Renaissance.* Paris: Champion, 2005.
LANDRY, D. *Origins of the Individual Self: Autobiography and Self-identity in England, 1591–1791.* Oxford: Polity Press, 1998.
LECOINTE, Jean. *L'idéal et la différence: la perception de la personnalité littéraire à la Renaissance.* Geneva: Droz, 1993.
LEICESTER, H. Marshall. *The Disenchanted Self: Representing the Subject in the Canterbury Tales.* University of California Press, 1990.
LÉVINAS, Emmanuel. *Le temps et l'autre.* Presses Universitaires de France, 1970.
—— *L'humanisme de l'autre homme.* Paris: Fata Morgana, 1987.
—— *Time and the Other,* trans. Richard Cohen. Duquesne University Press, 1987.
—— *De dieu qui vient à l'idée.* Paris: Vrin, 1998.
—— *Of God Who Comes to Mind,* trans. Bettina Bergo. Stanford University Press, 1998.
—— *Humanism of the Other,* trans. Nidra Poller. University of Illinois Press, 2003.
LEWIS, C. S. *The Allegory of Love.* Oxford University Press, 1936, reprinted 1972.
LIBÉRA, Alain de. *Archéologie du sujet, vol. I: Naissance du sujet.* Paris: Vrin, 2007.

Low, Anthony. *Aspects of Subjectivity – Society and Individuality: From the Middle Ages to Shakespeare and Milton.* Duquesne University Press, 2003.
Lowe, E. J. *Subject of Experience.* Cambridge University Press, 1996.
Marquard, Odo and Karlheinz Stierle, eds. *Identität.* Munich: Wilhelm Fink, 1979.
Martin, Luther H., H. Gutton and P. H. Hutton, eds. *Psychologies of the Self: A Seminar with Michel Foucault.* University of Massachusetts Press, 1988.
Melehy, H. *Writing Cogito: Descartes and the Institution of the Modern Subject.* State University of New York Press, 1997.
Meyerson, I. *Problèmes de la personne.* La Haye: Mouton, 1973.
Miller, Paul Allen. *Lyric Texts and Lyric Consciousness: The Birth of a Genre from Archaic Greece to Augustan Rome.* New York: Routledge, 1994.
Mizolle, Elisabeth. *Autobiographical Quests: Augustine, Montaigne, Rousseau and Wordsworth.* University Press of Virginia, 1992.
Morris, Colin. *The Discovery of the Individual, 1050–1200.* London: SCPK, 1972; Toronto University Press, 1995.
Nuttall, A. D. *Openings.* Oxford: Clarendon Press, 1992.
Onians, Richard Broxton. *The Origins of European Thought.* Cambridge University Press, 1991.
Oppenheimer, Paul. *The Birth of the Modern Mind: Self, Consciousness, and the Invention of the Sonnet.* Columbia University Press, 1980.
Pask, Kevin. *The Emergence of the English Author: Scripting the Life of the Poet in Early Modern England.* Cambridge University Press, 1996.
Pierre, A. J., ed. *Sixteenth Century Identities.* Manchester University Press, 2002.
Pintaric, Miha. *Le sentiment du temps dans la littérature française (XIIIe s.–fin du XVIe s.).* Paris: Champion, 2002.
Pironon, Jean. *Le luth et le blason: les sens, la sensation et le moi lyrique de Thomas Wyatt à Edmund Spenser.* Berne: Peter Lang, 2009.
Powell, Thomas. *Kant's Theory of Self-consciousness.* Oxford: Clarendon Press, 1990.
Quinones, Ricardo. *The Renaissance Discovery of Time.* Harvard University Press, 1972.
Renaut, Alain. *L'ère de l'individu: contribution à une histoire de la subjectivité.* Paris: Gallimard, 1989.
Ricoeur, Paul. *Temps et récit, vol. III: Le temps raconté.* Paris: Éditions du Seuil, 1985.
Ryan, Judith. *The Vanishing Subject.* University of Chicago Press, 1991.
Saeger, Paul. 'Silent reading: its impact on late medieval script and society'. *Viator*, 13 (1982), 367–414.
Saïd, Suzanne. 'La conscience de soi dans la tragédie grecque', in R. Ellrodt, ed., *Genèse de la conscience moderne.* Presses Universitaires de France, 1983.
Sartre, J.-P. *L'être et le néant.* Paris: Gallimard, 1943.

SHARPE, Kevin and Steven ZWICKER, eds. *Writing Lives: Biography and Textuality, Identity and Representation in Early Modern England.* Oxford University Press, 2008.

SHUGER, Deborah. *Habits of Thought in Renaissance England.* University of California Press, 1990.

SIMPSON, James. *Sciences and the Self in Medieval Poetry.* Cambridge University Press, 1995.

SINFIELD, Alan. *Faultlines: Cultural Materialism and the Politics of Dissident Reading.* Oxford: Clarendon Press, 1992.

SNELL, Bruno. *La découverte de l'esprit: la genèse de la pensée européenne chez les Grecs.* Paris: Éditions de l'Éclat, 1994.

SPEARING, A. C. *Medieval Autographies: The 'I' of the Text.* University of Notre Dame Press, 2014.

STONE, M. W. F. 'Conscience in Renaissance thought: a concept in transition'. *Renaissance Studies*, 23:4 (2009), 423–44.

STAROBINSKI, Jean. 'Sur quelques formes de critique de la notion d'identité (remarques historiques)', in O. Marquard and Karlheinz Stierle, eds, *Identität.* Munich: Wilhelm Fink, 1979.

TAYLOR, Charles. *The Sources of the Self.* Cambridge University Press, 1994.

TODOROV, Tzvetan. *Humanism of the Other.* Trans Nidra Poller. Duquesne University, 1987.

—— *Nous et les autres.* Paris: Seuil, 1989.

—— *Le jardin imparfait: la pensée humaniste en France.* Paris: Grasset, 1998.

—— *The Imperfect Garden: The Legacy of Humanism.* Trans. Carol Gosman. Princeton University Press, 2002.

TOLIVER, Stanley. *Poetry with a Purpose: Biblical Poetics and Interpretation.* Indiana University Press 1988.

TRINKHAUS, Charles. *In Our Image and Likeness: Humanity and Divinity in Italian Humanist Thought.* University of Notre Dame Press, 1995.

VALENCY, Maurice. *In Praise of Love.* London: Macmillan, 1958.

VERNANT, Jean-Pierre. *Mythe et pensée chez les Grecs.* Paris: Maspéro, 1969.

VEYNE, Paul. *L'élégie érotique romaine.* Paris: Seuil, 1983.

VICKERS, Brian. *Towards Greek Tragedy: Drama, Myth, Society.* London: Longman, 1973.

WALLER, Gary F. *The Strong Necessity of Time: The Philosophy of Time in Shakespeare and Elizabethan Literature.* La Haye: Mouton, 1976.

WEINTRAUB, Karl J. *The Value of the Individual: Self and Circumstance in Autobiography.* Chicago University Press, 1978.

WILCOX, Helen. '"The birth day of my selfe": John Donne, Martha Moulsworth and the emergence of individual identity', in A. J. Pierre, ed., *Sixteenth Century Identities.* Manchester University Press, 2002.

ZEEMAN, Nicolette. *'Piers Plowman' and the Medieval Discourse of Desire.* Cambridge University Press, 2006.

ZILBORG, Gregory. *A History of Medical Psychology.* New York: W. W. Norton, 1941.

ZINK, Michel. *La subjectivité littéraire*. Presses Universitaires de France, 1985.
ZUMTHOR, Paul. *Essai de poétique médiévale*. Paris: Seuil, 1972.
—— 'Le je de la chanson et le moi du poète', in *Langue, texte, énigme*. Paris: Seuil, 1975.

Index

The index lists the classical, medieval, Renaissance and early modern authors mentioned in connection with Montaigne and Shakespeare. It does not include Montaigne and Shakespeare, for the divisions of the book show that Montaigne is present throughout chapters 1 and 2, chapter 3, section 5, chapter 5, section 1, and chapter 6. So is Shakespeare in chapters 3 and 4, chapter 5, section 2, and chapter 6.

Abelard 42
Aeschylus 28,
Ambrose 95 n.3
Ames, William 62
Appius and Virginia 76
Aristotle 31, 37, 41
Arnaut, Daniel 44
Ascham, Roger 61
Aubigna d' (Agrippa) 47
Augustine 2, 32, 38–40, 41–2, 45, 128, 134, 147–8
Aquinas, Thomas 41, 128

Bacon, Francis 61,148
Ballads 59
Bernard, de Ventadour 44
Bernard, St 25, 42
Berni, Francesco 146
Bible 159
Boethius 54 n.111
Bright, Timothy 103

Callimachus 28
Calvin 38, 61–2

Cardan 46–7
Catullus 28, 33–4
Cavalcanti 45
Cellini 47
Chaucer, Geoffrey 59–60, 81, 143–4 n.62
Cicero 146, 161
Cornwallis, Sir W. 149
Crashaw, Richard 132

Daniel, Samuel 133, 150
Dante 45, 129, 133, 147–8
Davies, John 61
Descartes 65, 149
Dionysius (Pseudo) 31
Donne, John viii, ix, 1, 4, 6, 34, 44, 45, 63–5, 132–3, 135, 146, 149, 158
Duns Scotus 16, 41
Dyer, Sir Edward 63
Dyke, Samuel 67

Eckhart 42
Elyot, Sir Thomas 61
Epictetus 36, 39

Epicure 32
Erasmus 15–16, 48, 144, 157
Euripides 29
Everyman 75

Ficino 31

Gower, John 60
Greene, Robert 77
Gregory, of Nyssa 31
Gregory, the Great 36
Guinizelli, Guido 44–5

Harvey, Gabriel 62
Herbert, Edward 132
Herbert, George 132
Herodotus 30
Hesiod 26
Homer 27, 32–3
Horace 27, 34–5, 37
Hume, David 5–6

Jonson, Ben 66
Juvenal 35

Kyd, Thomas 77

Langland 43, 60
Lemaire de Belges, Jean 48
Lily, William 61
Locke, John 5–6
Lucilius, Gaius 27
Lucretius 27, 158
Luther 48

Machiavelli 129, 153
Marcabru 43
Marcus Aurelius 36, 39
Marlowe 62, 77–8, 133
Marot 48
Marston 62, 133
Martial 27

Marvell 132
Mirror for Magistrates 77

Occam 41, 129
Ovid 28, 33, 34, 136

Perkins, William 61
Persius 36–7
Petrarch 40, 44, 45, 129–30, 134, 137, 143 n.68
Plato 26, 30, 32, 126, 147, 153, 155–6
Plotinus 30–1, 127
Plutarch 30, 145, 165
Propertius 34
Prudentius 40–1, 42
Pyrrho 12, 147–8, 163

Rabelais 47, 130
Ronsard 15, 49, 130
Rutebeuf 129

Sackville, Thomas 77
Saint-Gelais, Octavien de 48
Sebond, Raymond 17, 160
Seneca 29–30, 36, 77, 164
Sextus Empiricus 32, 146, 162
Sidney, Sir Philip 61, 63, 65, 69, 142 n.45
Skelton 76
Socrates 25, 30, 39, 154
Sophocles 28–9
Spenser 15–16, 61, 69, 133–4, 138
Stoics 32, 35, 39

Thucydides 30
Troubadours 43–4
Villon 48
Virgil 32–3
Vives, Juan 66

Webster 62
Wyatt, Sir Thomas 62–3

EU authorised representative for GPSR:
Easy Access System Europe, Mustamäe tee 50,
10621 Tallinn, Estonia
gpsr.requests@easproject.com

www.ingramcontent.com/pod-product-compliance
Lightning Source LLC
Chambersburg PA
CBHW070357240426
43671CB00013BA/2535